S0-BLY-159

TRAVELLER WITHOUT
A MAP

BY THE SAME AUTHOR

Etching of a Tormented Age
China but not Cathay
The Spinners of Silk
Dragonbeards vs the Blueprints
A Harp with a Thousand Strings

TRAVELLER
WITHOUT
A MAP

HSIAO CH'IEN

TRANSLATED BY JEFFREY C. KINKLEY

STANFORD UNIVERSITY PRESS
Stanford, California

Copyright © Hsiao Ch'ien 1990
English translation copyright © Jeffrey C. Kinkley 1990

First published in Great Britain in 1990
by Hutchinson
First published in the United States in 1993
by Stanford University Press

Printed in the United States of America

Stanford University Press publications are distributed
exclusively by Stanford University Press within
the United States, Canada, and Mexico; they are
distributed exclusively by Cambridge University Press
throughout the rest of the world.

Library of Congress Cataloging-in-Publication Data

Hsiao, Ch'ien, 1910–
    Traveller without a map / Hsiao Ch'ien ; translated by
Jeffrey C. Kinkley.
        p.   cm.
    Translated from Chinese.
    Includes index.
ISBN 0–8047–2237–4 (cl.) — ISBN 0–8047–2238–2 (pa.)
    1. Hsiao, Ch'ien, 1910–   . 2. Authors, Chinese—20th
century—Biography. I. Kinkley, Jeffrey C., 1948–   .
II. Title.
PL2765.I33Z473   1993
895.1'351—dc20
93-28197 CIP

⊗ This book is printed on acid-free paper.

To
George Rylands
Harold Shadick
Sydney Bailey

And to the memory of
E. M. Forster
and
Arthur Waley

With gratitude and affection

Contents

List of Illustrations

Translator's Note

In this book Hsiao Ch'ien has reverted to the traditional Wade-Giles spelling of his name, the name under which he published his five previous books in England. The Pinyin romanisation system, which spells his name 'Xiao Qian', has been used for most other Chinese names and terms, except for famous persons and places that already have accepted English names.

This English edition of Hsiao Ch'ien's memoirs differs from all previous periodical and book versions in Chinese, including the 1988 Hong Kong book edition on which it is based. The present text has been abridged and adapted for the general Western reader. In some places, however (notably, Hsiao Ch'ien's account of his tribulations as a Rightist), it has been expanded to provide new names, dates, and places for the historical record.

Hsiao Ch'ien and I would like to express special thanks to Ewald Junge, Richard Cohen, Lee Ambrose, Gladys Yang, and Susan Williams-Ellis for their help with the English edition. I am grateful to Hsiao Ch'ien and Hutchinson editors for bringing my translations of Hsiao's own speech into line with the British English Hsiao used to speak in London and Cambridge (and indeed still does today). In fact, Hsiao Ch'ien patiently read and amended the entire English text two or three times. It was during this process that the book continued to evolve in the hands of the author, absorbing new personal reflections and turns of speech that moved him as he read. Still, this remains basically a translation, and all errors are my responsibility.

Acknowledgement is also due the Committee on Scholarly Communication with the People's Republic of China of the US National Academy of Sciences, and the US National Endowment for the Humanities, for funding a 1989 trip to China during which I conferred with the author on final textual revisons.

J. K.

1

My Childhood
(1910–1928)

Memory, I suppose, is one of the qualities that distinguishes human beings from other animals. Sometimes it is a heavy burden to the mind and sometimes an invaluable asset. A man may have travelled all over the world, but what often emerge in his recollections are not the famous mountains he has climbed nor the oceans he has crossed but the narrow, winding lanes he once passed through or the marshes where he used to catch frogs as a child.

To recollect one's early years in one's late seventies is like fumbling under dim lights with an old, dust-covered album of faded photographs. Many people seem to possess grand and elegant albums, but mine is just a makeshift old notebook. Between its covers are many snapshots taken in my earliest days. They show no glamour, no scenes of past glory, only hungry faces, squalor and misery. The self-portraits, moreover of all periods, reveal a particular characteristic (or ailment) of mine: a deep-seated insecurity about my relations with others, so that all too often some imagined criticism from earlier in the day returns to hurt me, or a succession of unrelated remarks link up to make a pattern of unfriendly comment that exists in my mind only.

But fortunately remembered pain is quite different from actual, present pain. It is like caressing a scar: one even feels a little proud of the smooth, shiny blotch. That is just how I feel about the north-eastern slums of Peking where I was born. Goat Shepherd Lane was in the poorest district in the city, but it occupies a unique place in my dreamland. Broken Tile Lane also, for that was where I started my long and chequered education. And Little Chrysan-themum Lane was on my way to work every morning in the rug shop; it was there, too, that my kind and gentle mother closed her eyes for the last time. Such, then, are the earliest snapshots in my album of memory. I kept them and their companions safe, thinking they would go to the grave with me. I never imagined there would come a day when I would bring them out into the lamplight of my room.

In China's old pre-revolutionary society to be poor was in itself a disgrace. Poverty brought not only physical suffering but also public scorn. I had no toys in my childhood and no picture books, but the degradation I was made to feel was far greater because my mother worked as a common servant. Yet it may well be that my handicaps were often only in my fancy. I was haunted by the feeling that, as the Chinese saying goes, I stood 'a head shorter' than other people.

My father died before I was born. There is nothing particularly shameful in that, yet I felt shame – possibly because my elders never mentioned it when I was around. I knew that all children except me had a papa, and that my mother had told me my father had died long ago, but for a considerable period I never thought to ask when he died, or how old I was at the time. And when I did finally question my mother, and she told me that he'd died a month before I was born, there was still nothing shameful about it, but that is not what I thought. Even when I wrote the afterword to my book *Chestnuts* in 1936, I was obviously still feeling uncomfortable with the truth. 'I did not have the good fortune of seeing my father', I wrote. 'When I was being born, he passed away.' It reads unclearly, as if the two things had happened at the same time.

People did not bother much with birth certificates in those days, of course, so there was always room for doubt in such matters. But every year, when the seventeenth day of the last lunar month came round, my elders would tell me I'd grown a year older. That meant it was time for me to 'kowtow' to all of them. First I bowed with my hands folded in front, and then I knelt, touching my head on the ground at least three times. Mama had me kowtow to my paternal aunt first, then to Venerable Elder Sister, then to Elder Cousin Number Three, and finally to her. To thank her for being so kind as to raise me I had to give the floor nine good whacks. So I knew the day and month of my birth quite early on, according to the lunar calendar.

And as to the year, in those days there were almanacs issued annually that told your fortune. They were an interesting pastime, but you had to know the year of your birth, so Mama provided that for me: 'You were born in the first year of the Xuantong Emperor [Puyi]' she told me. 'In the year of the chicken.'

Finally as to the hour of my birth, once after I'd poked around in an elm tree growing in the courtyard where we lived and so stirred up a nest of hornets that nobody dared step outdoors for the rest of the day, an aunt said crossly, 'Gracious, no wonder you noon-born cocks are called troublemakers!' (Roosters are supposed to disturb people in the morning, not at mid-day.) With that, I even knew what time of day I was born.

For a long time, then, I thought I knew everything necessary about the timing of my birth – until 1939, in fact, when I was in Hong Kong arranging my passport for travel to Britain, and the authorities insisted that I fill out my date of birth according to the Western calendar. For several seconds I stared at the form. There was no conversion table provided, so I simply had to choose a date. According to my mother I had been born during the reign of Puyi, the last emperor of China, who by then had been re-enthroned by the Japanese to head their puppet state of Manchukuo. I didn't want to be associated with him (although I wouldn't have minded being a subject of the earlier splendiforous Kangxi or Qianlong emperors!) so I put 1911 as my birth year, the first year of the Republic. For the month and day I put down 17 December, as if days and months in the Chinese and Western calendars were simply inter-changeable.

Once I had put it in writing I had to stick with it. During my seven years in the British Isles I used the date of birth in my passport whenever I applied for ration coupons or registered at a hotel. Then, when I got back to Peking in 1949 and went to register at the police station, I had another chance to work out my real birthday according to the Western calendar. But, from inertia, I just filled in what I always had before. When Peking was preparing for the first elections to the National People's Congress in 1958 I had yet another chance to get it right. A policeman carrying an enormous book came out on the street and shouted to the waiting people, 'Is anyone unclear about his date of birth according to the new calendar? If so, come to our station and we'll look it up.' I had half a notion to do just that, but by then I was accused of being a despicable Rightist, and a big-time Rightist at that, so I didn't even know if I were still considered a citizen with the right to vote. Why then should I start bothering about my date of birth again? Whether born under the empire or the old Republic, I still belonged to the leftovers from the reactionary class.

And so I let matters rest until, during the terrible Cultural Revolution, I was made to confess my past sins like all the other intellectuals. Having nearly exhausted my storehouse of possible indiscretions, one day I submitted a report confessing that I had 'cheated' on the date of my birth. Reprehensible though this was considered to be, still no one bothered to find out the real date. It wasn't until 1979, in fact, while visiting a Sinologist friend at Yale, that I finally cleared up the matter. Professor Hans Frankel took down a book of conversion tables from his shelf and pinpointed the date of my birth in the Western calendar as 27 January 1910. It took him only a minute or two but the information was very welcome. It came just in time for my seventieth birthday, which otherwise I might very well have missed.

My racial background, too, was for a long time uncertain. Being a Mongol, or at least part Mongolian, I could be called 'an ethnic', a fact I did not reveal until 1956 when I was writing an autobiographical sketch. This was another factor in my inferiority complex.

Actually, although nobody ever mentioned it, I had known since childhood that I was Mongolian on my father's side. Under the dusty yellow cloth which covered the ancestral shrine in the house of the cousin with whom we lived was a wooden board with a figure carved into it that looked like a herdsman. There was also a book of genealogical records in Mongolian script. At the lunar New Year, when all Chinese worshipped their ancestors, my cousin knelt on a low bench and reverently exposed the tablet. During the ceremony I remember millet porridge with cheese being offered also.

We couldn't read Mongolian, though, and today I don't even know if my ancestors were nomadic western Mongol herdsmen or Eastern Mongols who made their living hunting. But I must have decided as a child that they were hunters, for I often imagined them in large furry hats and wool-lined sleeveless jackets, going off into the primeval forest with guns on their shoulders to track wild beasts.

Once I started school, however, I discovered that students from minority peoples were often bullied. In those days the Chinese characters used to denote minority peoples were even prefaced with the ideograph for 'dog' (or 'wild beast'), and I often saw my Muslim schoolmates being chased and abused. Even students whose only crime was to speak with a southern accent would be called 'barbarian'. So I quickly learned to cover up my ancestry and fill in 'Han nationality' (majority of Chinese) on all the official forms and my mother was a Han anyway. I was expelled from high school just before graduation for being involved in movements, so when I eventually entered university in 1930, I was obliged to use a false diploma – and on this I was made out to be a native of Chaoyang, Guangdong, down at the southern end of China!

After Liberation (1949), most ethnic minorities were no longer discriminated against; they might even have certain privileges. Many people in fact did well out of their status as minority representatives, but I still did not wish to exploit my ethnicity so I kept filling in 'Han' on all the forms. Then, however, in the summer of 1956, after Hu Feng and his supporters had been thrown into jail, there was a thorough nationwide investigation of cadre backgrounds. I had already confessed every wart and blemish I could think of, but to prove that I was in agreement with the spirit of the campaign, I made a clean breast of the 'problem of my ethnic status'. Ever since then I've had to keep filling in 'Mongol'.

Still, I'm only a 'pseudo-Mongol', for I know nothing about Mongolian customs, and speak not a word of the language. Amusingly, on the tenth anniversary of the founding of the Inner Mongolian Autonomous Region in 1956, when the Chinese Writers' Association sent out a delegation of writers to inspire them to write literary pieces about the New Mongolia, one of the association secretaries, my old friend Yan Wenjing, took advantage of my newly confessed status to recommend me. On my return I dutifully churned out essays called 'Herding Sheep Across a Thousand Miles' and 'Scene from the Steppe', but I still think it is truer to call me a Han.

As to the father I never knew – I never saw so much as a photograph of him. Possibly he never had one taken. I tried to piece together a picture of him from the conversations of the adults. My father had served as a guard at the Dongzhi Gate, one of the nine gates in old Peking's city wall, and people said he never smiled his entire life. It was probably from his profession that I made him out to have been a big fellow, very tall, unlike myself, sitting up straight and grim on the *kang* (platform seat over a brick oven). Every time I went in or out of the city, I noticed that the doors he had guarded were thick and heavy: only a very strong man could have budged them.

I knew my mother much better, of course. She was a widow and I her only child, so naturally she loved me deeply. I remember that once, when Elder Cousin Number Three pointed a kitchen knife accusingly at my head, Mama clasped me tightly to her breast and cried out, 'This is the only flesh and blood I have left!' Later, however, when she had to get a job as a domestic servant, even though the house where she worked was not very far from our home, she was only allowed to visit us once a month. So, although I had a mother, it seemed that we had little time together. In those days I sometimes went to her place of work after school, either because I missed her or because I desperately needed money. I was obliged to wait outside the red gates. Occasionally a kind-hearted person might offer to inform her discreetly of my presence. She would slip out then, give me some coppers and a quick hug, then disappear back behind the gates. But such offers were rare. Usually I just had to suffer abuse from the other servants and still not get to see her.

My grandfather had three sons, of whom my father was the eldest. The elder of my two uncles lived apart from us in Cannon Street, which was named after the weapons that used to be made there. I can't remember ever having seen him, though I retain a vague image of his funeral in that district of old Peking.

My mother and I lived with my younger uncle (Uncle Number Three to me, the third of my grandfather's sons). He died when I was five. He passed away sitting in a chair and I clearly remember my aunt shaking his bald head back and forth and reproaching him bitterly: 'So that's it, you just move out. Leaving your wife and children with nothing!' Then she burst into tears. That was my first encounter with death.

This woman, Aunt Number Three, had married my uncle after the death of his first wife. She was left to care for four children, a daughter and a son from each marriage. Her grown-up step-daughter, unmarried, was almost a mother to me, so I grew to call her Venerable Elder Sister. She was short and fat, not pretty at all but with a heart of gold. Aunt Number Three's stepson was head of the house. He was my Elder Cousin Number Three, being third born among all the grandsons of our grandfather.

When she was at home I often heard Mother sobbing to herself. There were not many in the household, yet the relationships were always tense and complicated. The wife of Elder Cousin Number Three did not really want us under her roof; we had to go without food sometimes, and it was these circumstances that finally decided Mother to get a job as a servant in another house. I clearly remember her saying to Venerable Elder Sister, 'I'll be gone a lot, I'll have to leave the child with you. Take good care of him, for the sake of your departed uncle.' The kind woman swore to my mother that she would do her best. She did indeed. When Elder Cousin Number Three punished me by making me kneel for hours on end, she would slip me a cup of hot tea when he wasn't looking. When he beat me she would either beg for mercy on my behalf or even try to protect my body with hers. She washed and mended my clothes. It was also she who would have to wake me up before daybreak when I started going out to work.

She was also my first teacher, even though she was only semi-literate. She sang to me and told me stories from books. She could recite almost anything after a single hearing and she loved a work called *The Book of Adages*: 'It takes a long ride to know a horse; how then can one hope to know a man quickly?' There was one about snobbishness, too: 'A rich man is visited by distant relatives though he lives in the mountains; a poor man gets no callers though he lives in the centre of town.' Edifying or not, these scraps of philosophy were the first to come my way.

Elder Cousin Number Three himself was quite intelligent. He was good at the two-stringed fiddle, good enough to accompany himself as he sang Peking opera. He couldn't find work when he left school, so he entered Chaoyang University, hoping, although severely pock-marked, to become a lawyer. But no matter how hard he looked he still couldn't find work. His temper, bad to begin with, grew worse than ever. He became head of the house when his father died and he often took his anger out on me. I was scared of him. The moment he entered the yard, I would fetch his bicycle and busily start polishing it.

At the time of the Chinese New Year he would go to Northern New Bridge and set up a stand where he sold lucky New Year's couplets written to order in his expert calligraphy. I went as his little helper, grinding the ink for him to use. It was so icy cold that the backs of my hands cracked, and the blood from the sores froze.

I still had to smooth his red paper before he could write on it. The piercing wind played havoc with the paper, even blew holes in it if I wasn't careful. He'd give me ugly looks and curse me between his teeth: 'I'll settle with you when we get home!' When business was good, though, he'd pull out a few coppers and let me buy fritters and my favourite sweet, fried wheat cakes.

Later he found a relatively secure position in a Protestant church. His duties mostly involved propagating Christianity – there was a 'China Belongs to God' campaign on at the time – but actually, once at home he put his faith in just about everything *but* Christianity, from the *Diamond Sutra* to the Great Fox Spirit. But of these strange spirits and not so strange expediencies, more later.

My mother was a meek woman. My earliest memories are of her and my spinster cousin taking in sewing and laundry. Sometimes they sewed for the army supply depots. Piles of finished and unfinished uniforms and cotton wool for padding always lined our *kang*; the two women were seldom without needles in their hands. As I grew older I used to accompany them when they went to get new work and drop off the old. This is how my mother supported me before she went out to work – this and selling off what little remained of her dowry.

In those days dealers in secondhand goods could often be seen making rounds through the lanes and back alleys. They held a drumstick in one hand and a little tabor smaller than your palm in the other, which they rapped every few steps. Hence the towns-people called them 'drumbeaters'. To me they were no more than a very polished kind of robber. Even so, they put on airs, often wore the long gown associated with the upper classes, and had a blue money bag slung across their right shoulder. You had to chase after them and almost beg them to enter your house and inspect your belongings. This was one of the most humiliating errands my mother ever sent me on.

'Drumbeater, please come to our house. Won't you? Please?' Looking me over contemptuously and reckoning that the profit would be slight, he gave a little snort: 'What do you have for me today?'

What indeed? Mama's only pair of bracelets and a leather jacket Papa once wore were long gone. I remember when she sold our last piece of furniture – a little table that we used for eating and writing.

Pursing his lips, the drumbeater told her: 'That's not worth much – you'd be better off keeping it.' But Mama insisted. She pleaded and pleaded with him, for she wanted the money for my school tuition, and finally he parted with a few coppers.

Poor people can get by if they have rich relatives. Mother's oldest brother was a porter who often did furniture removals. In the winter he went around with his little push-cart, selling sweet potatoes, calling out 'Tasty as chestnuts! Tasty as chestnuts!' I'd stuff myself with his wares. Sometimes I watched him help people move house. He must have been immensely strong. He could bear a giant Dinner-for-Eight-Immortals table on top of his head.

My mother's other brother was a company commander under some warlord in the south of the country. I only saw him once when I was young, when he gave me a very ripe banana. I told him I wanted to see the south for myself, so he chucked me under my chin and teased me: 'Come with me, we'll make a soldier of you!' Immediately my mother clasped me to her bosom, as if afraid I might be press-ganged on the spot.

Whenever I eat roast duck I think of the mock Peking duck (bacon rolled up in delicious pancakes) of my childhood. My mother occasionally made this treat possible for me at her sister's home. Mama was earning three yuan a month, most of which she had to hand over to the household for our upkeep, but somehow she managed to leave a little with her sister, so that when I yearned for something special I could slip over and my aunt would make me pancakes and roll them round slices of bacon into the shape of a horn. My aunt never ate with me, but she enjoyed watching the food disappear. Feeling my bulging little belly, she would tell me, 'Now, child, grow up quickly so that you can support your poor mother.' Alas, on the very day that I earned my first real pay packet my mother passed away.

Houses in the north-eastern slums of Peking were old and in terrible condition. Some of them collapsed with every downpour of rain, crushing their occupants to death. When a roof leaked people couldn't afford to repair it, so they put a piece of matting over the crack in the tile, weighing it down with bricks.

One day one of those bricks flew loose while I was on my way to school. It was summer, so I was bare-chested. The brick scraped skin off both my forehead and my chest on its way down. A second earlier and I would have been killed.

This had given my poor mother a horrible fright, of course. For a long time afterwards, on the first and the fifteenth of each lunar month she went before the tutelary deity to burn incense on my behalf and perform a kowtow. She only stopped when a wise old man in our neighbourhood assured her, after feeling the back of my head to check my phrenology, 'This child has a long life expectancy.'

With the approach of winter, the Red Cross or some such organisation would set up soup kitchens. When my elder cousin was out of work, I would go with him to get some charity porridge. We had to make an early start, while the sky was still black. Our room felt as cold as the North Pole and my quilt seemed like a tent pitched beside an icy river, but I knew that every person in the queue would get a helping of gruel, and in the end I'd struggle out and up from my bed and throw on my clothes. There were no streetlights in Peking's maze of lanes in those days, so we groped our way along to the soup kitchen. A lot of people in our district depended on the charity porridge to get by, and in the darkness we could hear the clinking of many bowls.

The soup kitchen was in an open space at the end of Shepherd's Lane. I stood in line with my family, each of us clasping our own bowl. The queue was already long, but the doors of the kitchen remained firmly closed until the official opening time, which was at dawn.

Peking felt colder to me in those days. My eyes watered and the cold winds froze the mucus and tears on my face. We stamped our feet, rubbed our hands and sucked the air in warily through our teeth.

Most of all, we dreaded a long queue. As the sky turned from black to grey, we kept looking back anxiously to see how far the line went. There was only so much porridge to distribute, so if the servers saw the line lengthen, they had to water it down. One morning the queue was joined by a 'big nose' [a European]. This incident made a powerful impression on me.

When the guns of the Russian Revolution drove the Tsar's lords and nobles to flee with their valuables into comfortable exile in Paris and Vienna, their doormen, gardeners, cooks and valets fled too. After trudging wearily across the white expanses of Siberia, some of these poor White Russians landed up in China and came to live in Peking. A primary attraction for them was the onion-domed Eastern Orthodox Church that stood beside Dongzhi Gate in those days, complete with Russian monks intoning prayers and carrying lighted candles. When they first arrived, the White Russians went about selling the tapestries and other goods they had brought with them. Gradually they used up their capital, and then they had to beg. This particular big nose was one of these unfortunates.

After he'd slunk into the line, I heard someone yell, 'There's not enough for us Chinese. Get the big nose out of here.' But someone else said, 'Let the old man be. I'll put up with a little less.'

The argument raged. Perhaps it was a way of staying warm.

At dawn, the doors to the soup kitchen opened. People shoved forward expectantly. When I turned to look back, I saw that the old Russian had withdrawn from the line, taking his bowl with him in the direction of the Eastern Orthodox Church, wiping tears away with his sleeve as he walked.

As I was on my way home from school on Dongzhi Gate Street a few days later, I saw a crowd gathered around a mat-covered corpse by the wayside. Such cases were by no means rare; they even had a special name, *daowo*, which translates as 'the fallen down'. Ordinarily I would leave after a quick look, but this time I hung about. From what I could see protruding under the mat, the skin colour was unusual, thick hair covered the legs and the shoes were foreign-looking.

Soon the coroner arrived. When he lifted the mat, of course, it was the big nose who had turned away from the charity porridge line, with his emaciated face, jutting cheekbones, and sunken eyes. There was a chain around his neck, from which hung a little cross. His shirt had big holes at the elbows exposing his fleshless arms, and his trousers were held up by a frayed cord.

The coroner spoke out loud as he filled out the form: 'Name – unknown; nationality – unknown; relatives – unknown.' Two strong men then hung the body from a carrying pole of the sort usually used to lift coffins, and headed off with it in the direction of the city gate and the countryside beyond.

I had in fact seen my first foreigner some time before at about the age of five. Cigarettes had just been introduced to Peking. One afternoon, two rickshaws came into the neighbourhood, one bearing a big-nosed, brown-haired foreigner, the other a thin and bony Chinese with several cardboard boxes beneath his feet. The rickshaws stopped and the thin Chinese man started blowing on a sort of trumpet. He looked quite pitiful as he strained at it, his cheeks puffing in and out. Evidently the foreigner had hired him simply to attract a crowd. Then, once enough people had gathered, the foreigner opened up one of the cardboard boxes, a green one that had a picture of a swallow printed on it. He took cigarettes out of it, and distributed them to the onlookers. I remember the incident because then he suddenly picked me up from the crowd and hugged me, scaring me half to death.

I had another elder cousin, Number Four, who was the son of my older uncle. We never lived together, but he had a significant influence on my life. He had converted to Protestant Christianity. Hence he opposed the Buddhist practices in our home. One year on the twenty-third of the twelfth month, when we were making offerings to the kitchen god, he arrived and chased us all outside, saying he wanted to make the 'sacrifice' all by himself. To everyone's outrage he lit a fire instead, destroying the wooden shrine and all the sacrificial objects with it.

Being already something of a rebel myself, I secretly began to look up to him. He had attended Cheeloo (Qilu), a missionary university in Shandong, and even married an American missionary lady named Anna. That was quite a thing in those days, and there were serious repercussions. The American Consulate was dead against it; they warned Anna that if she married a Chinese, her American citizenship would be revoked. Her father wrote too, threatening to disown her. No one in their church dared stand up for them, either. But Anna was resolute, and eventually found a church whose pastor would marry them.

When she got married and moved into her husband's household, she lived just like a Chinese bride, with a mother-in-law above and sisters-in-law below. She spent her days washing and sewing. She also taught English for several decades, and her income was often the family's chief means of support. Yet she never breathed a word of complaint. After living half her life in China, being widowed and too old to support herself any more, she moved to America in 1972. Today she is ninety-five and living in Whittier, California.

It was through Elder Cousin Number Four that I first came into contact with the New Culture. It was also he who first got me into a modern school.

Although my long-suffering mother was not very literate, her life's wish had been for me to be educated. Even as she was dying, she made me promise to aim high and make something of myself, which was her way of asking me to get an education. When I was six years old, she had sent me to an old-fashioned, private, family-style school that was located inside a Buddhist convent at Xintaicang in Northern New Bridge.

The school was situated in a dark corner at the right side of the main hall of worship. About fifty of us squeezed in there, a desk built of layers of brick between each four of us. When I left for school in the morning, as well as my bookbag I carried two small copper coins, to be exchanged for sesame cakes or 'horseshoes', wheaten pancakes named after their shape. On the wall of the schoolroom was a crumpled rubbing from a stone tablet of 'Confucius, the Greatest Sage of All Ages' to which we had to bow three times before and after class. Each of us had a copy of the *Four Books* by Confucius and Mencius in front of him, and all day we would yell out passages from these ancient canons. A nursery rhyme says: 'It takes a tough backside to sit through the *Great Learning* and *The Doctrine of the Mean* [since the texts' difficulty entails many beatings].' I was black and blue before I was halfway through!

Before six months were up I had to leave school. We could not afford the baskets of goodies the teacher was supposed to receive whenever there was a festival; sometimes we couldn't even pay the monthly tuition. In punishment the teacher would knock my head with the metal bowl of his pipe, harder and harder each time until finally I left.

By then the May Fourth student protest movement of 1919 in Peking had been born and the new learning was blowing into the city like a fresh breeze. So my mother, who was now working as a servant, decided to send me to a private 'modern' school in Nine Turns Lane. It was on the west side of the road, with high stone steps up to the gate. Mama bought me a set of the new-fangled textbooks: lesson one taught the characters *man*, *hand*, *foot*, *knife*, and *ruler* with the help of illustrations. She sewed me a new long blue tunic for my first day of class and walked with me all the way to school, stopping often to smooth any wrinkles out of my tunic and to remind me, 'You're the only one left on our side of the family. You mustn't let your mama down, boy.'

The classrooms were in the east and west wings of the usual four-sided compound centred on a courtyard; on the northern side were the teacher's living quarters. When we entered, Mama unwrapped the handkerchief that held my tuition money, carefully saved out of her pitiful wages, and placed it humbly on a corner of the great Dinner-for-Eight-Immortals table. Then she said to the teacher, 'This is my only child. I beg you to make something useful out of him.'

For myself, I was anxious to find out just what this word 'modern' meant when it came to teaching methods. True, the textbooks were bound in the modern way, with the pages glued to a spine instead of laced together; they were so new that you could still smell the printer's ink on the pages. Also, instead of having to recite 'Confucius said this' and 'Confucius said that', I now had to read 'horse, cow, sheep, chicken, dog, pig'. But we were still expected simply to learn each passage by heart; just as before, the goal was to shout it out at the top of our voices, rather than actually to understand it. Another difference was that the tuition fees were higher, and there were lots more incidentals: gifts for the birthday of the teacher's wife, for the marriage of the teacher's sister and so on. Limited as we were by my mother's meagre earnings, I was soon *persona non grata* again. By this time, too, I had discovered another difference between the old and new systems. This teacher was younger, so his canings were heavier. Thick as his cane was, he even broke it once. When that happened he brought a new one from his drawer without batting an eyelid!

If I encountered anything at all that was really new, it was outside school. At twilight on summer evenings, I used to play with my friends in a meadow near Pocketbook Hollow. One evening while engaged in some game, we saw a group of students suddenly appear at the south end of the field and rest a flag against the wall. On the flag were written the words 'Society for the Promotion of Social Progress'. Probably this was an anti-illiteracy organisation set up by some public-spirited townspeople. A young man in a long grey gown and a young woman wearing a pale blue blouse and black skirt began holding forth to us about the hardships of being 'the sighted blind', and how Europe, America and Japan were strong because of their universal literacy. When they'd finished their speeches, they taught us a song, 'The Freedom Flower'. It may well have been the first time I heard the words 'freedom' or 'liberty'. Adopting the tune of a familiar North China folk song, 'Lovely is the jasmine flower', the students simply substituted the word freedom for jasmine. It was as if Scottish students had taken their own famous ballad and sung it thus:

O, freedom's like a red, red rose,
That's newly sprung in June.
O, freedom's like the melodie
That's sweetly played in tune.

I've sung that Chinese folk song very often in the years since. It was not only the beginning of my education in music; more importantly, it created in me a yearning for freedom itself. Only later did I discover how many men and women had laid down their lives for the idea expressed in that word.

Not long after I heard those students talking about literacy and freedom, Elder Cousin Number Four told my mother that a foreign missionary school called Truth Hall (Chongshi Xuetang), in the Anding Gate neighbourhood, was accepting new pupils. Boys there could study part-time and earn their keep by learning a trade the other half of the day. I remember my mother was very ill then. I never learned what her ailment was, I only knew she was unhappy and I often had to pound on her chest all night. When she got the news of the missionary school from my cousin, she begged him, tearfully, 'Could you be so good as to get this son of mine into that school? If he learns a trade, as well as how to read, then at least he won't starve if something should happen to me.'

My cousin agreed and made some enquiries. Finally one morning Mama dressed me up and my cousin led me off to Truth Hall. This was truly a new world. The school was situated in a five-storey building, foreign in architecture. Instead of piles of bricks, we had our little desks with drawers. There were big glass windows, an electric light bulb suspended from the ceiling, and a shiny floor beneath our feet.

Since I'd already been to the family-style school and studied some English, I was placed in the third form. Then they took me up to a rug-making workshop on the top floor, where I became apprenticed to a Master Pei. Thus began my work-study career.

British and American Protestant missionary education in China seemed to have been carefully thought out. Both the universities

and the missionary secondary schools were distributed system-
atically throughout the country. Peking had several secondary
schools in those days, each with its separate buildings for girls and
boys, and each operated by a particular denomination. In the
western end of the city, there were the Anglican-run schools
named Virtue and Earnest Endeavour. In the east end, there were
the Methodist-run Assembled Culture and Respecting Chastity
schools, plus the Congregationalist Educating Heroes and the
Bridgman Girls' schools. Truth Hall, my school, was operated by
the Presbyterian Church in the northern end of the city – we had
Mercy Hall also, a sister school for girls.

Truth Hall had two five-storey buildings. The North Building
was the student dormitory. The central heating only reached up to
the third floor; the top floor where I lived was as cold as an
icehouse. Mr Ma, the master of the dormitory, had a sideline apart
from his teaching: he exported pedigree puppies. Even the poorer
students could get into his good books if they supplied him with a
Pekingese puppy every so often. I couldn't manage this so he stuck
me up on the fifth floor. All I had was a very thin quilt handed
down from my mother, the cotton inside it long since wadded into
balls that left most of the quilt unpadded. Luckily my classmates
would help me by sneaking up after lights-out and putting their
greatcoats or padded jackets on top of me.

Because Truth Hall was a work-study school, as well as classes it
carried on three trades. It had a printing shop, a dairy farm and a
rug factory.

Though I wove rugs for several years, I developed no interest in
that line of work – in fact, I detested everything about rug-making.
To me, it was just a continuous process of being beaten. The novice
began by winding thread, then rolling the different-coloured yarns
into balls. This was done by two apprentices, with the younger
boy, usually me, stretching the yarn between his arms and the
more experienced one rolling it into a ball. The wool yarn was
crudely spun and uneven, so it often got stuck. Whenever that
happened, the older boy would give me a hard kick or whack.
Thus did apprentice take it out on fellow apprentice. After a year of
this I started actual rug-making, beginning with patternless pieces
woven from leftover yarn of many different lengths and colours.
While doing this work (as well as sweeping up and cleaning the
windows) I was still regarded as an apprentice and therefore still

subject to beatings. Rug-makers used three metal tools: knife, scissors and fork. All of them were sharp and all of them left scars on my body. Then, as soon as my apprenticeship was over, I was entitled to make life miserable for the next generation. It seemed a pointless way of getting revenge for what I had suffered before, so as soon as I'd finished my training and learned to weave Turkish-style rugs with embossed patterns, I left and went to work at the dairy farm.

The farm owned about forty smelly Swiss goats, and I herded these outside the Anding Gate on the slope of the city moat. While they grazed I would lean against a weeping willow and read. But I also had to milk them and deliver the milk to customers' doorsteps at the crack of dawn. I had to carry the milk, in bottles, from Northern New Bridge in the northern part of the city to the wealthy neighbourhoods down south, where the milk-drinkers lived. The actual weight of the milk was in fact less troublesome than my customers' dogs. When I exchanged a new bottle for the empty from the day before, the dogs always gave chase, yapping down the street. This regularly left me breathless and cross, and once with a tear in the back of my tunic.

Still, I liked the job of herdsman, for the goats were amiable enough despite their stench. Mama died at about this time, and after that, apart from Venerable Elder Sister, the only sense of affection and consolation I felt was when I pushed open the fence gate and forty bleating goats rushed out at me.

I always describe myself as having a poor educational background and this isn't for the sake of self-effacement or out of false modesty. Half the time other schoolchildren were at study, I was at work. And during my years at the rug shop, when I worked from daybreak until noon, all the major subjects such as arithmetic, algebra, and science were taught in the morning. In the afternoon, when I could attend, there were only courses like handicrafts, music and gymnastics.

I did all right in the English classes, taught by the principal, and although my Chinese wasn't nearly up to that of those who'd studied at home, Teacher Li Maoqing praised my compositions in class anyway. But my mathematics was horrible, and any interest I might have had in it was soon beaten out of me by the teacher we called 'The Pox'.

He always entered with a murderous look on his face, as if he were storming the classroom; his temper was like dry tinder, ready to burst into flames at the slightest spark. His standby was a switch made especially for beating children's palms. The pockmarks on his face were purple and he never smiled.

Now, our textbook was by a Mr Wentworth, very thick and costing more than one yuan. Every morning before setting off I would wrap it in a blue cloth and tuck it very carefully under my arm. One day, as I was going down Dongzhi Gate Street, a startled horse came charging up the street, right in my path. I rushed into the dark gateway of a funeral home. My blue parcel came undone. I gathered up the scattered contents in a panic. Only that night did I discover something horrible: my Wentworth was gone!

At school in the morning, after much persuasion, I got the pupil next to me to put his Wentworth between our two desks, but this did not go unnoticed by The Pox. He called me up, and it was some minutes later that I found myself back at my desk, eyes full of tears and palms all swollen and red.

'I'll beat you every day you come to the class without your textbook,' he roared at me as he stood on the dais, arms akimbo.

Fortunately it was the first of the month, time to pay the school for my board. The monthly fee was two yuan fifty. I persuaded the official in charge to let me eat just two meals a day, breakfast and supper, so I could buy another Wentworth with the one yuan that represented my lunch money.

For the next few weeks, therefore, while everybody else hurried towards the dining hall for lunch, I went into the basketball court by myself and listlessly shot baskets. One day a teacher, Mr Jia who taught geography to the upperclassmen, passed by. He didn't necessarily believe my sad story, but he made up my lunch money anyway, so that I wouldn't go hungry.

If I'd worked harder, I might perhaps have made up for my hours lost at rug-making, but instead I spent all my spare time at temple fairs. Peking had lots of them, all held on fixed days of the lunar month. On the first and fifteenth, there was a fair at Dongyue Temple, where the god of death was enthroned. On the seventh and eighth of the month, the Monastery Protecting the Kingdom celebrated with a fair. The Longfu Temple had its fairs on every day with a nine in it, (the ninth, nineteenth and twenty-ninth), and there were fairgrounds by the Bridge of Heaven and behind the Drum Tower.

These fairs were spectacular, far too busy and colourful for anyone to hope to take in everything. Just entering the temple compound was like stepping into fairyland. There were kites in the shape of eagles and goldfish and bright strings of red hawthorn berries to wear around your neck like the beads that bedecked high officials. I never tasted anything so good as the mung-bean cakes we called 'donkeys rolling on the ground', and for one copper you could get a bowl of delicious bean-curd milk. Peddlers sold fish glue for mending broken china and metal powders that could shine up the rustiest pots and pans. In one corner you could find songbirds, goldfish, rabbits and squirrels. In another corner people would be selling everything from rare flowers to the ubiquitous copper-a-bunch 'you-just-can't-kill-me' plants. There were fortune tellers and artists who would model your face in clay; there was a mighty wrestler called Bao San and an acrobat adept at swordplay and seventeen other martial arts.

But I particularly liked the ballad singers. Their theatre was little more than a shack covered with a tarpaulin and furnished with simple stools for the audience. There was no ticket for admission; at the end of each show, and sometimes during it, the proprietor would pass a plate or hold out a cap to solicit donations. Huddled right at the back, therefore, were two kinds of people, those who wanted to leave after a few minutes, and those like us who had no money. The price we paid was the angry glares we got. Sometimes I was chased away. But there were many other shows, so we would just slip out of one tent and into another.

My favourite act was a performer of *xiangsheng* comic cross-talk nicknamed Yun Li Fei (Flying in the Clouds). His brilliant extempore wit now strikes me as my first experience of the literature of satire. And the colourful vocabulary and vivid gestures of the *pingshu* (storytelling) actors had me so enthralled that on one occasion I went home without the jacket I was wearing – either someone had stolen it right off my back or I'd taken it off and simply dropped it.

Seemingly less of an influence on me were the lyrical *chaqu* folk songs often sung at these shows. However, having learned *The Boat Comes Home Midst Wind and Rain (Feng yu gui zhou)* by heart, I was to sing it later in life with serious consequences. My most momentous performance of it was in 1963, at a party hosted by the publishing house which employed me. My singing became a big crime in the summer of 1966, when people suspected I had been echoing a Ming dynasty verse that linked listening to the sounds of the wind and the rain with paying proper attention to difficult national problems. And even worse, the words 'wind and rain' had lately been used by Deng Tuo, chief editor of the *People's Daily*, who really did concern himself with affairs of state. The price he paid in 1966 for using those words was his life.

People expect natives of Peking like myself to be able to sing Peking opera, or at least to understand and tolerate it. This is not the case. For one thing, opera houses in those days were only for the rich. But for me there is another, more personal reason. When I was three or four years old, some relation took me to the Jixiang Theatre at Dong'an Market, which is still there today. I've long since forgotten what was performed. What intrigued me most were the long-spouted teapots carried by the attendants and the hot white towels which they tossed to customers over the heads of the audience. Then suddenly, during a battle on stage, while the actors paraded their long-feathered headdresses and brandished swords to the sound of drums and gongs, violence broke out all around me.

In those days soldiers of the local warlord could not only watch operas without paying but also demand special treatment from the management during the show. And if the service was the least bit slow, then they often started a riot. On this occasion the theatre was thrown into utter chaos as teapots, teacups, even stools and chairs came raining down from the balcony. People began screaming and crying. Fortunately we were near a window and my relation jumped out of it with me in his arms. Since then, I've never really liked Peking opera. Especially since the hot summer of 1966: I came to feel I was reliving the scene when Red Guards entered my house on a search-and-destroy mission.

One day in 1921, Elder Cousin Number Four took me to see an Englishman named Monroe, a pastor, and I ate my very first Western-style meal. My cousin had told me all about it beforehand, even giving me a little pamphlet in English called *Good Manners*. He told me how to use a knife and fork and explained that I must cut my meat before eating it, not lift it all up on my fork and take bites out of it, and that I must not put the knife up to my mouth.

I was nervous, of course, but our host was very friendly, and I soon settled down and was able to try out my English on him. When we sat down to eat, I didn't realise that I could pick up the bread roll off my plate. Instead I tried to cut its tough crust with my knife, and of course it slid off onto the floor. Nervous as I was, I managed to give my cousin a pained glance as if to say: Look, I did just as you told me, but what if the *food* doesn't mind *its* manners? Later that night we went to a cinema on East Chang'an Boulevard and saw Charlie Chaplin in *Gold Rush*. That was a first for me too; it expected nothing of me and I thoroughly enjoyed it.

I don't believe in gods or ghosts, but when I was little I was very credulous and superstitious. When I graduated from primary school, a photographer was invited to come take a composite rotating picture of the whole class with its teachers. But I'd heard someone say that a camera could capture your soul and shorten your life if it snapped you, so on the day of the picture, although I was made to sit cross-legged in the front row, when the lens got to us, I turned away and hid my face. When the picture was developed, I got a stern lecture from my teacher for spoiling it.

Another time, a friend invited me to take a tram ride with him. The trams were brand new to Peking; the line went from Northern New Bridge, where we got on, to Dongdan. It was fun to see the driver step on the bell pedal as we went ding–donging along. Suddenly one of the passengers started muttering, 'Electricity is so dangerous. I just hope it doesn't get out. If it does and passes through us, we'll all go blind.' I believed him, I'm afraid, and jumped off in a panic at the next stop.

Then again there was a student in my class who was clever and also very athletic. He got straight A's and was always the fastest runner at our annual track meetings. Suddenly he was absent, said to be in the hospital. Then came the explanation that he'd had to have his legs sawed off, because his father continually debauched himself with prostitutes. Later on I saw a syphilitic displayed at a medical exhibition, with his nose and much of the rest of his face all rotted away. The two events left a lasting impression on me. For the rest of my life I've not only stayed away from prostitutes, but even, whenever possible, from those who visit them.

Born into a Buddhist family and brought up in a Christian environment, I can say that conventional religion played an important part in my childhood. Even now in my seventies, I still thrill to the sound of bells in old churches or temples, and am particularly fond of religious music, including Christmas carols as well as the oratorios and masses of Bach, Handel and Mozart. I enjoy the smell of incense, the tranquillity of a chapel, and the sight of a Gothic spire on the distant horizon. But I have to admit that in my youth religion raised only doubt and resistance, and brought me far more oppression, humiliation and injury than comfort.

When I was five or six, a distant paternal aunt who was even poorer than we were turned up unexpectedly on our doorstep. Childless and having just lost her husband, she announced that she was turning to us for help. But Elder Cousin Number Three had just lost his job and the family was pawning and selling things daily, so she soon realised that she wouldn't be able to sit back and rely on our support.

Suddenly she told us she had found a backer – she had become the medium of an immortal called the Great Fox Spirit. Thereupon she went about curing every ailment in the district. First, while chanting, she burned a stick of incense. Then, putting the ashes into a bowl and adding water, she claimed she had created the miracle medicine of the Great Fox Immortal himself. I became very familiar with its taste. Before long she had changed from an unwelcome poor relation into a Living Bodhisattva, beaming celestial radiance up and down the street. And as well as faith healing, she picked up fortune telling too.

Although her position in the household stabilised, I was frightened to death of her, for I had to sleep on the same *kang* with her at night. For years afterwards I was afraid of the dark; this I owe partly to that aunt. To prove her close relationship with the Great Fox Spirit she would go into a trance every night at a certain hour. She made terrible noises, kowtowed and screamed, and then the god would possess her. I shivered under my quilt, well able to believe that a magical fanged monster had come among us.

When poverty and hardship push people to their wit's end, and when they are ignorant as well, they try to find something outside themselves to rely on. After trying his luck with the Great Fox Spirit, Elder Cousin Number Three went back to his Buddhism. That turned out to be yet another disaster for me.

In the daytime I had compulsory religion at school; they forced me to commit the Christian Bible to memory chapter by chapter. But in the courtyard my cousin was leading the whole family in monotonous kowtowing. Moreover, my aunt was not the only one who knew how to turn the supernatural to her own advantage. There came a beggar who suddenly started ranting in a dilapidated temple just outside the Dongzhi Gate. He claimed that the temple's deity had been reborn into his body, and the news spread far and wide. My cousin was interested in any god who might get him re-employed, so he decided to give this new beggar spirit a chance. He took me with him as he went to pay his respects with incense.

The temple was tiny and previously had been quite off the beaten track. Now its gable ends were covered with red and yellow banners bearing solemn phrases like 'If your belief in him is sincere, he will be efficacious', followed by the names of pious donors. We had to force our way through a huge crowd before we could reverently approach the great censer in the main entrance hall. Only after performing many deep kowtows were we fit to enter the throne room beyond, where the beggar was lazily reclining on a *kang*. I was certain he'd never had a bath in his life, for his skin was earth-coloured and greasy.

My cousin gave him a nudge, making me kneel down with him as he presented the box of cakes he had brought as his humble offering. I admired the beggar for his calm effrontery. Hardly bothering to look up, he lifted his dirty hand, broke off a piece of the apple he was eating and bestowed it upon my cousin, who accepted it as if it were a great treasure. Then he implored the beggar to intercede for him with the Bodhisattvas, so that he might find work again. He waited. The beggar god gave us an enigmatic grunt. We stood up and departed. At least my cousin treasured that piece of apple stained with the beggar's saliva too much to allow me to share it with him, for which I was very grateful.

My most genuinely interesting encounter with Buddhism was a pilgrimage I made to Miaofeng Shan, a sacred mountain roughly a day's journey north-west of Peking. It was the first long trip I ever took. I must have been ten or eleven years old at the time. It was around the time of the Duanwu Festival (the fifth of the fifth month). I travelled with an old man, well over seventy, who was going to redeem a past vow he'd made to the gods (they having answered his prayers in the meantime), and I had been sent to do the same on behalf of Elder Cousin Number Three, who was always making vows of one kind or another. We set out early in the morning from Dongzhi Gate, walking all the way across to the other side of the city. There were no trams or buses then, only rickshaws, which were beyond our means. At Xizhi Gate there was a tarpaulin-covered mule cart that would take us as far as the Summer Palace, about halfway, for a few coppers. After lifting me into the cart, the old man was obliged to find a place to sit on the running board, for the cart was already chock full of pilgrims. The road north-west in those days was made of big black flagstones. They made the ride extremely bumpy; it was continuous punishment for my backside, and sometimes I felt as if my heart was about to be shaken up into my throat.

Alighting from the cart at Green Dragon Bridge at the back of the Summer Palace, we resumed our march north-west. There were priests and monks all along the way, which was lined with graveyards. The distance was too much for us, and every now and then the old man would subside onto a tombstone. While he smoked, I looked round at the scenery and asked him how much farther we had to walk. He pointed to hills in the distance and said, 'Somewhere behind them, past the Black Dragon Pool.' It was quite dark by the time we reached the River of Northern Peace at the foot of the sacred mountain. We bought some sesame cakes at a little shop. Then, like all the other pilgrims, we bought ourselves torches to light the way up. Above us we could see the torch procession like a giant fire-dragon winding up towards the sky. Halfway up it grew dangerous – the path was narrow, with cliffs and an inky abyss below. 'I'm afraid!' I cried out. The other pilgrims didn't approve. 'If you are pious, your fear will go away,' one said. It was of little comfort at the time, but in later years this struck me as an apt characterisation of the power of belief.

We got to a level area just before dawn. It was customary for pilgrims to stop here for a rest, so as to be fresh later on in the day for the last short climb up to burn incense for Buddha. Innkeepers solicited customers there in the dim light: 'Our *kangs* are warm and our quilts are big. We don't have lice and we don't have bedbugs.' Actually there were both, and fleas to boot.

We went into one of the inns and laid down on the corner of the *kang*, where two strangers already lay snoring. I crawled over them and fell asleep the moment my head hit the greasy pillow.

The shrine on Miaofeng Mountain was made up of several temples. None was very large compared with the famous temples in town, but their incense and smoke sent vast white clouds billowing over the landscape. Each temple hall seemed to be dedicated to one particular profession, such as carpenters or bricklayers. The temple of the god of joy, patronised by people in the entertainment business, was decorated with the names of famous opera singers who had contributed.

Years later, I realised I had been present at a rare confluence of art and religion. The pilgrimage to Miaofeng Mountain was like a grand exhibition of North China folk arts and entertainments. In front of the temple and all the way back to the city there were stilt-walkers, all sorts of actors and dancers performing traditional skits, and stands draped in yellow cloth representing every trade imaginable. It was summer, just after the wheat harvest, and the peasants had dyed the new wheat straw many different colours and from it had woven marvellous straw hats, lanterns and all sorts of simple toys. When a pilgrim bought one of these it was called 'taking some good fortune back home'.

Though strangers from all parts of North China, the pilgrims somehow formed a community of their own. Belief linked them together. Many tradesmen had pledged to Buddha that they would set up shelters along the way, where weary pilgrims would have a place to sit and rest, and at some places they even offered free hot cups of porridge and white bread. I had a hole in my shoe, but the cobblers were doing service for Buddha, too, so I got it repaired for nothing.

What disturbed me about the pilgrimage was its masochistic side. The believers had come, mostly on foot, from provinces as far away as Henan and Shandong, either to beg for dispensations for themselves, or to redeem pledges for critically ill family members at home. Many tortured themselves cruelly in order to please the gods and show their piety. I saw one pilgrim who had been stopping every two or three steps to strike his head on the ground for the last hundred miles or more. Then there was a man who had crawled on his knees through the hot sun all the way from Henan, wearing a mock shell on his back to suggest that he was a turtle (a cuckold). His knees were a mess of blood – even the bones seemed to be exposed. He was accompanied by a little boy, his son, who carried a kettle of water for the old man when he grew thirsty. I was told that both were good examples of filial devotion. When the older man's mother had fallen ill, he had promised Buddha that he would crawl all the way to Miaofeng Mountain if she got well. That was not the worst. There were those who had promised to jump off a cliff at the back of the temple to show their piety. Some crippled themselves, some met their death. I thought of this when reading of the mass suicides in Jonestown, Guyana.

My first Christmas at Truth Hall was very happy. In the days leading up to it, we made coloured decorations and sang the traditional carols. The coloured lightbulbs on the little Christmas tree filled my lonely heart with a special joy. I was moved also by the story of little Jesus, born in the manger, the son of a carpenter who bravely took on the oppressive empire of Rome. And I admired the way he drove the money-changers out of the temple, thinking that he might be something of a revolutionary too. Many other Bible stories (especially those in the Old Testament) fascinated me, like the story of Joseph and his coat of many colours. The poetry of the book of Psalms, Proverbs and the Song of Solomon, and the exposition of a philosophy of love in First Corinthians, Chapter 13, left a very deep impression on me.

My antipathy to Christianity did not come from the faith itself. It was Elder Cousin Number Three's practice I despised, the way he propagated Christianity during the day and worshipped the Buddha at night. And sadly, after entering the missionary school, I discovered that there were a lot of people like him, just using religion as their rice bowl. The dormitory master at the Presbyterian school had two faces: there was the mask he wore for the principal, and the one for less important people; the mask he wore before the wealthier students, and the mask for the poorer ones. During religious services he spoke of love and more love, but in fact he loved no one but himself.

After some reading in the history of art and literature, I came to understand Christianity's important cultural legacy all across the globe. The Old Testament is a treasury of the Jewish people's poetry and history, accumulated across a vast span of centuries. Regardless of his divinity, Christ has clearly inspired great writers and artists from Dante, Leonardo da Vinci, Bach and Milton, right down to today. The theses accusing the Vatican which Martin Luther nailed up in 1517 fuelled the Renaissance that ended the darkness of the Middle Ages and culminated in a great intellectual liberation for humankind. And Jesus was a true proletarian, for his disciples were fishermen, shepherds and labourers.

Unfortunately, the only Christians I knew in my childhood,

including even Anna, of whom I was so fond, were extreme fundamentalists. In one rural Chinese village, (in Xianghe county, I think), I even came upon a shocking service of so-called worship by a Pentecostal sect called the God Summoners (*Shenzhaohui*). About fifty believers knelt in a compound outside the church, each with a small pile of bricks in front of him. They bashed their heads against the bricks during prayer until their foreheads were bruised and bloody, and then began screaming gibberish like madmen. They said they were speaking in tongues in all the languages of the world.

Admittedly I personally was much better off in a missionary school like Truth Hall than I had been in the Chinese convent. After all, regardless of their religious motives, the schools and hospitals which the churches had been running since the nineteenth century played an undeniable role in both China's modernisation and mine. But the religious instruction I received at Truth Hall was completely under duress. We had services in the school early every morning, and on Sundays lined up to march to church – always after a roll-call had been taken. I had to memorise the Collects just as I had memorised the words of Confucius before. And if I failed, just as before I'd get smacked.

The pastor said we must close our eyes during prayer. But I was a rebellious child. The more they told me to close my eyes, the more I refused to, and I was not the only one. Teacher was furious. While the pastor led us in prayer, Teacher would walk down the aisle, checking to see that we had our eyes shut. If he caught us, he'd sentence us to several hours of detention out in the yard once the service was over, so we learned to close our eyes the moment he drew near, and then open them again when we heard him walking away. Perhaps this may be counted as my first act of political resistance.

Some of the other practices at the school were even sillier. There was a girl student in Mercy Hall, an orphan like me, who was really rather pretty, and a boy at Truth Hall was so taken with her that he wrote her a letter. It was intercepted and ripped open by the dormitory house mother. The whole affair was hardly the poor girl's fault – she didn't even know the correspondent – but the house mother considered it a grave offence, and scrubbed the girl's lips and neck with harsh kitchen soap for several days running, until she was bleeding. It was the purge of the girl of her sin, the woman said. Again, as up on Miaofeng Mountain, I saw religion as cruel.

As I grew older, still more questions began to trouble me.

On Sundays we lined up and walked to church in file, passing through the big cantonment reserved for the mission's foreign teachers. The paved path was lined with pine trees, but you could see past them to the lush green lawns and the grand two-storey houses, each with its own garden and its own swing and sand pit – I noted the blond and blue-eyed children at play. When we passed through the compound again after the service, delicious smells of roast beef wafted out towards us. There were verandas with potted plants, cooks in white uniforms, gardeners and *amahs* – it was a life of luxury and extravagance a world apart from ours. I went back to my cousin's house, to sip watery corn porridge. If the Christians' God really existed, I wondered, how could He be so unjust? Did He love the white people better than us?

Later I learned about the political and historical background to the Church in China. Foreign preachers wouldn't have been able to enter China had it not been for the humiliating treaties negotiated by the Qing dynasty – especially the corrupt emperor, with his eunuchs and sycophantic officials, who virtually gave away our sovereignty. Frankly Christianity had entered China in the wake of British gunboats and that is why, in my eyes, missionaries and their converts have always represented a relationship of the strong over the weak. I was particularly influenced by the May Thirtieth Incident of 1925, when students demonstrating in Shanghai were shot dead by British troops. After that, whenever a preacher pointed at us and called us sinners, I always asked myself, '*Who* is the sinner?'

Love is the central tenet of Christianity – 'Whosoever shall smite thee on thy right cheek, turn to him the other also.' Why, then, did the Christian nations force China to pay reparations for attacks upon their merchants? They retaliated as fiercely as the so-called pagans! How did they dare preach this doctrine of submissiveness in a country under their rule when they didn't practise it themselves?

I finally had a falling out with Elder Cousin Number Three (which is to say, since my mother was dead by then, with my only remaining family in the household). He was urging me to become a postman, for he considered it an iron ricebowl (a job for life), one that would enable me to support him. He even got me a letter of introduction from an Anglican bishop, as China's postal system was then in the hands of the British. I had no desire to be a postman, for I'd heard that they mostly sat around translating into Chinese the addresses that people abroad had written in foreign languages.

My cousin was angry, and made wild threats: 'If you don't do what I say, I'll break both your legs!'

But I was no longer one to take such things without protest. I rebelled against him. I wrote him a long letter, more than three thousand words, all in red ink. I can still recall my solemn, innocent words at the end:

'Enough of your nagging. Enough of your anger. You'll have no chance to break my legs – I'll use them to walk my own way.'

With that I ended my dependent life and at the age of fourteen became the captain of my own little ship.

Every day I read the classified 'help wanted' columns in the newspapers. I first applied to become newspaper apprentice at the *World Daily* (*Shijie ribao*), but they did not hire me. I heard it was because I was too short. But I kept an eye out and continued answering the advertisements. Finally I was taken on as a trainee at the Beixin Book Company.

The Beixin Book Company was located in a traditional square compound off Azure Lane. It occupied three rooms on the south side of the inner courtyard, two of which were interconnecting and served as the salesroom. The editorial department occupied a single room on the east side. Li Xiaofeng, the proprietor, and his wife, lived in other rooms off the courtyard. Yuan Jiahua (who today works in China's Languages Institute) was the sole editor.

It was a modern press devoted to post–May Fourth ideals. At its nucleus was a group of like-minded friends, mostly professors at Peking University, headed by Lu Xun (Zhou Shuren). Other key personnel were his younger brother Zhou Zuoren, Liu Bannong, Jiang Shaoyuan and Xu Zuzheng. The press also published a periodical called *Threads of Talk* (*Yusi*).

The company printed a great deal of the New Fiction, but the proprietor smoked a traditional water pipe, like a gentleman of the old school, and he always had an abacus at his elbow, its beads black from printer's ink. When I reported to him on the first morning he raised his head slowly and I sensed a man who would not suffer fools gladly. He was only middle-aged, but his long, thin

face was sharp and filled with wrinkles put there by his philis-
tinism.

'Oh, so there you are. Take these proofs and correct them!'

I went and sat down at a small desk against the wall and began.
The work was wholly new to me, and I imagined the boss checking
up on me out of the corner of his eye, between the hisses of his pipe.
Too nervous to think sensibly, I just went down the manuscript
character by character, so mechanically that I didn't get the overall
sense of the piece, my head reeling with the noxious smell of
printer's ink. But I must have done a reasonable job because
nobody ever complained and I was given a lot of proofreading after
that.

A list of the writers who came and went in Azure Lane would
virtually comprise a literary history of the era. In those days, Zhou
Zuoren was still writing elegiac couplets for the martyrs of 18
March and polemicising with Lu Xun against the narrow-minded
teachers at the Peking Women's Normal College. In 1936 when I
was a writer myself, and I got to see Lu Xun again in Shanghai, I
asked him if he still remembered the little errand-boy who used to
deliver royalties and manuscripts to him. After a long hard stare, he
recognised me and broke into a friendly smile.

I saw a lot of authors on that job. The poet Liu Bannong visited
often, speaking in his stentorian voice and chain-smoking; there
was the romantic writer Zhang Yiping, tall and thin and always
dressed in a silken long gown; Xu Zuzheng, author of China's first
modern love story, *The Diary of Younger Brother Lansheng*;
Zhang Jingsheng, just back from Paris, who had written a book
most considered pornographic, *The History of Sex*; the writer of
metaphysical fiction Feng Wenbing; the anthropologist Jiang
Shaoyuan; the linguist Qian Xuantong; and many others.

I was mostly occupied with odd jobs. I ran errands by bicycle to
the post office, the printing press, and the homes of the authors. I
proofread *Threads of Talk* and books on all sorts of subjects,
fighting off nausea from the printer's ink. I was particularly scared
of delivering royalties – such thick wads of banknotes, how could I
ever make it up if I were to lose one? Each time I would ask my
fellow workers to tie the money to my wrist in a handkerchief, so
that I could keep my eye on it as I cycled.

One day the manager gave me a new errand; to go and copy out
by hand books from the Peking University Library. 'Don't skip or

miswrite a single character. Don't even change a single dot of punctuation.'

This was my first literary training, a chance to get to know some fine works in detail. Going through the *Short Story Monthly* and *Modern Critic* I copied out every translated work in what was to become Xu Zhimo's *Short Stories by Katherine Mansfield*. It was the first time I had closely read a text.

When scholars abroad ask me which foreign authors have influenced me most, I answer as follows. A writer reads much as he plans his dinner: he wants greens and fat, starches and proteins, native foods and imported ones. (The staple food is his own experience.) They all turn into calories after they're eaten and digested, but you can't be sure which calorie was produced by which food. The first works by a modern author that I really got to know were those short tales by the delicate New Zealander, Katherine Mansfield. To me, they read like vignettes from the Song dynasty. The people in them were ordinary enough, and the plots were simple, but the underlying emotions were so deep and the pathos so intense that I was profoundly touched.

The books displayed on the Beixin salesroom counter were marvellously varied. I roared with laughter over *Hedian*, Zhang Nanzhuang's satiric late-Qing novel in Suzhou dialect, and shed many a tear over Goethe's *The Sorrows of Young Werther* and Theodor Storm's *Immensée*. I loved the legends about Xu Wenchang collected by a Chinese woman, 'Miss C F', and was fascinated by the documents from the Taiping Rebellion copied by Liu Bannong from the Louvre. There was no time for reading during the day, of course, but I was allowed to borrow one or two books from the rack to take home overnight.

The Beixin bookshop was in a sense another school for me. I discovered all sorts of May Fourth intellectual influences and ideologies, and got a taste of some of the new literary works. The book that had the biggest impact on my moral and intellectual values was Hua Lin's *Neo-Heroism* (*Xin yingxiongzhuyi*). I must have read that little book a dozen times or more. Before I came into contact with it, my ideal was simply to strive for myself and win glory for my ancestors. *Neo-heroism*, though it strikes me now as muddled and platitudinous, did lead me to a more selfless level. I began to think of my fellow countrymen, and even of humankind as a whole. Another work I read very avidly was Ibsen's *An Enemy of the People*, translated by Pan Jiaxun. I wrote out the last sentence in the play, 'the strongest is the loneliest', on a slip of paper and pinned it on the wall as my motto (it gave me comfort to think of it again when I was branded a Rightist in 1957). My mind must have been quite a hodge-podge of influences in those days!

There were two apprentices about the same age as I at Beixin, one dark and rough, the other fair-skinned and delicate like a girl. As a trainee, I was paid a little more than these apprentices, five silver yuan a month, and treated much better. They had to sleep on the office desks at night, while I was given a room to myself opposite the Red Building of Peking University (then located in the centre of town). I also ate my lunch with the boss and his family; the apprentices were summoned to the table for the leftovers only after we had eaten.

I remember how the dark-faced one came up during my first day on the job and said, 'lunch is ready, sir.' Dropping my work and weighing the pages down, I went into the dining room.

During the meal, the boss inquired about my schooling and vaguely promised to give me a raise after a year if I did well. It was then that I timidly asked him for permission to borrow some books to read after work. He nodded.

As we ate, the two apprentices were busy outside the shop tying up bundles of books. The boss called them in after we had finished. While he paced watchfully up and down the room, the apprentices fed on our leavings.

'I must eat less and spare more food for them,' I told myself, suddenly understanding how things worked.

Gradually I became accustomed to the place. Every day after work I would borrow a book to occupy my evening. Sometimes the other two boys would drop in to my room for a chat, and we became friends. I learned that the fair boy was an only son, much doted on by his widowed mother. He was only thirteen; he had lost his father as he was about to enter secondary school, so he'd had to come to work instead – most folk considered this work quite exalted. Still, his mother missed him. She came to see him every other day, talking nineteen to the dozen and bringing him homemade cakes. My envy of him because of her made me miserable.

The darker boy was young too, but very ambitious. He kept his little kerosene lamp burning till midnight, studying in the hope of being able to enter a military academy. He was not in good favour with the boss, but he had a strong body and an equally strong will. He was very conscientious about his work, even worrying over mail-order receipts until they were safely posted in the mailbox. He'd return soaked with sweat and didn't have sense enough to change; on a hot day he'd be pretty unapproachable. But it didn't bother me too much, for it was a sign of his dedication and honest simplicity.

One of the manuscripts I had to proofread was a little book about socialism. The company was going all-out to promote it. It helped crystallise certain ideas in my mind which previously had been vague and disorganised. I began to realise that society was divided into classes; that they came about due to differences in economic interests and that there was a struggle between them. A chapter dealing with strikes especially caught my attention, particularly since we had just received a pamphlet from Shanghai about how to organise a strike. A light went on in my little mind.

One evening I showed the booklet to the apprentices. 'We are all labourers,' I told them. 'We have the right to demand equal treatment from the boss.'

Next day the three of us left our work at eleven in the morning and stealthily crept out of the printing room. Before we left I wrote a note to the proprietor saying, 'We demand that the apprentices eat at the same table as the family and are not given leftovers. We also demand every other Sunday off.' Grinning at each other, we signed it 'Your Labourers', adding our three names in full underneath.

It was very pleasant to leave that dim, stuffy room and come out into the fresh air. But where were we to go now? Only the fair-skinned one had a home to return to, and he didn't dare. Without fully realising what we'd done, we still felt a vague dread, like children who were playing hookey.

With the sun on our backs so warm that we soon began to itch, we stood watching the traffic. It was diverting, but not enough to make us forget our worries. We hurried out to one of the major thoroughfares and wandered along the pavement, trying to enjoy our freedom. We stopped at a fortune-teller's stall, asked him a question and listened as he mumbled some unintelligible reply. Then we squatted down alongside a secondhand goods dealer, gazing at some of the treasures he displayed.

By noon we were hungry. Even after pooling our resources we didn't have enough for a proper meal, so we went to a stall selling bean-curd soup. We had one bowl apiece and pretended to be satisfied. It was then that the fair-skinned one asked me, with tears in his eyes, 'When do you think we should go back to the shop?' Frankly, I'd no idea.

At dusk, when we could wait no longer, we went back for our reply.

We found the boss sitting on the steps with his legs crossed, smoking his waterpipe as usual, watching over two new boys in the compound who were doing the work we used to do. He did not even look at us.

We were mortified.

After the fiasco, the dark-faced lad was enrolled in the Whampoa Military Academy that was training the officers who would reunite China in 1927. The fair one probably just went home. I went back to Truth Hall, looking for a job. The new school year had just begun and luckily the school office needed someone to handle their mimeograph machine. So I returned to printer's ink.

I had been too young to take part in the May Fourth movement, which surfaced when I was barely nine. I had however become politically aware by the time of the May Thirtieth massacre in 1925. The books I had read at Beixin and some of the iniquities I'd witnessed at the missionary school had filled me with strong nationalistic feelings. The blood shed on May Thirtieth in Shanghai on Nanjing Road joined with my own misery to become a mighty torrent inside me. And I was but one small drop within a flood that was bigger still.

In 1925, after the British massacre, a campaign committee to support the Shanghai strikers was formed and all the students in Peking, including those in missionary schools, went on strike. It turned into a great movement against British imperialism. The principal of Truth Hall, who was a foreigner, naturally sympathised with the British, and at first he tried to prevent the students from striking. When he failed in that, he tried to discipline us poorer students who were receiving aid from the school. But we too refused to obey – the slaves of yesterday had become rebels overnight. Ultimately, as the storm mounted, he and his family had to take refuge in the seaside resort of Beidaihe.

I still rose before daybreak, but no longer to go to work. Instead I rushed to the school, where we made little flags with slogans written on coloured paper for the demonstrators. Then I joined a small group going from street to street shouting anti-imperialist propaganda. I was still very short and had to climb up on the stone slab beneath the Dongsi Arch to get myself seen and heard.

'Don't buy these Japanese Jintan pills! Buy our own herbal medicine, *biwensan* (fever breaker) and *wanyingding* (all purpose tablets) instead!'

I also joined the demonstrators who were marching and shouting slogans out on the main streets. When we passed the Legation Quarter off Chang'an Boulevard, machine guns were in place to meet us, along with soldiers in foreign uniforms who from time to time would point their rifles at us, as if to say: The massacres of your people in Nanjing Road, Shameen, and Wanxian could easily be repeated here. What these oppressors didn't realise was that their guns served only to strengthen our determination and deepen our hatred.

It was at this time that I made the acquaintance of Li Anzhai, a college mate of Cousin Number Four. He lent me some radical pamphlets from his own collection, some about humiliating treaties negotiated by the Qing dynasty, some about more abstruse matters such as historical materialism and the liberation of humankind. Each time I visited him to return the booklets, he would briefly discuss their contents with me and encourage me to pass them around to the other students – to 'our brothers in poverty', as he put it. Thus it was that, without going through any initiation or filling out any form, I found myself a member of the Communist Youth Organisation.

In our talks I often attacked religion, but Anzhai persuaded me to use Christianity as a cover for our activities. I organised a Mutual Help Corps at Truth Hall and, with help from Anzhai, joined a committee with ten members of other Peking high schools. At Truth Hall, we pretended our meetings were Bible study classes. My letters to comrades in other schools too, were full of fake Bible talk. On holidays I attended meetings at Tiger Cave (Laohudong) in Haidian, where Li Anzhai lived. One day he told me he was going on a trip – only later did I find that it was to Ulan Bator, a Soviet satellite and one of the main sources of communism in the Far East. Meanwhile he turned me over to Yu Daoquan, the man

who would recommend me to teach at the School of Oriental and
African Studies in England in 1939.

I spent that winter vacation with Zhong Yiyan, a radical
Cantonese schoolmate. His home was in Qinghe, near Peking. His
father, who had studied in England, was chief engineer of the
nearby woollen textile factory. They had a very large compound
with a vegetable garden at one end and a fishpond at the other.
They also kept twenty beehives and a beautiful flower garden.
Yiyan's father was affable and full of good humour. While tending
his bees, he would discuss with me from behind his apiarist's veil
the question of how to liberate China. He thought the answer was
education and heavy industry. I know now that the old man was
trying to induce me to study something practical. After getting no
response, he suddenly cast a sidelong glance at me and asked
pointblank, 'Bing Qian (for that was my name then), what do you
want to be when you grow up?'

I'd never thought about that before. 'I want to be a revolutionary!' I blurted out. At this, Yiyan's father laughed and laughed. He
said I had no idea of what that meant. And to tell the truth, I didn't.

But I was soon to find out.

Peking was at that time under the rule of Zhang Zuolin, a
warlord based in Manchuria whom the Western press called 'The
Old Marshal'. He was so terrified of being inundated by a red tide
that he even banned *Master Ma's Introduction to Grammar*, a
nineteenth-century textbook by Ma Jianzhong, because he thought
Master Ma might be a cover for Mr Marx.

Zhang had three different police branches under his control: the
regular police, a Public Security Corps, and a secret Detective
Corps with special responsibility for tracking down reds. Little did
I realise that the father of one of my classmates, Peng, was head of
the last group. His specific responsibility was to expose reds in the
classroom.

One day, at dusk, I was playing with some friends making caves
by Sand Dune Pond. Just as a group of bats swooped down over
our heads, a boy suddenly ran up to me. Dragging me behind the
handball court, he whispered, 'Bing Qian, something awful –
they're coming to arrest you.'

'But what for?' I asked, my hands on my hips.

In fact I didn't really understand the word 'arrest'. But we used it
to mean 'you lose' when we played hide-and-seek, so I guessed it
must mean something unpleasant.

Later someone told me on the sly that the detectives had already chosen their informer, my classmate Peng. Although in his teens, he was short, and scrawny as a chicken. But we were usually friendly with each other. I couldn't believe it, so I sought him out and asked him,

'Would you ever do anything to hurt me?'

He smiled quite calmly and shook his head. That was enough for me.

The next Saturday, when I was all alone on the playground reading my books, Peng suddenly ran up to me.

'Bing Qian, there's a telephone call for you in the porter's lounge.'

Weekends were the worst time for a homeless child like me. A little warmth was just what my soul ached for, so I went there quite unsuspectingly.

But there was no call for me, and the old doorman was nowhere to be seen, either. Instead there were two plainclothes policemen with fierce faces.

'Now Mr Hsiao, come with us and have a cup of tea,' they said, smiling contemptuously.

Peng had disappeared.

'I don't know you', I said.

'Come on!' One of them grabbed my arm and the other pushed me out. I remember it as if it were yesterday: one with a goatee beard wore a short, grey, padded jacket and had bound his legs with silk; the other wore a black long gown and dark glasses – he was missing an eye. Struggle as I might, I was unable to escape from their rough hands.

They dragged me onto a tram, and that night I found myself locked in a room with sixteen or seventeen others, squatting with them on a *kang* not six feet wide. No talking was allowed. My belt and even my shoelaces had been taken from me, lest I attempt suicide. I used my shoes for a pillow, like all the other prisoners.

Who could sleep on a night like that? My heart was pounding wildly and I had no idea what might happen to me.

The guards talked loudly the whole night long, warming themselves at the stove. Some talked of the prostitutes they'd visited during the daytime, others of their luck at *yabao*, the game of gambling with dice under a dish. From their conversation I also learned how much they had got for catching each of us: five silver yuan.

This detention centre was in Baofang Lane, quite near the city's pork market, where pigs were butchered before daybreak. I listened to them shrieking and imagined the butchers (half naked, I was once told) attacking the poor animals with their sharp knives. I had eaten pork many times, but this was the first time I felt sympathy for the pigs.

Come dawn and at the blast of a whistle all seventeen of us had to get up. Half an hour was allowed for the latrine, after which we all silently squatted back down on the *kang* again for the rest of the day.

I discovered that there was a nine-year-old boy among us political prisoners. He smiled at me and soon we were friends. For talking to him I got a whipping, but on the sly we managed to play the finger-guessing game of 'stone, scissors, paper' anyway.

We were having so much fun that it seemed to make the older prisoners even more depressed.

One of them I still remember well. He was a middle-aged man with whiskers. Later I learned that he was a well-known scholar who had studied economics in Paris for eight years. He and his wife returned to China with their newborn baby, hoping to serve their country with the help of what they had learned abroad. But when they landed at Tianjin a couple of mildly radical books were discovered in their trunks and they were immediately arrested. They were sent to separate prisons and the man had no idea how his wife and baby were faring.

Every day we just sat and watched the shadows that fell across our paper window move from one end of it to the other. We were waiting to be tried. We wanted a chance to defend ourselves, to tell our own tales, and to find out where they meant to send us.

But nothing would happen all day long.

We all started making wild guesses. Some said we might be paraded through the streets and then shot, or perhaps just be shot without ceremony in the back yard at midnight. Others said we'd be chained together and marched over to police headquarters for torturing.

One night I was summoned at midnight.

'What's your name?'

The man who had spoken was the middle one of three. He wore

a big black beard,, like the King of Hell. The ones on either side seemed to be his assistants.

'My name is . . .' It was a big, dark room. Suddenly I shuddered.

'Speak up little boy. Confess and we'll let you go.'

I told them that according to the Bible I had sinned, but then so had everybody.

'I'm not really guilty. I don't know anything.'

'You don't know? Is that so?' he said leaning forward. 'In that case, you're going to get beaten until your memory improves.'

But I really had nothing to tell. Even though they whipped me I couldn't invent something.

After that they dragged me back to my cell. My back was so bruised that I could hardly crawl up on the *kang*. When I tried to lie down, hoping for a short respite, I felt the lash of the whip again.

I couldn't help sobbing.

I was questioned three times in all, always by the same three interrogators. The chief, in the middle, liked to try to intimidate me. 'Let's shoot this little runt!' he'd mutter. One of the assistants took notes all the time. The other pretended to be on my side. He smiled and told me 'I have a kid just your age. I wouldn't want him to die like you.' They wanted to know who was directing me, who was my superior.

My political consciousness was in fact quite vague, but I could count: Yu and Li were my big brothers and the sacrifice of one person was better than that of three. I was guided simply by a traditional sense of loyalty. I'd rather die than hand them over. I doggedly insisted that I knew only the pastors in the church and the teachers in the school. I was a devout Christian who had only organised a Bible study class. I tried to prove it to them by reciting one long passage after another from the Good Book.

On the third day, just as I was repeating what a devout Christian I was, the chief interrogator produced a mimeographed booklet he said had been found during a search of another school. It seemed to be a list of all the members of the Communist Youth in Peking (or maybe just of the East City area), with names, ages, native places, and even brief appraisals of them. My name was of course on the list. At the sight of it, I was stupefied. Inwardly I blamed the organisation for having let the list fall into enemy hands, indeed for having printed such a list in the first place, but now that I think about it, the list might not have been genuine.

Naturally I still insisted I was just a pious Christian and denied having joined anything. So they kicked me a few more times and took me back to the cell.

Back on the *kang*, the littlest political criminal wanted me to play games with him again, but I couldn't concentrate any more. I kept worrying about whether letters from my committee had fallen into their hands. If they had, what had I written in them, and how could I explain it?

At night we had to sleep on our sides; there was no room to turn over. I was far too preoccupied to sleep, anyway. I overheard the guards by the stove saying we would soon be sent under guard to Swallows Alley, by the Drum Tower. 'Then they'll get to meet their maker!' I began to wonder how they'd escort us – all in one chain gang, or in groups? Would any of my classmates see me along the way? For the first time in my life death was real and I had trouble facing it. I tried to recall passages I had read in *Neo-Heroism* and to instil in myself a martyr's courage. But I also felt regret for having to die so young, before I could repay my mother for her suffering on my behalf. Two days later I was still working out the possibilities in my mind. None of them was good.

I was summoned to the interrogation room again. I had thought I was on my way to Swallows Alley for sure, but instead I saw the principal of Truth Hall, Mr William Gleysteen, talking to the superintendent. He had come to bail me out. The conditions, laid down by the superintendent in my presence, were that I was to be under house arrest at the school (I couldn't leave the grounds), subject to further interrogation if summoned, and barred from participation in all political activities.

Later I learned that my Little Cousin Number Six had chanced to see me being forced onto the tram by the undercover men. He ran to tell Elder Cousin Number Four, and his American wife, Anna, who rushed to the school and pleaded with the principal to save me, stressing that I was an orphan and the sole issue of the eldest branch of the family.

My departure from the detention centre was also my first ride in a motor car. Once we were outside, the principal asked me if I knew why I had been arrested and I told him I was a socialist. Surprisingly he did not reproach me but only said, 'You're too young for politics. Why not leave it alone for a few more years?'

During the period of my house arrest in the school grounds, my American relative came with some fellow church members to see me nearly every Sunday. They would sing hymns, and then pray for me. In their prayers they referred to me as a lamb who had strayed, but who was forgiven and spared by God. This failed to win me over. There was an even younger lamb still in the detention centre. Why had God not saved him? Clearly I had been saved simply because I had a foreign relative who could appeal to a foreign principal.

My release left me with feelings of guilt and I tried to console myself by remembering that my release had been arranged without my consent and not because I had broken or confessed during the interrogations.

My house arrest did not last long. June 1928 saw great changes in Peking. The National Revolutionary Army [the forces of the Kuomintang and its allies] captured the ancient city, and the warlord Zhang Zuolin was forced back into his old Manchurian base, where he was ultimately blown up in his own private railway car, by Japanese army officers.

Now the streets of Peking were filled with banners saying 'Down with the Great Powers', 'Abolish the Unequal Treaties', and 'Celebrate the Success of the Northern Expedition of the National Revolutionary Army'. The principal and dean of Truth Hall now smiled when they met me, and my classmates dared to speak to me. Sadly, this would prove to be only the first in a succession of drastic public re-evaluations of me.

Originally the only student organisation allowed in missionary schools had been the YMCA, which was run by converts, a minority of the students. Non-Christians in the student body had always resented this. When the revolutionary army reached Peking, each missionary school was ordered to establish its own student committee, and Truth Hall was of course no exception. Suddenly I was a hero: elected chairman of the student committee by acclamation, and editor-in-chief of the school magazine. As such, I was able to attend a great celebratory outdoor meeting in Nankou. On the dais were Chiang Kai-shek and his warlord allies of the time, Yan Xishan, Li Zongren and Feng Yuxiang. I was very excited. I really believed that the revolution had succeeded: that China, antiquated, feudal and divided as she was, had in the twinkling of an eye become a united and progressive democratic nation.

There was a great night-time procession, in which we all marched in the streets carrying lanterns. We paraded our lights through all the old government quarters, through Beihai and Zhongnanhai down to the Gate of Heavenly Peace, shouting slogans until we lost our voices.

The school principal was convinced that China had turned Red. For safety's sake, he fled with his family to Beidaihe and handed over the school administration to the stout old dean (a Chinese we all called Fatso).

I went back to my work at the mimeograph machine in the school office. One day the portly acting principal came up to me all smiles and asked me to put down my work for a moment. He gave me a heart-to-heart talk. Evidently he wanted me, the new head of the student body, firmly on the side of the school administration.

'Your Elder Cousin Number Four is a graduate of Cheeloo University,' he reminded me. 'If you watch your step, later on we can recommend your admission there, too. After that, who knows, maybe you'll go on to America the way I did.'

At first I found myself intrigued. But then he asked me to resist student pressures to disband the YMCA. He warned me against consorting with the wrong people and ended on a threatening note: 'Don't fool yourself that everything has changed now.'

Our student committee held a big meeting. Although I knew everybody there, since they were my classmates, it was the first meeting I'd ever chaired. Some of them gave impassioned speeches denouncing the YMCA as simply a mouthpiece of the school administration and biased against the poorer students. There was a motion to disband the organisation and let our own student committee take over its office on the school grounds. When this motion was put to a vote, every hand in the hall went up.

That evening I wrote a letter to a friend of mine, Zhao Cheng, detailing all that had happened that day. Zhao was a Chinese from Vietnam who'd been at Truth Hall and had just been admitted to Yanjing University. In a flash of anger at the end, I wrote: 'Fatso wants to buy me off, but I'll never give in.'

Sometimes people are incredibly naive. I had absolutely no sense of how dangerous I had become in the eyes of the school administration. Since I was no longer under house arrest it never occurred to me that I might still be under surveillance. In the past I'd never bought stamps for myself. To mail a letter, I'd simply sealed it and handed it through the window to the school porter with two cents for postage. And that's what I did with my letter to Zhao.

It wasn't long before I found myself called into the principal's office. The moment I walked in I could see that the acting principal's fat face was livid with rage. On his desk lay the letter I'd sent off to Zhao – ripped open.

'The school gave you the opportunity to study and pay us back through work. Is this how you reward us?'

'What right have you to open other people's mail?' I retorted, feeling very self-righteous.

'I can not only read your mail, I can expel you,' he sneered. Then he went on about how I didn't know what was good for me.

I had wrongly assessed the situation. Believing that the national revolution had really succeeded, I had assumed that everybody now had rights as citizens. I told him I would sue him.

'Fine, fine – go to it.' He pointed to the door. 'But first you've got to move yourself off school property.'

I was up the creek. Where would I sleep tonight? I no longer had a home at Elder Cousin Number Three's place. Biting my lip, I left the office.

By this time the stairs outside Fatso's office were crowded with students trying to listen in. On hearing that I was expelled, several boys who lived at home shouted 'Come to my house!' I discovered that I wasn't as alone as I had thought. 'OK, I'll stay with you,' I gratefully told a friend called Zhang who lived in Fragrant Cakes Lane.

I walked out of Truth Hall. The real world was a lot different from how I had imagined it. I was reminded of what the acting principal had told me: 'Don't fool yourself that everything has changed now.'

The old five-bar flag of the early Republic might be gone for good but, far from the country having turned Red, everything even touched with the colour was fair game for the secret police who still remained. Though I was absolutely determined to go to the municipal offices to plead my case, friends wiser than I persuaded me that I would just be setting myself up. The Kuomintang had apparently inherited the black list of the outgoing warlords, so I was in serious danger of arrest again.

Just then Zhao Cheng, the student to whom I had written the fatal letter, got a telegram telling him that his mother was seriously ill; he was about to leave for his ancestral home down south in Swatow and he generously offered to take me with him.

2

Into the Wider World
(1928–1939)

Before the age of eighteen I'd never ventured beyond the confines of metropolitan Peking, except for one autumn hike to the Great Wall. Now, all of a sudden, I was going off to China's south-eastern corner – to Swatow (Shantou), in Guangdong province. I had no idea what I'd do there. I was both curious and anxious about the future, but most of all I felt a strong urge simply to break out. The year was 1928.

Just before we departed, my classmate Zhao Cheng, the Vietnamese Chinese, noticed that I'd worn holes through the soles of my shoes. He presented me with a new pair that his family had bought for him. I was embarrassed to accept them. 'Come on, put them on,' he said. 'We Pekingese can't let the southerners look down on us.' Another classmate gave me a blue cotton gown. It was rather worn, but he had washed and starched it till it was neat and clean. After that, they went with me to the Eastern Railway Station. My friend Zhao was waiting for me at the station entrance. All my worldly property fitted into a blue cloth bundle.

Our journey started with a three-day train ride to Shanghai. When we got there, we put up in an inn near the Great Chime Clock to wait for the ship to Swatow. I'd read about Shanghai's foreign settlement, but now I saw it with my own eyes. I'd never seen so many tall buildings, or *any* as tall as this, for that matter. Some had domes and some had steeples; some were Victorian, others rococo. There were neon advertisements in all the colours of the rainbow and line after line of automobiles crawling down the river embankment road. Everywhere we went I saw the shop signs of foreign firms, from New York, Yokohama and Amsterdam, as if the shrewd merchants of all the world had gathered here. Foreign gunboats and merchant ships lay at anchor in the Huangpu

River. But there were no Chinese ships on this Chinese river, and the policemen patrolling the streets with their billyclubs were red-turbaned Sikhs.

We purchased two tickets for fourth-class berths on a Butterfield and Swire Line steamer plying the coastal ports that was moored beside a foreign warship. It would weigh anchor the next morning, and just now its deck was in utter chaos. Coolies in a long line carried trunks of merchandise on their backs down into the hold.

In the morning, as we emerged from the Huangpu River into the Yangtze at the Wusong estuary, I caught my first glimpse of the sea. I had had no idea that its horizon would be so broad and vast.

On the third day, flocks of seagulls began to circle over the prow of the boat. Land loomed in the distance. The steamer threaded its way between two islands and into the harbour; on the right bank was the city of Swatow. Hundreds of fishing boats were moored along the shoreline, some of them with little red flags flying from their masts.

When we went on shore, my friend found us temporary lodging in a little fruit shop. He then placed a long-distance call home, only to learn that his sick mother had already passed away. He set off immediately for his village, which was outside Chaoyang, to attend the funeral.

The fruit shop had just a one-bay street frontage. Business was conducted on the ground floor and the family lived upstairs, in a loft permeated with the sweet smell of the fruit. The proprietor was a middle-aged fellow with high cheekbones. He always held a gurgling water pipe and blew out white smoke between his words. For the first time it was brought home to me that China was divided not just by politics, but by language as well. Since he did not speak Mandarin he could only point at the wooden cot in the corridor that I must sleep on. Thus began a strange new life of communicating through motions and gestures. When it was time to eat he mimed raking food into his mouth with his two forefingers. But a lot of things in life can't be expressed through gestures. We just had to stare at each other, fretting and frustrated.

The fruit shop was off a little alley. Rickshaws and bicycles streamed by without cease, adding a constant clang of bells to the brisk clopping of wooden clogs. Sometimes a food pedlar would pass by, beating his clappers and shouting out his wares in a hoarse voice. Then, at about the hour when the lamps were lit, there came the clear and melodious sounds of a flute from an upstairs window. It made me homesick.

I longed for Peking and for my friends. I ached to return to the little streets and alleys of the neighbourhood by the Dongzhi Gate. Above all, I wanted to live with people who shared my language.

When my friend, Zhao Cheng, had finished with his mother's funeral arrangements, he returned to Swatow. I felt as if I'd found a long-lost relative. But he'd taken me away from Peking without any thought for the future and now he had to find some work for me.

Just like a salesman, he took me all over the city, trying to unload me. One shop actually did need an accountant. But they lost interest when they learned that I couldn't speak a word of the local dialect.

Later my friend learned that a Baptist mission school across the bay at Jiaoshi was looking for a Mandarin instructor. He got someone to recommend me to them. The school was delighted to hear that I had just come from Peking, the home of standard Mandarin. Then they asked about my credentials, indicating that they hoped I had at least graduated from a technical school. My friend bragged that I had taken the special training course in Chinese at Peking's Yanjing (Yen-ching) University – which was in reality *his* university. So I got the position by passing myself off as a Yanjing graduate.

Thus I moved to a school in a fertile valley in the Wugongling (Centipede Hills) and became a twenty-five-dollar-a-month Mandarin instructor. And it was there that I experienced my first love – a very sweet but, in the end, a very tragic passion.

When I had read about love at the Beixin Book Company, as in *The Sorrows of Young Werther*, some of the descriptions and the lines of dialogue had set me to quivering. But I'd never had any intimate contact with the opposite sex. One Christmas, admittedly, in a skit performed at Mercy Hall, the girls' school, I'd been bowled over by a little girl playing the part of an angel, but I had never even found out her name.

The school where I now worked was divided into a primary school and a junior middle school. I taught twenty-odd classes a week, from seventh grade to twelfth; some of the students were older than I was. We used Y R Chao's (Zhao Yuanren's) *Mandarin Primer*, and to lighten the classes and even get the students actually to like Mandarin, I filled out the time with some little songs I selected from a series of children's operas by Li Jinhui.

In the beginning, some of the students weren't too keen on studying another kind of Chinese. They would have preferred to learn Cantonese, for it would be of more practical value to them in their future professions. But those little songs soon helped me to overcome this prejudice.

When the students' indifference towards Mandarin began to change, I helped them organise a Celestial Voice Troupe, the purpose of which was to promote the use of the language. And it was during one of the troupe's performances that I began to feel a decidedly unteacherly affection for one of the girl students, Hsiao Shuwen.

And then, at the celebration following the successful performance, one by one the students came forward to sing their own song, do a dance, or tell a joke, to entertain the others. It was almost over when someone insisted that I perform something, too. I had nothing prepared, so I sang a song that Venerable Elder Sister had taught me, about the tragic life of an orphan. I remember that there was a hazy moon that night; the party was held on the school lawn. And before I got to the end, I could hear sobbing. It was Hsiao Shuwen. Later I learned that she was as good as an orphan, too. When her father, a doctor of traditional herbal medicine, took a new wife after his first wife died, the family couldn't afford to continue her schooling past primary school, so she was sent to be a salesgirl in a department store. She was only in school now because one day the former principal of her primary school happened to go by the shop, and when he spotted her there he insisted on paying her way through junior high.

It was our common misfortune that drew us together. We quickly began to feel an affection for each other based on mutual commiseration. Guangdong custom strictly forbade marriage between boys and girls of the same family name, so our common name became our camouflage. We would steal out to the beach for a stroll under the moonlight, there to share our innermost feelings. After finding a lonely spot among the boulders at the foot of the hills, we would sit on a stone to hug and kiss. Girls often go barefoot in South China. I touched her soft, white foot once and said, 'What a pity, northern girls always keep this beautiful part of the body tightly wrapped up.' Pretending to be annoyed, she answered, 'They have to, with men like you around.'

Often we stared down at the steamboats moored in the harbour, dreaming that one day we could board one and sail far, far away into the South Seas – for that was our idea of paradise.

Westerners call love 'the tender trap', 'the wisdom of fools'. To me it was a delicious honey-coated fruit, but one that was bitter inside. I quickly came to the bitter part.

This began with my departure. By June, our strolls on the beach were no longer so carefree. I *had* to leave, for I couldn't continue teaching with false credentials. I felt guilty and was constantly afraid of being exposed. Colleagues on the faculty often cross-examined me about my supposed time at Yanjing. One day a student in the very course I'd claimed to have graduated from returned home from Peking. My colleagues informed me excitedly that I could meet him at the dining table at noon. I broke out into a cold sweat. In the end I had to pretend that I'd come down with an acute illness; I went hungry that day.

Meanwhile, in the summer of 1929 I had decided to return to Peking and actually enter that class, and so make good the lie. This would of course also give me genuine qualifications to work as a teacher, and since for her part Shuwen had decided to transfer to Hanshan Normal University in nearby Chaoyang, so that she too could become a teacher, we would then be able to go to South East Asia together.

But a gaping monster was lying in wait, ready to gobble her up. The school principal who had paid her tuition was not a philanthropist after all – he had planned to take her for his concubine all along. When I got back to Peking, I passed the entrance examinations for the special course for Chinese teachers, and our dreams seemed to be coming true. But, at the principal's direction, all of my letters to Shuwen were confiscated before she got them. He would not allow her to write to me, either.

In the early summer of 1930, I realised that something was wrong. I put aside my studies in Peking, borrowed money for the boat ticket, and returned alone to Swatow. After combing the nearby countryside, I found her teaching in a village school. The principal was now putting pressure on her not only as a suitor but also as a creditor. I insisted on taking her luggage back to Swatow and there I bought boat tickets for two, so that we could go north together.

But on the morning we were to board she disappeared. She left me only a short letter, telling me to go without her. Believing that she no longer loved me, I obeyed her. But I was very bitter – so much so that in 1937, when I wrote my autobiographical novel *Meng zhi gu (Valley of Dreams)* its ending made her out to be a callous, hard-hearted woman.

Then, half a century later, in February 1987 when I passed through Swatow on my way back from a lecture tour at the Chinese University of Hong Kong, I finally learned the truth: the jealous principal had threatened her with my death. 'If you two board the boat together,' he'd told her, 'I'll kill that young fool.' He was a powerful man in those parts, and had in fact made arrangements to do me in on the docks that day if Shuwen was with me. So she had stayed away, and had written that seemingly heartless letter only to save my life. My novel wronged her. She had abandoned me only out of love.

I soon found the special course at Yanjing University not to my taste. One needed a firm foundation in the Chinese classics to study epigraphy, phonology, and the history of ancient literary criticism, and I had very little.

That year I was drawn to modern literature instead. The lecturer was a visiting professor from Qinghua University, Yang Zhensheng, who had been a trailblazer in the May Fourth movement, as author of the novel *Yujun*. He spoke on Chinese literature during the first term, and on foreign literature in the second. He was quite tall, and he spoke very slowly and methodically. Perhaps because he had specialised in educational psychology when he studied abroad, his lectures were fascinating. It was from him that I got my first sketchy impressions of Chinese literature since the May Fourth movement. He also inspired me to read Tolstoy, Turgenev, and Chekhov, as well as Thomas Hardy.

I attended another class in the English department on 'The English Novel'. There Grace Boynton proved to be another inspirational teacher. She concentrated on the Victorian novelists – George Eliot, the Brontë sisters, and Dickens – but also introduced modernists like James Joyce and Virginia Woolf.

Yanjing University had a student welfare committee, one of the purposes of which was to find spare time jobs for poor students. I was one of them. The rule was that you were paid twenty-five cents an hour, regardless of the nature of the work.

I mowed the lawn around the professors' residences and babysat for three little Scottish children. Sometimes I was also a guide for visiting foreigners, such as the American writer John Phillips Marquand. But my most interesting work, which I qualified for as a Pekingese, was teaching Chinese as a foreign language. I taught the Czech Sinologist Jaroslav Průšek and J W N Munthe, the Scandinavian wife of the British police chief in Peking at that time, who went on to write respectively books about Chinese literature and a biography of the Jiaqing Emperor. I also worked with a young American named William Allen.

I first met Allen as his Chinese instructor. He was twenty-four or twenty-five, and on a round-the-world trip financed by his mother. Once in China he fell in love with our ancient nation. After class I would often tell him what I had learned that day from Professor Yang about China's New Literature movement. The subject began to excite him. Shanghai in those days put out a very successful English journal called *Millard's Review of the Far East*, so he decided to sink all his remaining money in founding a new rival journal called *China in Brief*. I was put in charge of the contemporary Chinese literature section, and selected excerpts from the works of writers such as Lu Xun, Mao Dun, Guo Moruo, Wen Yiduo and Yu Dafu. One issue was specially devoted to Shen Congwen, the great humanitarian satirical author, and included a long interview with him.

In those days the foreigners in Peking were mostly diplomats or missionaries. Their interests ran mainly to golf and horse racing; none cared a fig about modern Chinese literature. So the journal only lasted for eight issues, by which time Allen had used up all his money. He had to go home without completing his trip around the globe.

While taking the short course for teachers of Chinese at Yanjing University, I met Yang Gang (then named Yang Bin), a young woman majoring in English who was to have a significant influence on my life. We met at a poetry-reading meeting in Professor Boynton's house. Grace Boynton, who was from New England, convened one of these meetings every Friday. She would sit on a sofa by the fireplace, a colourful scarf thrown across her thin shoulders, and recite Victorian poetry (such as Tennyson's) in her high, piercing voice. Sometimes when she got tired, she would call on a student to continue the reading.

Yang Gang, the daughter of a big landlord, had entered the Communist Party in 1928, but that had not affected her love of English romantic poetry. She always sat at Grace Boynton's side, sometimes continuing her readings and sometimes using her newly-acquired materialist viewpoint to question the professor's interpretations.

As a rule I cowered in a far corner, listening eagerly but not daring to chip in, and it was Yang Gang who took the initiative in getting to know me when she learned that I had been arrested back in 1926 for work on behalf of the Communist Youth. I lived in the second men's dormitory and she lived in the third courtyard of the girls' school. She wrote me more than a hundred letters, hoping to lead me back onto the revolutionary path. Each began by addressing me as 'Younger Brother' and then proceeded to propagate some revolutionary truth or other.

In those days I wanted only to sail down to the South Seas and lead a bohemian life. My enthusiasm for revolution had long since cooled. Yang Gang earnestly lent me one book after another, full of the theories of Lunacharsky and Plekhanov and such, but no matter how I forced myself, I just could not get through them.

Once as we were strolling by the ruins of the Yuanmingyuan palace, she took me to task: 'These theories are so important. Why won't you read them? These aren't just any old books, these are the revolutionary truth!'

I objected that the sentences in the translations were too long, and the content was too abstruse. Pretentiously, I said, 'Theory, theory . . . it's like a map – it's no substitute for actually going there. I want to experience this strange and complicated world for myself! I want to know life at first hand.'

'So you're simply going to blunder about? You're not going to read a map first?' she asked.

'You can travel without a map. It's much more interesting and exciting without one.'

'Be careful not to fall into an abyss,' she warned me, 'or get lost in a forest. You may be eaten by a tiger.'

How cruel the class struggle can be. That revolutionary who carried a map with her all her life was driven to commit suicide in October 1957.

Besides revolution, however, I often discussed literature with Yang Gang. And when, in 1930, I told her I wanted to take regular college courses and start my studies all over again, she helped me enter Furen University. A cousin of hers was head registrar there.

Furen was a Roman Catholic university, newly established by American Benedictine fathers. I majored in English. The chair of the department was a short, fat, bespectacled Irish-American priest who came from the American Midwest. He was extremely learned and he wrote very well. Often he invited me over in the evening to hear love poems he'd written himself. He cried to himself as he read them. He was sensitive and yet not very well-balanced. Often he would get extremely angry for no particular reason. But we got on, and soon he asked me to be his assistant, to help him grade examination papers.

He also encouraged me to translate some modern Chinese literature for the English-language *Furen Magazine*. Altogether I translated and published three plays: *Wang Zhaojun* by Guo Moruo, *The Tragedy on the Lake* by Tian Han and *The Artist* by Xiong Foxi. At his urging, I did a lot of reading of Irish-American authors, particularly Eugene O'Neill – and the stories about his wanderings in the Caribbean only intensified my desire to escape to the South Sea islands.

Since I was now assistant to the department head and occasionally taught Chinese to foreigners, I was fairly well off financially. I was crazy about Hollywood films. Some Sundays I would bicycle to three different movie houses and see three different films in one day. I watched some of them five or six times, like *The Love Parade* with Jeanette MacDonald and Maurice Chevalier. I also bought sheet music for the title songs, so as to be able to play them on the harmonica, and I memorised many of the wittier lines of dialogue. I can still recite some of them today.

In the summer of 1932, my Yanjing classmate Lin Guande planned to return to Fuzhou in the south, to be dean of a mission high school. He invited me to join the teaching staff, but I said no. Then, a few days later, the department head flew into one of his inexplicable rages. I immediately telephoned my friend Lin to say that I would join him after all. When I told the department head, he could not stop apologising. He wanted me to stay. But I had made up my mind.

★ ★ ★

This was the third time I had left Peking for the south-east. When the steamer reached Mawei, we boarded a barge to thread through the 'Ninety-Nine Turns' of the Min River. Large ships were unable to make it up to Fuzhou, perhaps because of the Ninety-Nine Turns. Of all the nation's coastal cities, Fuzhou was the most Chinese-looking. By the same token it was dirty and disorderly, but it offered picturesque and romantic views of green hills and clear blue waters. The Anglo-Chinese (Ying Hua) College, a high school run by the American Methodist Church across from Nantai on Cangqian Mountain, was set in delightful scenery, bordering the beautiful waters of the River Min.

There I became a Mandarin teacher again.

At the faculty meeting the first day of class, two colleagues quietly showed me scars on their heads and necks. They advised me not to be too harsh in grading the students, lest I suffer similar violence myself. I thanked them for the warning, but it did not scare me. During the first term I failed several of my students.

The school had very strict rules. Sunday (the Lord's Day) was reserved for silent prayer. Ball playing was forbidden. Being a newcomer, I was unaware of this regulation. So one Sunday I got up a basketball game with a group of students about my age. Just as we were dashing about and struggling for the ball, a pastor suddenly appeared. He glared at me and insisted on taking the ball away. The students told me that if I, a teacher newly arrived from the north, hadn't been there, they would have been severely punished.

One day I met an American woman teacher in the faculty lounge. Her face was unusually flushed, so I asked her what was the matter.

She said that she had asked her students in class, 'Am I your teacher?' 'Yes!' they all yelled in unison. But when she followed up with the question, 'Am I your friend?' they all called out 'No.'

She asked me, 'In North China, would the students give the same answer?'

'Yes,' I said. 'According to the Confucian conception, to call a teacher a friend is most improper and irreverent, for the teacher is supposed to be one generation above, an elder, while the student is only a junior.'

She asked again, 'Then parents and children can't be friends, either?'

'Correct,' I said, with a nod.

She went away, still upset.

Fuzhou left me with many beautiful memories. I often went at dusk to stroll among the banyan trees. Wildflowers were everywhere, very beautiful. Most unforgettable was a camping trip out on the Luohan Ridge of Mount Gu. Five of us went, taking along a tent, cooking utensils, and Fuzhou's special dry noodles. Below the ridge flowed the River Min. We spent six nights under the moonlight. One fellow strummed the guitar; I was just learning to play tunes on the musical saw. We gathered firewood and boiled our noodles, then ate and sang our hearts out as we leaned against the rugged crags.

During the winter vacation, I took a boat to Swatow to visit friends. It was a cargo ship and it tied up for several hours in Amoy for loading. I went ashore to take a look around. I entered a park where I found a maze fashioned from thickly planted pine trees. After taking a few turns inside, I couldn't find my way out again. For passers-by looking down from a roadway above, it must have been good entertainment to see me keep running into walls, but the time of the ship's departure was getting nearer and nearer. Finally a kindly person pointed out a gap between the pines where I could crawl out. It was another entry for my growing list of close calls.

When school ended for the summer, I handed in my resignation and again bought a ticket on a ship to return north. Transferring from Furen to Yanjing, I became a third-year student in the department of journalism. Becoming a journalist was entirely my own idea. I thought that journalism would broaden my perspective on life. And why go on studying English when I wanted to write in my own language?

In those days the Yanjing journalism department was a branch of the University of Missouri School of Journalism. Vernon Nash, the chairman, and several of the other professors were straight from Missouri. Edgar Snow, future author of *Red Star Over China*, was one of them.

In 1928, Edgar Snow came as a young man to China from Kansas City, planning to stay just six weeks. While on a trip to the great Chinese North West he learned that five million people had died from a drought there. He saw China's backwardness, but he also saw her exciting potential for progress, so he changed his mind and decided to stay – for thirteen years, as it turned out. And for two of those years, while serving as a foreign correspondent in China, he also taught in the Yanjing University journalism department. Fortunately that coincided with my last two years in that college.

Right from the very first day of class he seemed different from the others. He told us, with a grin, 'I've come not to teach, but to learn.' On getting to know him I discovered that he truly wanted to get to know the reality of China through personal contacts with its people.

Most foreigners in China in those days, whether diplomats, businessmen, or missionaries, were supporters of the old order. Perhaps that was because it was in their personal interest. But there were rebels among them, and Snow was one of them. His emphasis was not on exposing the misdeeds of the great European powers in China. Instead he gave his sympathy and support to the Chinese people's own efforts to cast off their backwardness. And his interest in China was not limited to politics and the economy. He quickly got to know something about China's New Literature movement.

Soon after we were introduced, he learned that in 1930 William Allen and I had edited *China in Brief*. He wanted to translate some works by modern Chinese authors and for me to help him as I had helped William Allen. I noticed that he didn't care for some of the slick and fashionable stories that were being printed in *Xiandai* (*Les Contemporains*, a journal devoted to modernism). He wanted realistic stories that exposed and condemned society.

I would translate the piece into English and Snow would polish it. Sometimes he would simply retype it and the text would be ready for the press. Often I stood behind him to watch him revise my drafts. It was more educational than any class in translation.

When I transferred to Yanjing in 1933, I started writing short stories in my time outside of class. 'Can' (Silkworms) was my first story. Shen Congwen published it in the Literature Supplement he edited for the Tianjin *Dagongbao*, a liberal, non-partisan daily newspaper. After that, I wrote one or two pieces every month. Later other literary journals published my stories one after another. That's how I became a writer.

To simplify things, literary historians often divide Chinese authors of the 1930s into the Peking School and the Shanghai School. In fact the distinction between the two was blurred once Ba

Jin, Zheng Zhenduo and Jin Yi came north. I felt myself lucky to have begun my literary career at a time when the Peking and Shanghai schools had merged their differences in the common goal of resisting Japan.

I met Ba Jin in 1933 when he was living at Yanjing University (today, Peking University) with Xia Yun in the Weixiuyuan, one of the many former gardens on the campus site that used to belong to the nobility. That was three years after I met Shen Congwen. I admired Shen Congwen's erudition and his prose style, and he gave me much guidance and support as I became a writer. Ba Jin's influence on me was broader. I was constantly encouraged and inspired by his concern for the state of the universe and the fate of humankind, his breadth of vision, and the way he spoke directly to his readers with his soul, instead of using flowery words. During the fifty-five years of our friendship, Ba Jin has always treated me lovingly and protectively, as if he were my elder brother. When I was in political trouble, he never disowned me.

Edgar Snow took an interest in my writing career, too. When he heard that I had written a short story called 'The Conversion' about the Salvation Army, he immediately had it translated for *Living China*. And when the book came out, he told me that American critics had taken special note of my piece, since it examined Chinese reactions to the pressures of Western culture.

Sometimes Snow published these translations in *Asia* magazine. Once he tried to give me an envelope stuffed with bank notes, saying that it was my share of the royalties. I refused to take it. I told him that I'd gained much more working for him than I'd given. When I graduated in July 1935, he gave me a leather suitcase bulging with English books by famous British and American authors, including the complete works of George Bernard Shaw. It was the first library I'd ever possessed. In 1937 I left them in the house of a friend who lived in the French concession at Hankou. They were of course destroyed during the war.

Besides writing fiction, during the summer vacation of 1933 I took a trip on the Peking-Suiyuan Railway. My friend Meng Yangxian was a freight handler on the line. Often he had to ride on the train to guard the cargo, so he took me along too. We rode in the caboose. The train stopped for a day or two at the big stations. In those days opium was grown everywhere, and the cities were filled with prostitutes. I published my first piece of reportage literature, *Ping Sui suoji (Notes from the Peking-Suiyuan Line)*, based on my observations and experiences during that summer.

By chance, that piece brought me an opportunity to meet with the man who ruled Inner Mongolia, the land of my ancestors. General Fu Zuoyi, having read my *Notes*, asked my teacher in the department of journalism, Wu Wenzao, to set up a meeting between us. Perhaps as a gesture of respect, General Fu offered me a minor official post. But it was precisely that courtesy which scared me away. I had long ago decided never to become a bureaucrat.

On 9 December 1935, a vast student movement erupted in Peking to protest against Japan's new incursions in North China. Japan wanted to establish another puppet regime like Manchukuo. In fact they already had Eastern Hebei province well in hand. Edgar Snow and his wife Helen took an active part in the demonstration, marching at the head of the parade. I had already graduated and was working in Tianjin at the time. When I hastened back to Peking the next day, I found that the movement had been suppressed by the government. I went with the Snows to the hospitals to comfort the wounded students. The Chinese authorities tried to suppress all news of the incident, but the Snows made the true facts known to the whole world.

Edgar Snow's excellence as a reporter lay in his dissatisfaction with official reports and surface statistics. He saw through to the real essence of things, to the mind and the will of the people. He knew what they were for and what they were against.

On 28 January 1932, when the Nineteenth Route Army resisted the Japanese incursion in Shanghai, he had seen that the Chinese people would be invincible if only they were united in the defence of their country. As early as 6 June 1936, he predicted, in the *Saturday Evening Post*, that Japan in China would 'shortly provoke an effort of resistance that will astound the world'. In 1948, when Yugoslavia declared its independence of Moscow and the Chinese Communists joined in the chorus denouncing Tito, Snow wrote on 18 December in the same magazine that China had been the first to spurn direction from Moscow. And on 9 April 1949, he surmised that 'in the long run the Chinese Communist Party probably cannot and will not subordinate the national interests of China to the interests of the Kremlin'. For that, he could not revisit China until 1960, when the break had actually occurred.

I kept up my contact with the Snows after I graduated from Yanjing and went to work for the *Dagongbao*. In the spring of 1936 I went to interview General Feng Yuxiang, who was known as 'The Christian General'. Chiang Kai-shek, then leader of the Northern Expeditionary Force that had overthrown the warlords of the north, had summoned him down from his retirement on Mount Tai to become vice chairman of the Military Affairs Commission in Nanking. But Feng opposed Chiang's policy of dealing with inner dissent before resisting outer aggression – in other words, suppressing the communists before fighting the Japanese. During our interview the general commended the December Ninth student movement, calling for the immediate release of the imprisoned student leaders. He also spoke of his support for writing Chinese with the Roman alphabet instead of traditional characters.

I transcribed the interview that very night and mailed it back to Tianjin. I had been used to having my despatches printed as written, but this one was heavily censored. The words in support of the students were deleted and really all that was left was the part about romanising the Chinese language. I was furious.

My last meeting with Edgar Snow was in Paris in 1944, just after the city had been liberated. We were both war correspondents at the time. As we chatted in a hotel bar – a table away from Hemingway – he told me how much he missed China and wished that it could become a democratic country after the war.

It was no accident that I went to work for the *Dagongbao*. My first short story had been published in that paper, in October 1933, and my 1933 travelogue, *Notes from the Peking-Suiyuan Line*, was published in a magazine printed by the same parent news company in Tianjin. The *Dagongbao* was known in the thirties and forties as the *Manchester Guardian* of China. I joined its staff in July 1935, immediately after graduation, and served the paper for fifteen years, counting the five years in England when I was a part-time correspondent. The paper thus allowed me to realise many of my dreams, the most important of which was to see the country and have a wide experience of human life, as fuel for my writing. To me journalism was always a means, never an end. Practically all serious Chinese writers in those days had to have another job to earn their living. I preferred being a journalist in Tianjin to teaching English in a high school or serving as a petty official.

It was my first time in that North China port city. The bustling crowds and chaos outside Tianjin station were about the same as those outside Peking Station. But the streets were much narrower, and the people talked much louder.

My rickshaw rounded the corner and we were in the British concession. Immediately everything was neater and cleaner. But, as in Shanghai, Sikh policemen in red turbans and full beards patrolled the street corners. Another turn and we were in the Japanese concession. Its narrow alleys were filled with signs bearing the trade names of prostitutes. One more turn and we were in the French concession. The rickshaw drew up outside number 30, an undistinguished two-storey grey brick building, not even set back from the street. I raised my head and saw a sign that read *Tianjin Dagongbao*.

I'd imagined that the paper would be housed in a magnificent office block: surely such a great paper did not function in such lowly surroundings. The editorial office was up on the first floor, just one big long room, with three-drawer desks arranged in five continuous rows. The two rows closest to the door handled major news and editorials; next was the row for international news; then the metropolitan section. The supplements, sports page and so forth took up the last row and were at the end of the paper – hence they were derogatorily called the *bao pigu*, the paper's arse. Proofreaders and cable decoders were crowded into the corners.

Manager Hu Lin introduced me to the staff. It was the afternoon, so the day staff were all present and the night shift was beginning to show up. We all shook hands and took each other's measure.

The editorial offices at that time were thick with smoke and coal dust, for they were right across from the French concession's electricity generator. They also reeked with the smell of printing presses. Having just come from the pure, green scenery by the banks of Weiming Lake on the Yanjing campus, I had a hard time adjusting to my new environment.

The newspaper's dormitory rooms were square, with a bed in each corner and one shared writing desk in the middle. I met my roommates that evening. Each of us was from a different university: Nankai, Qinghua, Peking and my own Yanjing. Being all about the same age and having similar backgrounds, we got along well enough. They explained the general structure of the publishing house to me: Wu Dingchang, the final boss, had just left his job to take up a post with the Nationalist government in Nanking as Minister of Industry and Commerce. They had only seen him once. That left Hu Lin and Zhang Jiluan. Hu was the general manager while Zhang was the chief editor, although divisions of labour were not rigid: the managers sometimes wrote editorials and the editors occasionally enquired into business affairs. The editorial staff appeared to be divided into a Hu clique and a Zhang clique, but my roommates tried to stay above such matters. They didn't go to office birthday parties or play mah-jong with the boys. I agreed completely with their attitude. In effect we became our own clique – the collegiate clique.

Just before dawn I was startled awake by a roar that set my plank bed shaking. Thinking that there was an earthquake, I jumped up and shook awake the Peking University roommate who was sleeping across from me.

'They're only starting up the presses downstairs to run off the papers,' he mumbled, rubbing his eyes and drifting back to sleep.

I was of course relieved to learn that it was not an earthquake, but it occurred to me that since I worked for a daily paper, the presses would be rolling like this in the small hours of every morning. Eventually I got used to the noise by imagining myself to be on an ocean voyage, travelling in steerage.

On assuming editorship of my domain, the 'Little Public Garden', a section aimed at ordinary townspeople, and looking at the pile of manuscripts on my desk, I was immediately confronted with a dilemma. I only now realised that the supplement was devoted to traditional art forms such as comic dialogues, folk stories and articles about Peking opera librettos. I neither understood such things nor was in the least interested in them. When Mr Hu asked me how I was coming along, I truthfully told him that I feared that I was not the right person for this particular supplement.

I still remember the words he used to set me straight:

'If you think you're not right for it then you're just the man. I myself find that supplement horribly old-fashioned. The *Dagong-bao* isn't in print just for old codgers who raise birds in cages to show each other in the park. I wanted you on board so you could sit down and wholly remake it. Any changes you come up with are fine with me. I'll support you.'

That really excited me. But then I remembered how many of

these geriatric manuscripts were already accepted and waiting to be printed. I asked him what to do.

'There's always got to be a transition between the new and the old,' he said. 'Tell you what, print them at the bottom where they won't be noticed. And while you're publishing them, you can announce your new editorial policy. When people see that there's a new editor and that changes are in store, the old-style pieces will stop coming.'

Mr Hu was a bold entrepreneur, and he had found himself an impetuous youth – me, still in my twenties.

It wasn't that easy to turn a supplement for old fogies into one for young people. I wanted to make the 'Little Public Garden' into a garden for literary youth, yet I could not be too lax in my standards. Therefore, in a letter 'To Writers', I first expressed my full understanding of the submitters' predicament, as one who had been there myself. Then I discussed my standards of selection: 'Writing is not like dry goods; there are no fixed measures for it . .

But the fact that you can't measure it out doesn't mean that anything goes. A good piece of writing is like any good work of art. You know it when you see it. Like porcelain from a famous factory, good writing has a lustre: perhaps from the penetrating quality of its thought, or the boldness of its imagination, or the dazzle of its language.'

A lot of manuscripts were submitted after the changing of the guard. Several dozen arrived daily, but most of them were at the level of high-school compositions. Some were not even coherent. I grew anxious as I read on. I bluntly stated that articles submitted must achieve a certain level of literariness: 'Literature is clearly something quite different from journalism. The "Little Public Garden" is not the place to send your notes on your travels. If you're a local correspondent reporting on a famous pagoda, the number of steps to the top is something you'll want to get right. But what matters for a writer of literature is his own impression of the pagoda and, still more, how he relates it to other fragments of life, how he selects, trims and arranges his words to create from it a complete and unique experience.'

Thus did I develop my still very immature aesthetic views. What I wanted was for writing to be more than just accurate – for it to be *true*.

In those days many supplement editors discarded works by

unknown authors the moment they arrived. I had probably suffered that fate myself at one time. Therefore in my announcement I promised my contributors that I would read all submissions. I had a lot of energy then. I could read a hundred thousand characters of manuscript a day besides managing my editing, and I made a point of sending a proper letter back even with the rejections. Working without an assistant, I wrote twenty or thirty letters an afternoon. 'I see each of your anxious faces in your letters, pleading for a quick reply. You're afraid that the post office brought your manuscript to the wrong address, or that the editor will doze off in his chair and forget to read your piece. Friends, although I can't be so rash as to guarantee the faithfulness of the postman, your editor will not overlook your manuscript. If only your article imparts a little something of value to the readers (a little beauty or a little inspiration) then the editor will print it. He is but a go–between for authors and readers. His conscience will not allow him to bury contributions of merit. . . . If the writer spares no effort, then the editor will try to be a good fisherman, and let no worthwhile work slip through his net.' (4 July 1935.)

This letter, which took up most of the page, provoked a strong and immediate reaction. Many readers sent me letters agreeing with what I'd said and guaranteeing their support.

I made two major innovations in the supplement. First I created a 'letters to the editor' column, so that young people could express themselves. I soon found myself receiving double the number of letters I had before. They were about literature, whether or not to go on to college, about love, about the sorry plight of young people, and I answered in whatever space might be left over at the bottom of the page that day.

I also tried to popularise book reviews, which were sadly lacking in China at the time, by organising a team of critics and carrying their reviews regularly. Without book reviews, I thought, good authors lacked one source of needed support. After all, my own thesis when I graduated from Yanjing University in 1935 had been entitled 'A Study of Book Reviewing'; while still an undergraduate I had heard I A Richards lecture in Peking, and I was particularly influenced by his *Practical Criticism*. So we helped to introduce Lao She's *Divorce* and Pearl Buck's *Exile*, organised round-table criticism of Cao Yu's play *Sunrise* and Sun Yutang's epic poem *The Precious Horse*. Besides reviews of new books, I put together critical evaluations by scholars in the field for authors such as Dostoevsky, Balzac, Dickens, Hardy and Gorky.

The 'Little Public Garden' was invigorated, but the differences between it and the daily Literature Supplement had become blurred, so it was handed over to me to edit also, and when the Shanghai edition of the *Dagongbao* was founded in 1936, the Sunday Literature Supplement became my responsibility, too. I composed travelogues while editing both the Tianjin and the Shanghai supplements, trying to steer clear of polemics between conservatives and leftists and among the Marxists themselves. And I even obeyed the official policy of that time that we could not say 'Japanese' in a critical context, only the more tactful '*Dong yang ren*', literally 'foreigner from the East'.

In the autumn of 1935 a terrible flood struck western Shandong. News of it dominated the paper. One day Mr Hu called me into his office. There I saw a man with a long, gaunt face and a tall, skinny body. He was the painter Zhao Wangyun. The boss wanted us to enter the famine area and cover the news together; I would write and Zhao would illustrate my despatches.

We got on well. The painter told me about his life as we rode down on the train. Raised in a destitute family in Shulu county, Hebei, he was largely self-taught. A country squire had helped with his learning. Zhao Wangyun's opinion was that if Chinese painting limited itself to flowers and landscapes, it would have no future. He was particularly derisive about the traditionalist painters who still dressed in ancient clothes. I found this most inspiring and told him that I felt similarly about literature. Essays from the Ming and Qing dynasties were all the rage then in Peking literary circles, but I disliked them. Other authors were dabbling in the occult, doing their best to evade reality. On the other hand, I didn't approve of the sloganeering political articles, either. The key to finding both a topic and a style lay in opening one's heart to the people. Wangyun agreed with all I said. His aim on this trip was to realise his own ideal, he said: to use native Chinese-style ink painting to expose the suffering of the famine victims.

By the time we reached Yanzhou, signs of the disaster were already evident. In Jining, refugees suddenly surrounded us. In the train stations, along the roads, in the fields, on the paths between them, wandering in the cemeteries and the wilds, the refugees were everywhere, their eyes sunken in their sockets. They had lost the will to live.

We worked in our little room at the inn that night. One painted, one wrote. Soon our articles and illustrations appeared in Tianjin. The newspaper commended us: donations were coming in to the office from everywhere. The paper then began officially to solicit contributions for the disaster area; the two of us worked even harder, staying up all night.

One night lewd talk came from next door at the inn. When I asked a steward in the morning, he said that the top officials in the county government had been having a prostitute party. I was so angry that I wanted to fire off a 'Comparative Look at Misery and Merry-making', but Wangyun's wiser head prevailed. He reminded me that the district we were in was under their jurisdiction. If the paper printed my story, we would have to leave, and that would only hurt the victims of the famine. Wangyun was ten years older than I and more experienced in the world. I had always hated senior government officials, but from that time forward I realised that they had less conscience than anyone else on earth.

After the worst of the flood in western Shandong, the boss sent me to Pei county in northern Jiangsu. There I saw the effects of regional separatism. While the Yellow River still rushed through Shandong like a mad beast, Jiangsu built a dyke along the boundary between the two provinces, hoping to avoid any major share in the disaster. After several months of being under water, the people of Shandong could stand it no longer. They sent a large number of conscript labourers to stealthily pull down the dyke during the night. Armed warfare between the provinces began. I realised that China could have no future without powerful centralised government.

While I was out covering the flood, the publishers of the *Dagongbao* were already planning to set up a Shanghai edition. I was one of the employees selected in 1936 to go there to make advance arrangements. The Shanghai office was on King Edward Road, not far from the Great Chime Clock. I was married now and our flat was in a three-storey building on the Avenue Vallon, in the French concession. But sadly the marriage was not happy. My wife went to work in Tokyo and I moved into bachelor quarters in Shanghai's White Russian Quarter.

September 1936 was the tenth anniversary of the Xinji

Company, owner of the *Dagongbao*, so the newspaper planned major commemorative activities. One day in July, the boss asked me to begin a nationwide hunt for manuscripts in commemoration. But how could I possibly read the vast number of submissions that would result? Suddenly I remembered something from my classes at Yanjing. Columbia University had established an annual Pulitzer Prize, and given it to completed works that had already won some critical notice. That would be easier to manage. I suggested to the boss that we follow Columbia's example and set up Dagongbao Literary Prizes and publish the winning works. He immediately agreed with the plan, proposing a Science Prize, too. This was the origin of the first literary prize in China. The publishers decided to award three literary prizes of 1,000 yuan and four science prizes of 2,000 yuan – for Hu Lin was prejudiced in favour of science.

In July 1937 the Sino-Japanese War started with the Marco Polo Bridge Incident outside Peking. The newspaper sent me north to Peking for a tour with other journalists. Not long after my return to Shanghai, the Japanese attack of 13 August took place in that city, beginning the full-scale war. I went to the war zones in Zhabei and Dachang with the other reporters and saw Chinese airplanes bomb the Japanese flagship *Izumo Maru* on the Huangpu River.

At the start of the war, the *Dagongbao* shrank from sixteen pages to only four. Only the most important national, international, and metropolitan sections survived the cuts. I was out of work.

Subsequently, after the fall of Shanghai, the *Dagongbao* was re-established in Wuhan, but the supplement was taken over by Chen Jiying, who had better connections at the paper than I. I visited the Wuhan office only once. I felt unwelcome, like a stranger.

Some of my friends had gone to the Communist capital at Yan'an, while others had joined the Kuomintang. But fortunately Yang Zhensheng and Shen Congwen, having fled Peking to Wuhan, took me on as an assistant in their new project, editing secondary and primary school textbooks.

At the start of 1938, we moved to Kunming. There I received a letter from Hu Lin in Wuhan, saying that readers were asking for my restoration to the Literature Supplement. He wanted me to edit and send in the supplement from Kunming. Remembering how abruptly I had been dismissed in Shanghai, I wanted at first to refuse. Now that I had another way of making a living, he could find someone else. On the other hand, I had not imagined that readers would miss my supplement in those war-torn days. I couldn't take my spite out on them – a supplement was not the same thing as its publisher or manager.

So I accepted. For a time my friends sent manuscripts from all over China: from behind enemy lines, from the guerrilla areas, and from the Communist districts of northern Shaanxi. Things got very exciting at my little desk in Kunming. But gradually, either because more space was needed for advertisements, or because the top levels of the newspaper were divided in their opinions, my Literature Supplement became an irregular item. Sometimes it was given only a half page, sometimes just two or three columns.

In August 1938, I suddenly received a telegram and then an air letter from Mr Hu. First he apologised for my dismissal the year before. Then he spoke of his determination to publish the *Dagongbao* in Hong Kong, stressing its role as an outpost for China's war propaganda. He wanted me to go there post haste, to help with the planning. Shortly afterwards he wired travelling expenses.

I had been terribly restless in Kunming. I had to admit that editing textbooks was not for me, not after three exciting years in the newspaper business. I thought of how so many of my friends had already accomplished something, while I, an Oblomov, was just a tramp steamer that had run aground. After seeing off a friend on his way to join the [Communist] New Fourth Army, I seriously considered following him. People warned me that there were Kuomintang checkpoints all along the way. Once stopped, I would be sent to a concentration camp and tortured. I was, of course, a coward. Having gone on for years about the arrival of a 'great era', now that it was finally at hand, I was of no use. That left me sleepless and melancholy. One day I even brought home a bottle of tablets for my depression and took several. Only afterwards did I think to read the instructions: they were for women who were having their period!

A few days later I found a travelling companion, Shi Zhecun. We went to Hong Kong together by the established, long, safe route, via Annam.

When, after the three-day ocean voyage, I finally arrived at the editorial offices on Queen's Road, Hong Kong and saw my old friends again, it was a great boost to my confidence. I was back at my old job: editing both the Literature Supplement and a lighter entertainment supplement. If I had any energy left over, I could go looking for news in the interior.

The first step for regrouping our forces was for me to establish contact with friends behind enemy lines in the guerrilla areas, at Yan'an and in Shanghai. (Some districts in Shanghai were not yet occupied by Japan because they were under the protection of foreign countries not yet at war in Asia.) Several hundred letters went out. Ultimately the supplement, under me and my successor Yang Gang, published over a hundred pieces from Yan'an. But first I had to establish the supplement under the ideologically objective standards of 1938. In my editor's introduction, I pointed out that not all submissions had to be about fighting the Japanese, for articles on the home front were important, too. The supplement maintained its old tradition of printing book reviews, and established columns like 'Letters from the Battlefields' and 'Whereabouts of the Authors'. But it also became more international in outlook, and it added a Miscellany page devoted to military, political and economic subjects – anything that would stiffen our resolve to defeat the enemy, particularly accounts revealing Japan's weakness in her home islands. Thus the supplement enlarged the boundaries of pure literature.

When I returned to Hong Kong in 1939 from a trip to Burma to report on the Burma Road, an amazing letter from the School of Oriental and African Studies at the University of London was waiting for me. They wanted me as a lecturer in the Chinese department; I had been recommended by Yu Daoquan, who was already on the faculty.

Yu Daoquan had been my superior in the Communist Youth in 1926, but we had lost all contact in the years since. When I was arrested all those years ago, he had entered the Yonghegong temple in Peking. There he studied Tibetan with the lamas, ending up as one of China's foremost Tibetologists. I had no idea when he went to England, but evidently he was a reader of the *Dagongbao* and had learned of my whereabouts from the paper.

From childhood I had wanted to venture to the South Seas. I wanted to go to America, too, for the prestige of it. The idea of going to England had never really occurred to me. But I had read

A main street in Peking, seen from the city wall.

During my early career as a goatherd, 1925.

The market at the south-east corner of the city wall.

Top left: Joining the Communist Youth, 1926.

Shortly before being expelled from school, 1929. The characters in the background read 'Revolutionary Youth'.

Bottom left: Taken in 1930 following the tragic end of my first love affair.

Graduating from Yanjing University, June 1935.

Smoky, a kitten of Rhea, in the company of Kingsley Martin and Dorothy Woodman to whom I gave Rhea as a present.

Happy days: Cambridge 1943.

King's College as I knew it – the Chapel and Gibbs building seen from the Backs.

My great friend, Margery Fry.

Bertrand Russell at Trinity College Cambridge, 1945.

The writer, E.M. Forster, with whom I enjoyed an extended correspondence on the subjects of literature and our cats.

English literature for several years and had made tours of the British Isles long ago in my imagination through the novels of Dickens and Hardy. I felt emotionally more at home with that nation than any other outside China. And a long foreign voyage was particularly attractive to me in 1939, when I was suffering family problems and was in an emotional maelstrom from which I could not extricate myself. I was in love again, and still alienated from my wife, but she would not divorce me. This posting would release me. The only problem was the salary, only £250 a year, with no guarantee of continuation. What made me hesitate even more was the problem of travelling expenses. How could I raise them? And even if I did, how could I afford to return after a year if my contract was not renewed? Friends who considered themselves British experts all shook their heads at the salary and said that I'd have to pay a large portion even of that as income tax. Every one of them poured cold water on my hopes.

Little did I know that my newspaper boss, Hu Lin, had heard about the letter and already knew all the details. He called me into his office. Smiling at me, he said, 'A gift comes down to you from Heaven and you're still undecided? You must send them your acceptance immediately. The newspaper will advance you your travelling expenses. You can pay us back by sending off regular articles.'

When he saw that I was still hesitating, he made the following political forecast: 'Hitler has already swallowed up Austria and now he's encroaching on Czechoslovakia. That man is going to be hard to satisfy. A big war is inevitable. For us in the news business, this will be a once-in-a-lifetime opportunity. I was just thinking of sending a reporter out on our own money, but we couldn't guarantee that Britain would grant him a visa. You're invited! What are you scared of? I'll have the accounts office buy your boat ticket and have Xu in the business office apply for your passport!'

He had made my decision for me.

Procedures were simpler then; within a few days I had my passport and visas. I received them together with a few dozen pounds sterling for spending money to get me by in England until my salary started arriving. In those days the newspaper's dormitory was in the mid-levels of Victoria Peak, on Robinson Road. I lived on the fifth floor, but a taller building across the street looked directly into my flat. Evidently someone up there saw the foreign bank notes as I packed my bags the day before the departure. The next morning when I awoke, my belongings were strewn all over the room and the foreign currency was gone. The boss made up the difference, relieved that my travel documents had not been taken also.

So I was on my way to Britain to teach Chinese and serve as a foreign correspondent. Then, as my ship sailed through the Gulf of Tonkin, Britain and France declared war on Germany. I would be a war correspondent, too.

Today people speak of reporters in China as being 'bred' by their newspapers. At the same time, they wonder why no truly great ones have come out of our country in the last forty years. The case of the *Dagongbao* proves that great reporters cannot be 'bred'. The *Dagongbao* had no training classes – in fact the boss never gave any of us a single day off for extra preparation.

Of course, Hu Lin did not really send me to England to school me in the European situation, or to develop my powers as a war correspondent. My going to Europe was purely by chance; the boss was just taking advantage of an opportunity. But he was enthusiastic about my trip to England and he gave me a free hand to write what I wanted to write and to explore what I wanted to explore. Great reporters don't get to be that way sitting around, they must be forced to go out into the world. There are no short cuts. Reliance on one's own understanding is precisely the quality that is lacking under the present socialist 'iron rice bowl' system.

I continually hear young reporters in China complain that they lack the proper training and background. My lifelong motto has been that with effort you can achieve anything. You create your own qualifications. If the time they spent regretting their lack of qualifications were used instead to strengthen their abilities, they would be better able to seize the opportunity when it came.

When I took over the 'Little Public Garden', I privately looked down on it. I was wrong. I didn't then realise the important function of newspaper literary supplements. I of all people should have realised it, for if I had not been given a push by one, perhaps I would never have become a writer. Feuilletons are cradles for young literary people. They have served as an important means of promoting Chinese literature.

People have often asked me how to write travelogues that are artistic while being newsworthy. I have thought continually about that question and pursued that goal for more than half my life. Edgar Snow taught me that one should read superior contemporary reportage, but that it is more important to read great works of literature – old and new, domestic and foreign. You can't improve the quality of your own reportage if you read only other reportage.

Reporters are particularly mindful of their readers. Nothing gives journalism more vitality than bearing one's readers in mind. And a news writer also needs a sense of history. That means not just a grasp of the background to events, but a sense of the pulse of the era. Snow had it. He could see that fascism was destined to fail because it could not win the people's hearts, and he could see the strength of China beneath its outer weakness. Today the sparring between the forces of reform and conservatism and between democracy and feudalism are a severe test for all of us, journalists in particular. The problem we face now is the same as in Snow's day: how correctly to assess and measure something for which no measure has yet been invented – the will of the people.

Everything that is worth doing in life calls for resourcefulness, courage and devotion. Journalism is no exception. If I had another life to live, I'd be a journalist all over again.

3

My Life in Wartime Britain
(1939–1944)

It was dusk that winter day in 1939 when I first stepped on English soil – so dark in the blackout that I couldn't even see the faces of the other travellers in my compartment on the train I took to London. As we rattled and lurched towards Victoria Station, I finally spoke a few words in the dark to the passenger across from me. He told me his bride was in the seat beside him, returning with him from their honeymoon in the south of Italy. They were to change trains that night and travel on up to their home in Scotland. Then he would enlist.

In wartime, people are like shadows passing on the wall, detailed but insubstantial.

After getting off the train, I wandered around the vast, gloomy station for some time. Finally I found a porter who directed me to a 'good but reasonable' hotel, the Wilton.

Relieved of my baggage, I decided to go out for a stroll, hoping to see the Tower of London by starlight. I turned back after only a few groping steps. I realised that even if I found the Tower, I'd have no hope at all of getting back to the hotel in the blackout. Also, it was past nine o'clock and I still hadn't eaten supper. My stomach was keeping going on a glass of cider and two skimpy sandwich halves I'd purchased in Paris at the Gare du Nord.

Soon after I'd taken a small table in the corner of the hotel dining hall, a dark-skinned young woman came in and sat down at a nearby table. We were both of us people of colour, so we nodded. She seemed very elegant and sophisticated.

When I went to listen to the radio after supper, she came in again and we got talking. She was on a pleasure trip and planned to leave the next day. I asked what part of Africa she was from. She told me she was from the Bahamas. My geography was terrible, so I asked how far the Bahamas were from the first landfall of Columbus. She said he landed precisely *on* them. Then she told me about the islands. I particularly remember that originally blacks had had to ride at the back of Bahamian trolley cars with whites in front, but then there'd been a road accident that injured all the whites at the front and left the blacks in the rear safe and sound. After that, the seating was reversed.

I saw her off at the station early the next morning. She said she'd be safe as far as Liverpool and her ship; after that, she was in the Lord's hands. This was wartime.

The next morning I boarded a train bound for Cambridge. When the University of London was evacuated at the beginning of the war, its School of Oriental and African Studies had relocated in Cambridge at Christ College – the Alma Mater of the great Milton. There I started a new page in the history of my life. As well as my work as a reporter for the Chungking *Dagongbao*, I began to teach Chinese.

A Sanscritologist was director at SOAS; the faculty included famous professors and also lecturers who'd merely spent some time in the Orient. E D Edwards, head of the Chinese department, had been a missionary in my country, as had E R Hughes, head of the Chinese department at Oxford. The man in the department who taught Malay was a former colonial official in Singapore. A Russian, Minorsky, was the professor of Persian: he had been ambassador to Persia for the tsar. When the time came to defend the Russian motherland, the Soviet Union exhorted those who had emigrated after the revolution to return home. One day Minorsky came by to shake hands with all of us and take his leave. He was a scholar, not a soldier. Even so, he was returning to his roots, to defend his ancestral land.

Besides E D Edwards, who did not teach, there were four of us in the Chinese department. One was senior lecturer Dr Walter Simon, a German Jew who had fled the Nazis. Another was Mrs Whitaker, a Cantonese married to an Englishman. Yu Daoquan – the man who had encouraged me for a while when I was a Communist Youth member in 1926 – was a Tibetologist, but nobody wanted to study his subject so he taught Classical Chinese instead. My subject was modern Chinese.

All British institutions of higher education were hit by low enrolment in those days, for most of the students had been called up – except in fields of study that could be directly related to the war effort, such as physics and medicine. Consequently I had an easy time of it. One of my pupils was the manager of a Scottish chemical fertiliser factory who considered learning a little Chinese in his spare time to be a high-class hobby; and there was a young lady in love with a Hong Kong colonial official who thought that understanding a bit of Chinese would be of use to her some day as a housewife. Midway through the term she stopped coming. Someone brought me a letter of explanation: she'd broken with the man stationed in Hong Kong and now was in love with a colonial official in Ghana. Therefore she was going to learn 'African'.

Perhaps it was simply nostalgia, but Cambridge from the start reminded me of my old home, Peking. My favourite haunts in the ancient Chinese city had been its temples and monuments: the Monastery of Prosperity and Good Fortune, the Monastery Protecting the Kingdom, the Temple of the Eastern Peaks. Cambridge, too, had churches and many historical landmarks.

I was particularly charmed by the English city's unhurried and tranquil atmosphere. I loved the copses and knolls down by the river; the Bridge of Sighs behind St John's College; the livestock market and a gypsy camp in the surrounding verdant fields.

Therefore I felt at home in Cambridge. Cities with a bit of the village in them seem to appeal to me. My first delight was discovering that I could ride a bicycle there; I purchased one just a few days after my arrival. I'd wanted to ride a bicycle to the office when I walked in Shanghai in 1936, but a local had laughed at me, claiming that only postmen rode them. In Cambridge practically everyone had one, complete with a rustic basket suspended from the handlebars. Students and professors filled their baskets with books, shuttling back and forth between colleges, lecture rooms and the library.

Like all Chinese in England, save those from Malaya who were British subjects, I was classed an 'enemy alien'. According to the regulations of the Home Office, even an accredited journalist such as myself was under curfew from eight in the evening to six o'clock in the morning. But at least I was just an 'enemy alien', not a 'belligerent enemy alien', and in that subtle distinction lay the difference between internment and relative freedom. I was allowed unlimited travel, except within five miles of the coast, and my only official responsibility was to report to the local police station once weekly, no doubt to show that I had not fled underground. No one could really explain why these regulations existed; perhaps they were a carry-over from the Anglo-Japanese naval alliance of 1902.

In those days, it was difficult to find a barber willing to cut the hair of an Oriental, and renting a room was virtually impossible. Wanting to spend my first Christmas in London, I consulted the rental ads in the papers ahead of time and wrote from Cambridge to reserve lodging in an apartment house across from Hyde Park. After getting off the train at Liverpool Street, I even rang the management from the station to confirm our arrangement. The lady on the other end of the line said, 'Come along over, the room has been reserved for you.' I found the address, carrying my little suitcase and rang the bell. When the door opened, the woman who'd been so encouraging over the telephone sized me up in an instant. 'So sorry,' she said, 'the room has just been let.' The door closed with a clunk. I wrote a letter to the *New Statesman and Nation* protesting about this and they printed it.

In point of fact I've experienced several sudden re-evaluations in my life. After Pearl Harbor, I abruptly became a member of the grand alliance, rather than an enemy alien, all because of a sneak attack by the Japanese. And from then on the Chinese section in SOAS became very busy, not only because China had become an ally, but because of the possibility that British troops might fight in the Far East one day. (No doubt they were already hoping to recapture Malaya!)

After all, not long before, Churchill, in a desperate effort to keep the British Empire intact, had sought the favour of the Japanese by sealing off the Burma Road, the lifeline into China that Chinese labourers had built with the sweat of their brows. So even the statesman I most admired could cast all principles aside when it came to national self-interest. Since I had gone as a journalist to visit that lifeline of ours and report on it, I was invited to several English cities to lecture about it. I also participated in a People's Congress organised by the British Communist Party that called for the immediate opening of a second front. Afterwards a London plain-clothes policeman paid me a visit. Very politely, and in a terribly roundabout way, he interrogated me for more than an hour. I don't know what he discovered, but I never heard anything more.

By then I had transferred to King's College Cambridge, as a

research student. A story was going round there that the War Office had asked an English Sinologist to suggest a Chinese phrase to be sewn onto the uniforms of British pilots, so that if their planes were shot down by the Japanese over Malaya, local people of Chinese background might be persuaded to assist them. No doubt the Sinologist was very learned in his field of ancient Chinese. He wrote out a four-character phrase for the ministry: 'Detainest-thou not this honourable pilot of ye Airborne Dragon'. Someone should have told him that even the Chinese had moved on in the last two thousand years.

It was now that China began to exist in the eyes of the British. Publishers asked me to write books and a film studio invited me to script a film called *The Chinese in England*; they filmed me giving my commentary in a mock-up of my study at King's College, built in the studio. Naturally the BBC went into action, too. They invited reporters from allied countries living in London to broadcast to their own peoples in their native tongues, giving reports on the European war and the war effort of the English. I was chosen for China and was asked to speak to Chungking every Tuesday.

By then the war in Europe and in Asia had become virtually a single front, so I cast my net wide. I submitted my reports for censorship a day in advance and was always able to read them in their entirety the next day without any complications, expressing my private opinion of the war situation as well as my impressions of wartime Britain. All went very smoothly for several months.

On one occasion, however, I mentioned the independence movement in India. Since arriving in England I had become good friends with the Indian author Mulk Raj Anand, and I had got into several arguments with Englishmen over the question of Indian independence. The first time, as I recall, was in the SOAS senior common room. When a colleague who had served in India as a colonial official heard me say it was inevitable that India would one day be independent, he completely forgot his gentleman's upbringing. I never went into that fusty old common room again.

My broadcast script mentioned the friendship between the two ancient nations of China and India and expressed evident sympathy for the Indian movement. I translated it into English as usual and sent it to the studio the day before the broadcast. Not long afterwards, the BBC deputed someone to return my script to me in person, accompanied by a letter politely requesting that I delete the section about Indian independence. They had written another paragraph to replace it.

Since the commentary was intended as my own personal opinion, I considered this unreasonable. I wrote a letter in reply, suggesting that if His Majesty's government wanted to comment on the Indian question, it could do so in its own name: I did not intend to be a spokesperson for that government.

After writing the letter, I presented it to the BBC's reception office on the ground floor. Then I went home. I later heard that they filled in my time with music. And from then on the BBC's current affairs department halted all broadcasts of individual opinion and changed over to the reading by radio announcers of scripts approved by the Corporation. Later George Orwell, as head of the BBC's Far Eastern division, invited me to do several special broadcasts to the Indians and Americans, but strictly on the subject of literature.

I'll never forget one incident that occurrred on the day after Pearl Harbor. I was sitting on a bus going down the Strand. Suddenly a drunken passenger behind me shouted out 'tough luck you bet on the wrong horse!' He went on shouting, growing more and more excited. Eventually it dawned on me that he was yelling at me. I turned round, stared at him, and asked him why he was being so rude. 'Because you're a dirty Jap!' he said. I corrected him: 'No sir, I am a Chinese!'

That made things worse. He immediately got up and sat next to me. First came a long torrent of apologies. Then he gave me a clumsy salute, shouting 'A tribute to the great nation of China!' At that all the other passengers in the bus began to echo their respects. The bus continued down the narrow London streets, but now there seemed to be a pro-China symphony orchestra aboard it, with the wino sitting next to me as the soloist. The longer he continued his shouting, the closer he moved to me, almost as if he wanted to hug me. Finally I could stand it no longer – the alcohol on his breath nearly asphyxiated me. I struggled free of him and got off at the next stop. When the bus started up again he was still pressing his flushed face against the window and enthusiastically waving his workman's cap at me. As I watched him driven away down the road, I was overcome with embarrassment at my unworthiness: in an instant I had become, even if only in the eyes of some poor drunk, the incarnation of all the glory of my nation, and I hadn't been able to handle it.

A person abroad quite often is not simply himself, but a reflection of his country's position in the eyes of others. One is made to bear not just one's own character, but one's national character as well.

England had long relied on imports for its food. From the start of the war German submarines patrolled the high seas with deadly efficiency. A land army was established so that conscientious objectors and those unfit for active service could contribute by growing food. At one time even the lawn in front of the entrance to the Houses of Parliament was dug up and planted with potatoes. If you didn't farm there were other things you could do to help. In 1941 the Society of Friends organised forty young English lads into an ambulance unit, with the aim of rendering medical aid at the front in China. I was to have a hand in that enterprise.

The ambulance unit asked the School of Oriental and African Studies to prepare a short training course for them before they left. They wanted us to teach them practical Chinese and the basics of Chinese geography and history in three or four months. The school appointed a colleague of mine, Dr Simon, and myself to the task. The classes were held in a warehouse of the Quaker-owned Cadbury Company outside Birmingham. The young students came from every part of England and every social class, and all were conscientious objectors.

These conscientious objectors fell into one of three categories: religious: all Friends were forbidden to kill; moral: some simply believed killing to be immoral or inhumane; and political: before the entry of the Soviet Union into the war, British Communists accepted the party line that the war was between imperialists and they therefore refused to fight. After receiving their call-up papers conscientious objectors could appeal individually to the courts for exemption. If the courts judged them sincere, they were approved for non-combat duty.

I ate and slept with those forty young lads in the ambulance unit and they greatly increased my understanding of England. When I asked them why they'd chosen to do their relief work in China, they answered, 'The Chinese are a peace-loving people. The Japanese took advantage of that quality: their bullying and aggression began back in 1931. So we want to do something to help the Chinese.' In other words they wanted to go out and right a wrong.

Their attitude meant that relations between us had to be more than the ordinary one between teacher and student. Filled with gratitude, I taught them all I possibly could of my country's language, history and customs.

After completing their course, they went off to China, most of them to the front along the Burma Road. When I returned to China in 1946, before the People's Republic was established, I lived in the Jiangwan district north of Shanghai. The Friends' headquarters in China happened to be there, so I was able to see them often. I learned that the Quakers had taken many risks to help us. Some of the forty I'd known were war casualties, while others had contracted diseases that would cripple them for the rest of their lives. Some volunteered to stay in China after the war, to help with the industrial cooperative movement, and some of those worked in the Communist base areas. In 1948 I invited one of the latter to lecture about conditions in those liberated areas in a class I taught at Fudan University. Since he was British and spoke in English, the school authorities didn't interfere; Chiang Kai-shek's officials outside the university were none the wiser. Peter Townsend (one of the forty) even stayed on in China after the nationwide Communist Liberation in 1949 and remained until 1952 as a foreign expert. Today he edits the *Art Monthly* in England.

One day in the early 1950s, the *People's Daily* devoted a full page to a translated transcript of a meeting between Stalin and a Quaker delegation led by Duncan Wood. He, too, had been among my original forty young men. It was from the transcript of that meeting that I came fully to understand the importance of this pacifist organisation in the world peace movement.

The social reformer Margery Fry, who died in 1958, was the Quaker I knew best. In the winter of 1940 she invited me to stay the weekend at her cottage in Aylesbury. In the evening she brought out a stack of old newspapers and magazines. 'Flip through them,' she told me, 'and you'll discover another side of England.' I read them carefully by lamplight. Among them was a report of proceedings in the House of Commons from about 1840. She'd circled a passage for my benefit. Her great-great-grandfather, during debate, had vociferously opposed the 'unjust war with

China'. He asked: 'Why must we sell this narcotic opium in China? China forbids it; why then do we so brazenly take up arms against her?' It was a long and impassioned speech, very moving.

She asked me for my reaction. I said, 'Of course I admire your great-great-grandfather's willingness to speak out. Still, his speech wasn't able to block a single shell from the British artillerymen who assaulted Canton, much less the war of invasion.' My meaning was that Parliament was just a place to let off steam, not to determine national policy.

The Friends' international peace advocate Dr Sydney Bailey invited me to lecture on China when I visited England again in 1984 and 1986; we talked of old times to our hearts' content. By then the Society of Friends had organised a diplomatic friendship association to ease tensions between East and West.

When I first went to Cambridge at the start of 1939, I lived for a time in a little house in Milton village. My old friend Yu Daoquan lived in the flat below, and I in the one above. I had only a table and chairs and a convertible sofa-bed, so my room was quite bare. But outside my window was a grove of trees and a meadow on which were pastured cattle and sheep. I could see the church steeple in town far in the distance and, closer by, the Golden Deer pub.

Why then did I move out? It's a sad story. Yu Daoquan had become interested in demonology. His bookshelves were filled with volumes on the subject, like *Speaking to Loved Ones Who Are Forty Years in the Grave* and so forth. I didn't believe in spirits, but my frightening childhood experiences with the aunt who claimed she was a medium had left me with a phobia about being in the dark. And when I began to hear muttered mumbo-jumbo every night downstairs, I trembled in my bed and couldn't get to sleep. I had to move.

I moved in with the Vancillis, an Italian family. My fellow roomer was Kenneth Lo (Luo Xiaojian), today the proprietor of the Memories of China restaurant in London. Mr and Mrs Vancilli had a little boy and a little girl. Mr Vancilli taught Italian at the university. He was a Tory, and his wife was an extreme Communist – whether a party member or not, I don't know. She kept up with current affairs and liked to express her views, nearly all of which came straight from the Kremlin. Every meal after the dessert Mr Vancilli would perform his single household chore: he would measure out his coffee beans, and put them into a hand grinder. As he turned the handle, he would bicker with his wife: the debates would begin amid the heady smell of coffee. Out of respect for us, they would begin in English, most of which we could understand. Said Mrs Vancilli: 'This is an inexcusable war between two greedy imperialists.' Mr Vancilli: 'If Stalin hadn't signed that immoral pact with Hitler, there'd have been no war in the first place.' Mrs Vancilli: 'Do you call Chamberlain moral? Why did he sell out Czechoslovakia?'

From there they went on to stronger language, like 'Balls' and 'That's a bloody lie!' By the time the coffee was brewed and ready for drinking, their English vocabulary of abuse was exhausted so they went at it in Italian. They swore so loudly and looked so fierce that I often feared they would actually come to blows.

There were families all over this college town who were willing to invite foreign students into their homes to live. You found them in the classified ads of the *Cambridge News*. Some of them offered three meals a day, some only bed and breakfast. Now it happened that such rooms with a family usually came with a landlady's daughter, too, or an LL.D as they were called in jest. But these 'doctors of law' were a very mixed bunch. The Vancillis' daughter Elisa was only thirteen years old. And worse, every day after school she had to sit down at the piano and practise for at least an hour. I can still remember some of her exercises today, for I lived in the very next room. Other LL.Ds were older and without musical ambitions. They'd go out to the cinema with a different man every Saturday night. Some just saw the film for the fun of it, then parted after a quick good-night cuddle. Others went further.

An LL.D called Lucy crossed over the line. When I went to stay for a few days on the coast at Barmouth, I found a former classmate of mine from Hubei, Mike Zhang, and Lucy living like married folk in a flat nearby. I often ran into them strolling along the shore at dusk. It didn't worry Lucy, but Mike kept trying to explain: 'We're really in love – we're going to marry and go live in China'. I teased Lucy, 'Can you bear to leave England?' Nestling into Mike's embrace she answered, 'Wherever he goes, I'll follow!'

It was no wonder that this willowy, green-eyed, golden-haired English girl had fallen in love with Mike. He really was talented and attractive, an amusing talker, an excellent violinist and an ace on the tennis court. In Cambridge, sculling ability was another male requirement and not only could Mike scull, he could also pole punts and he was the only Oriental on a college rowing team. He took Lucy to Henley when he competed against Oxford. Lucy stood on the shore, jumping wildly up and down and cheering. With the Cambridge boat in the lead the whole way and her Mike one of the oarsmen, how could she restrain herself? Mike had even joined the university debating society, where he proved himself learned and quick-witted. After a debate I once saw Lucy in high spirits waiting at the foot of the stairs. She embraced Mike the moment he came down.

Mike graduated just before the beginning of the blitz. He had to return home immediately, by order of the Chinese Ministry of Education. I gave him a farewell dinner shortly before his departure and naturally invited Lucy too. I roasted a duck and made noodles as best I could, with Italian macaroni. As we ate I said, enviously, 'Soon you'll be able to eat real Chinese noodles'.

One day about a month after Mike left, Lucy came to see me, a mournful look on her face. 'Has Mike written to you?' she asked. 'No,' I said. She sat for a while, then made me promise as she left, 'If you hear from Mike, for heaven's sake tell me.' I tried to comfort her: 'In wartime you can't count on the mail. I bet you'll hear from him before I do.'

She came five or six more times after that but Mike never wrote. He could have made one final contact, if only to say 'We're finished'. I wanted to comfort Lucy, but could think of nothing to say. As Mike's fellow countryman, I was embarrassed even to see her.

Several years later I happened to read in the papers that Mike had taken an appointment at a Chinese university. They even printed a photo of him with his wife and little baby. For all I know, he may well have been married or betrothed before he went to England.

One other thing happened in my life as a roomer that is hard to forget. When my institute moved back to London in 1940, I rented a large basement room in Hampstead. Once settled in I discovered that not a soul lived on the four floors above me. I was the only resident in the building. Puzzled, I asked my landlady the reason for this the next time I paid my rent.

'The upper floors are all reserved by Russians,' she explained, 'but they haven't arrived yet.'

When I had first arrived in England, everyone except the British Communist Party was cursing the Soviet Union. People said the whole war had been brought on by the Nazi-Soviet Pact. Then, after Hitler turned around and attacked the Soviet Union in June 1941, the British and the Soviets of course became allies. For a time Britain was Russia's arsenal. Fleets of transport ships unloaded every sort of armament, heavy and light, at Murmansk, and many a British sailor lost his life in the convoys. The Soviets sent team after team of munitions experts to advise British factories on how to make arms the Russians could best use. One day several large limousines drew up to the front door of my building. Twenty-four Soviets moved in, wearing their fur hats and down-filled leather parkas. They could hardly speak a word of English and I spoke no Russian, but when they learned that I was a Chinese, they warmly shook my hand.

Soon they went their separate ways to Sheffield, Coventry and other cities known for their armaments factories, but every Saturday they returned to spend the weekend together.

If there is an international language it's music, particularly songs. We had no common language between us, but I'd learned quite a few old Russian and more recent Soviet songs back in Shanghai during the thirties. When they came down to my basement to see me, after they'd got out their 'Hellos' and I'd poured tea, we'd continue the conversation with those songs. Judging by how fast our friendship grew, songs are better than mere spoken language. We sang songs from before the October Revolution, such as 'The Song of the Volga Boatmen', and post-revolutionary songs too, such as 'On the Wide Plain of the Ukraine', 'Life Flows Like Mud' and the Soviet national anthem. Whatever the song and whatever the words, I only had to hum a few bars for them to pick it up and insist on singing it through to the end.

As we got to know each other, their English graduated from the 'Hello' stage. A young fellow named Sasha even wrote love letters. It seems each of them in their own factory had a young British war worker for a girlfriend. Sasha's was called Kate. The Russians' places of work rotated and Sasha not only wrote to his girl when they were apart, but rang her up long distance. He was terribly conscientious. Before placing his call, he always prepared what he would say and carefully wrote it out on paper. Unfortunately his vocabulary was still very limited, so he asked me to help him compose his conversations, and also to correct his pronunciation.

The telephone was on the ground floor, just above my basement. He spoke very loudly, so I could always hear when he was improvising beyond the script we'd prepared. Furthermore, he punctuated every other sentence with stentorian 'darlings' and the prolonged smacking of his lips for kisses.

My room was very big, so they asked me if I would help them throw a dance there one weekend. I invited some neighbours too. 'Fine,' the Russians said, 'with us two great allies throwing a party, how can the young ladies resist!' Dusk fell on the appointed day. A dozen young women arrived dressed in the finest their ration books would allow. They had expected the party to be like most in wartime England – that it would run until ten at the latest, and then they could go home. They (indeed, I also) had underestimated the depths of Slavic passion. The young women tried to take their leave several times after ten o'clock, but the Russians wouldn't let them go. And they were growing more boisterous, singing as they danced. The girls were tossed about as the Russians clasped them close, then whirled them around with their feet off the ground. One fellow, probably from the Ukraine, also did a lively traditional dance, kicking his legs out from the squatting position. The party went on until dawn.

That got me into trouble. The next day the neighbours got together and protested. I also got a warning from the landlady. Personally I felt hard done by, for I'd not learned any of the dances – I'd only attended to the refreshments.

Later on, fearing I might get rheumatism in that damp basement, I moved. The following year I happened to run into Sasha in Hyde Park with a little wife on his arm. 'Hello Kate,' I said not thinking. Sasha's face tensed up. His English had grown quite fluent; very solemnly he introduced me to her: 'May I present to you my wife, Zoya.'

The Kremlin had sent them a planeload of their families.

Being aware of events in China and an experienced reporter too, I became intimately involved with the China Campaign Committee soon after my arrival in Britain. Indeed I became their principal speaker.

The China Campaign Committee was a society organised by a group of progressive Englishmen at the end of the thirties to lobby on behalf of China in her War of Resistance Against Japan. Its principal organisers were Victor Gollancz, publisher and head of the Left Book Club, Kingsley Martin, editor of the *New Statesman and Nation*, the feminist and social activist Margery Fry, Harold Laski, the Labour Party theorist and Arthur Clegg, reporter on foreign affairs for the British Communist Party organ, the *Daily Worker*. Dorothy Woodman, a political writer who specialised in Pacific affairs, was in charge of the day-to-day management. The committee was able to send many shipments of medicine and medical instruments to China, always insisting that they be evenly divided between the Nationalists at Chungking and the Communists at Yan'an. For that reason they were always in trouble with the Kuomintang, and particularly the Nationalist ambassador to St James's. They knew all about the New Fourth Army Incident [when Chiang Kai-shek's armies attacked allied Chinese Communist armies, ending the truce between them] and the atrocities committed by Dai Li's secret police network in the Nationalist-controlled areas. Indeed they organised a letter-writing campaign in which the more famous society members made anti-Nationalist protests in the London papers. When in 1941 Churchill appeased the Japanese by closing the Burma Road, the committee was again active in protesting. Later in the war, they supported the industrial cooperative movement INDUSCO, which particularly flourished in the Communist-held areas of China. The committee issued certificates of shares in the co-ops to us contributors. I kept my certificate as a souvenir until 1985, when I donated it to the industrial cooperative general office in Peking.

The committee's propaganda work included not only distributing pamphlets about China's War of Resistance Against Japan, but organising Chinese and others knowledgeable about the war (professors who had taught in China, doctors who had practised medicine there, etc.) to go on tour throughout Britain to lecture. I was the only mainland Chinese to arrive in England after the beginning of the war and before Pearl Harbor. When war broke out in Asia, the Chinese students already studying abroad had returned home in a stream.

Outside the University of London, then, I had more contact with the China Campaign Committee during my first years in England than with any other organisation; Dorothy Woodman and Kingsley Martin, the man she lived with, became my closest friends. I visited them several times in their country cottage in Essex, often went to plays with them, and once attended a music festival at Dartington Hall with them. Martin enjoyed chess, which unfortunately was not my game, but our tastes in art were very similar – or, more accurately, they initiated me into similar tastes.

Dorothy Woodman had got in touch with me as soon as I reached England in 1939, and at her prompting I delivered several dozen lectures on the war in China. Some talks were in London, most in outlying areas. It turned out to be a marvellous way for me to get to know British people, from villagers in Welsh mining districts to Scottish highlanders. The China Campaign Committee bought me my round-trip train tickets in advance. On arrival, there was always a hospitable local representative to shepherd me round and take care of my meals and lodging. Since I was propagandising on behalf of my own country, I naturally accepted no remuneration whatsoever, and this helped me to make friends with men and women from all classes of society. Some struck up correspondences with me that continued even after I left England in 1944. In 1949, on the eve of my final departure from Hong Kong to Peking, I broke off relations with all my friends overseas. After 1979, however, I was happily able to restore communications with several British friends who turned out to be still alive and in good health.

What a pity that all of my diaries were destroyed in the Cultural Revolution (1966–7). Otherwise I could write a worthwhile book about my lecture tours on China in England. Still, some of the memories from those years are still clear in my mind.

I remember the time I stayed overnight with the curator of the Nottingham Museum following a lecture there. He had become interested in *objets d'art*, and indeed knew a great deal more about Han pottery and Song porcelain than did I. But it was only after hearing my lecture 'China Is No Longer Cathay' that he realised that my country was more than a vast antique shop – that since the nineteenth century it had been struggling to throw off the burden of its past, to catch up with the times. From there he quickly developed a keen interest in China's efforts to modernise, and thenceforth we corresponded regularly. When in 1942 he learned that I was lecturing at the gallery housing the Wallace Collection in London, he travelled all that way just to hear me. His one complaint against China was that we put too many of our birds in cages.

The day I went to Leicester, I stayed in the home of a Mr Groves who ran a sock-knitting factory. His was a model middle-class family. In those days Leicester was a small town, but in ancient times it had been the site of a major Roman encampment. Mr Groves showed me the fourteenth-century town hall, and braving the rain we saw where Lady Jane Grey had been beheaded in the sixteenth century. He sighed the whole way there and back about how such a talented seventeen-year-old maiden had been queen for only nine days before being executed by Mary Tudor. She only went to the block because of her father, he said, who'd joined the opposing forces. I was often astonished by the average British citizen's sense of history.

My home was stripped during the Cultural Revolution, but by some miracle a tin candy box he gave me with my name and his address embossed in its top survived.

On my trip to Aberdeen, I was hosted by the Gordon family – descendants of the General Gordon who met his end in Khartoum, after helping Zeng Guofan beat the Taiping rebels in the mid-nineteenth century. A great lawn led up to a three-storey red-brick mansion, behind which was an old castle-like structure and a family chapel. I slept in a great sandalwood bed with carved railings and painted posts said to have been constructed for a visit to the manor by George V. His Majesty must have been a large man, I thought, for his bed felt as big as a swimming pool. After breakfast Mrs Gordon invited me to see her family's cattle. She'd retained her maiden name after marriage. Her husband was a tall, blond Scandinavian, who seemed to me like a high-class butler.

We crossed the lawn to the cowsheds. Evidently in order to honour her clan's old link to China, each of the cows was named after a Chinese city. She called out to a brown one: 'Jiujiang! Come meet a visitor from home!' Then she yelled over to a black one: 'Come here, Chungking!' No doubt her intention was to put me at ease, but when I saw those two huge beasts coming at me with their sharp horns, I felt no national affinity with them at all. Notwithstanding Zhuang Zi's famous 'Treatise on Everything Being Created Equal', we Chinese have never had much time for the cause of equality with animals.

There was one occasion, in Canterbury, that really angered me, a lecture given to accompany an exhibition of ancient Chinese bronzes and porcelain. It was of course a glorious thing to see objects from one's own country displayed in a famous historical and cultural city of another country, and to see them admired by thousands of visitors. What upset me was hearing how those treasures had been obtained. The owner of the collection had been a physician on a British warship that took part in the expedition to punish the Boxers for their 1900 uprising. I learned that this well-bred gentleman had taken his treasures as a looter amid the chaos of war. For me, then, the exhibition lost its charm; it was a reminder of my country's tragic past. At the same time I wondered how the spoils of war could be exhibited openly as an expression of friendship.

There was one other embarrassing incident, at a small town in the Midlands. As I stepped off the train I was met by a blonde young woman in a light-coloured dustcoat who pushed a child's pram. She asked my name with a smile, then introduced herself: 'I'm Mary. My husband, Brian, is a fighter pilot at the Middle Eastern front.' She then pointed to a curly-haired young man by her side: 'This is Johnny, my husband's younger brother.' They took me to their home. It was an exquisite little country cottage with a parlour, dining room and kitchen on the ground floor, and three bedrooms upstairs. She left me in the guest room so that I could come down to dinner after I had unpacked.

While my hostess was busy in the kitchen, Johnny, the young man of the house, chatted with me. He was a conscientious objector, a pacifist who had been allowed to do war service on a neighbouring farm.

'If there's a moon tonight, I'll have to go out again after supper and get on with cutting the farmer's hay,' he said, looking at his watch.

The thought suddenly occurred to me: if he went out that would leave Mary and me alone in the house together. How awkward! But she seemed quite a proper young woman, so I didn't really worry.

She was a good cook and the dinner was delicious. She kept the dishes coming and asked me all the usual questions about China. She asked if men and women really got equal pay for equal work, and if several generations of a Chinese family really lived under the same roof. She asked about China's war effort too. I got these sorts of questions after every lecture, so at least I had my answers ready.

After dinner, Johnny pushed back his chair and got up. Putting on his cap, he said, 'See you in the morning,' shouldered a pitchfork that was propped up next to the door, and went off to make hay.

The moment Johnny was gone, bottles of sherry and gin appeared on the dinner table. Both were scarce items in Britain at the time. I began to be on my guard. I reminded myself that I was here to raise support on behalf of the war in China, and that her husband was a comrade-in-arms, fighting far away in the Middle East. I kept shaking my head and telling her I didn't drink – which was not exactly true.

Paying no attention she poured out two glasses of sherry.

'This is the famous Bristol Cream. A GI gave it to me. Here, have a taste!'

I felt obliged to accept.

Just then the baby upstairs began to cry. She had to put down her glass and hurry upstairs, clump, clump, clump. I relaxed a little. I regretted coming here, but at least it was no fault of mine – my lodgings were always arranged by the people inviting me to speak. And besides, who would have expected that the man of the house would be out making hay all night?

She came down with the baby in her arms, and picked up her glass to toast me. Taking advantage of this to remind her of who we were, I quickly lifted my glass to meet hers: 'To our quick victory over Japan, and your quick victory over Hitler! May your husband be home soon!'

She downed her sherry in one swallow. Holding her baby in one hand, she poured herself another glass with the other. I quickly covered my own glass with my hand. Whether from her eagerness or my politeness, the wine spilled onto my fingers and ran down them into the glass.

Rocking her baby, she asked me if Chinese men were allowed more than one wife. I told her they were allowed only one. She contradicted me: 'Nonsense, you're fibbing. The books say the Emperor of China had dozens of concubines. I borrowed *The Golden Lotus* from the library and the man in it has five wives.' That was more than a thousand years ago, I told her.

Now she wanted me to hold the baby for a while so that she could wash the dishes. That I was quite willing to do. Though I wasn't a father, I'd always loved babies. The chubby little bundle went to sleep quite sweetly in my arms. As I looked at him, an image of his father flashed through my mind. He wore a short leather jacket and goggles pushed up on his forehead.

After Mary had washed the dishes she took the baby from my arms, looked at me sideways, and asked me, 'Wouldn't you like to be a papa?' I was so embarrassed I couldn't look at her. Then came a real shocker. 'How I'd love to have a baby with a Chinese man,' she whispered.

Pretending to have got a headache from the wine, I wished her good night and headed for the stairs. My heart had begun to thump. I was no saint. I was a young man, just turned thirty, with sexual desires. Even so, as I reached the head of the stairs, I quickly called out good night again and plunged into my room.

It seemed to be a combination guest room and storage room. There were several chests of drawers and a row of wardrobes. On the wall was a wedding picture of the mistress of the house, clasping a young man in morning dress, the husband who was now so far away.

I breathed a sigh of relief as I locked the door. I changed into my pyjamas, staring at the photograph all the while, reminding myself that the husband was my comrade-in-arms. My comrade-in-arms!

I got into bed and turned off the light. Just then there came three light taps on my door. I heard her voice: 'Are you asleep?' 'Excuse me, I was', I replied. A few moments passed, and then again, tap, tap, tap. 'What's the matter?' I asked. She said, 'The baby has colic. He needs some medicine and it's in your room.'

As a guest in the house, I could hardly prevent her from entering to get her things – particularly when it was medicine for her child. I crawled out of bed, opened the door, and hurried back under the bedclothes.

'Excuse me,' she said, going over to the chests and pulling out one of the drawers. She appeared to be looking for the medicine, but then she turned and sat down on the side of my bed. I pulled the blankets up to my chin.

'You mustn't be so shy,' she said. Then she told me, 'You're not the first Chinese man I've known.' She told me about a Chinese from Southeast Asia with whom she'd been friendly.

'My husband is hairy all over, just like a gorilla'. She reached out and stroked my face. 'You Chinese men have skin that is soft and smooth, like satin.'

Jesus, God, Confucius, Mohammed . . . *somebody* come and

save me. I'm too weak to overcome a temptation like this. After my face, she began to fondle my neck. She bent forward and said, 'You're shivering!' I said, 'I'm afraid.' 'Afraid of me?' 'No, of myself.'

She laughed softly and took hold of the edge of the blanket, easing it down.

Just when my fate was hanging by a thread, there came a pounding at the front door. 'Mary? Mary!' It was Johnny.

Mary quickly went downstairs and opened the door. I heard her and her brother-in-law whisper a few words, then come up the stairs together. I heard Johnny say out on the landing, 'Just as we started work it came on to rain.' That was timely rain indeed.

From the time that England declared war on Germany in September 1939 until the Nazi invasion of Denmark in April of the following year, the Western front was completely quiet, though at sea German submarines were sinking merchant ships. France entrusted its entire defence to its Maginot Line; it was reported that the soldiers played poker within the bunkers and basketball outside them. You had to pay for your own gas mask in Paris – one hundred francs. No wonder people called this the phoney war.

Britain and France seemed to be under the impression that a naval blockade would be sufficient to bring Germany to her knees. But at the end of 1939, Berlin actually increased its civilian food rations: the meat allowance, for example, went up from one pound monthly to three pounds. Even with Western Europe blockaded, Germans could still buy in Eastern Europe. And when their sources of natural rubber were cut off, the Germans made synthetic rubber. Germany could still buy most of the petrol it needed from the United States. Capitalist merchants pursued profits wherever they could find them, regardless of principle. Japan was still buying military supplies from America too. Who knows but that the petrol used to fuel the planes that bombed Pearl Harbor was drilled in Texas?

Because of the lull in the war, in the spring of 1940 I went on an eleven-day trip to the Lake District with the famous translators Yang Xianyi and Gladys Taylor (they were not yet married) and several fellow Chinese students who were soon to return home. Shouldering backpacks, we climbed the hills and admired the magnificent scenery.

By the time I returned to Cambridge, the phoney war was over.

In April the Nazi armies took Norway and their troops advanced
on the Low Countries. In May, Holland and Belgium surrendered
in succession. England was thrown into a panic. Chamberlain,
leader of the appeasement faction, had to resign. Churchill
delivered his moving 13 May speech to the House of Commons,
telling his countrymen 'I have nothing to offer but blood, toil, tears
and sweat'. The Conservative and Labour parties established a
joint war cabinet so they could cooperate in defeating the enemy.
On 10 June, Mussolini entered the war on Hitler's side. France was
now under attack on two fronts. The Nazi Panzer divisions cut
through France, battling their way to the coast. France found her
Wang Jingwei [leader of the Chinese puppet regime] in the person
of Marshal Pétain.

I was in Cambridge at the time of the critical retreat from
Dunkirk in May 1940. Early one morning I went out and saw the
streets full of soldiers who had escaped from France. Some were
leaning wearily against walls, while others sat on the ground. All
were covered with mud. Yet they were still singing popular
patriotic songs, showing their contempt for Hitler and his forces
on the other side of the Channel.

At such moments spiritual strength is the decisive factor in
determining the survival of a nation. Those 300,000 survivors of
the great Allied rout in 1940 were to become the backbone of the
Allied counterattack in 1944.

My admiration for the capacity of the British to endure in the
face of the greatest adversity knew no bounds. Perseverance was in
fact victory.

After the fall of most of Western Europe, England was truly
under siege. Rumours came thick and fast. Everyone was discuss-
ing not whether the Nazis were coming, but how soon, and by
what route: by air, or by amphibious landing boats. British
reconnaissance planes detected large numbers of German troops
along the opposite shore training at scaling cliffs. I was astonished
that at this critical time for the fate of their nation the English did
not lose their sense of humour. Instead of hysteria in the face of the
crisis, one still heard funny stories about the coming attack.

According to reports from Dutch refugees, Nazi paratroopers
disguised themselves as people from all walks of life – businessmen, women, even nuns. One day a rather stout middle-aged
spinster, whom I happened to know personally, was surrounded

by people who suspected that she was a paratrooper. They insisted that she was a man in disguise, and she had a hard time before they let her go. The gear required by paratroopers was also diverse. Some newspapers depicted them in search of bicycles. Therefore, on 13 May, I handed in my dear old iron donkey. A friend who went with me jokingly asked the impatient constable, 'How about our roller skates and tricycles – will you be needing them, too?' Said he, 'It depends on how the parachutists disguise themselves, doesn't it?'

One day a child in Cambridge suddenly ran home yelling 'Parachutists! The German parachutists have come, they've landed in the willow grove across the river!' But, on examination, it turned out only to be some poor soul who'd hanged himself.

Perhaps because the British Isles were not home to me, I remained fairly uninvolved. When people began selling off their rare books in the open-air market at Cambridge, I bought one after another. That was when I developed an interest in collecting English prints and illustrations. I also went on holiday with some Chinese friends to Barmouth, a prosperous summer resort on the Welsh coast beneath Snowdon. It was there, oddly enough, that I fell in love with Western music.

When we arrived, the three of us presented our food ration cards at the grocers. It wasn't a very large shop. There was a proprietor, about fifty years old and his lame assistant – both of them exempt from war service. The owner greeted us with a smile every time we entered. Before we ordered our food, he'd wipe his hands on his apron and shake hands with us. He was extremely friendly and also well informed about the war in China.

One Friday when we'd bought our provisions and were about to leave he called after us: 'Might I have the pleasure of the company of you three Chinese gentlemen in my home tomorrow night for a cup of coffee?' Pointing at the ceiling, he said 'I live upstairs'. We gladly said yes.

Perhaps he had a wife up there and many children? And most British families liked to grow flowers and raise cats and dogs. But we discovered he lived alone, no wives or dogs, or even flowers. Instead, his walls were lined with albums of gramophone records. And in the corner of the room was a gramophone with a huge horn speaker.

He'd changed into a dark blue suit and wore a bow tie beneath the collar of his snowy white shirt. After expressing an apology for his ignorance of Chinese music, he brought over a stack of record catalogues and asked what we'd like to hear – a symphony, concerto, opera or lyric song. This put us in an awkward position. We'd only heard folk songs like 'Santa Lucia' and 'The Last Rose of Summer'. Finally he selected a piece by Debussy for us, *'L'après-midi d'un faune'*. He said this music fitted best with his impressions of the Orient.

With all the piety of a priest setting out sacrificial objects on an altar, he lightly placed the first record on the turntable. From the great papier mâché gramophone horn came music that was by turns slow and fast – suddenly distant and then very near at hand; at times graceful and melodious, at times thundering and vehement.

We Chinese consider marriage to be one of the most essential parts of life. A man of marriageable age who remains a bachelor is suspected of being physically defective or mentally abnormal. This old shopkeeper brought me to understand the nobility of celibacy. Ever since then, except for the ten dark years from 1966 to 1976, though I have never really understood the theory of European classical music, I have listened to it regularly and as piously as he.

Another rather less happy incident occurred during our holiday. My two friends were living in a beach-front hotel, while I had rented a flat on a side street. The landlady, Mrs Jones, was a childless widow in her sixties, and her apartment house was the sole means of livelihood left her by her husband. She was very welcoming. She said that since she was little, she'd always heard that the Chinese were a very polite and cultured people. I was the first Chinese person she'd ever met, and she felt honoured to have me as her guest.

One day, one of my friends, Wu Yuanli, received a package from a friend in San Francisco that contained all sorts of Chinese delicacies. Wu generously suggested that we all share them to make a proper Chinese meal. It was a most enticing offer. I had nothing to contribute, so I said, 'You can't very well cook in your hotel room, but there's a paraffin stove in my flat, so we can do it there.' Eager to accept, Wu and his colleague brought over the rice noodles, bamboo shoots and a tin of Chinese pickled herring. I borrowed a frying pan and stirring ladle from the landlady. She even provided us with dishes for three place settings.

We agreed that we should fry the herring first. I volunteered to man the skillet. I rolled up my sleeves and poured the oil into the frying pan first. Then came the pickled herring, in several pieces. The aroma had us all drooling. It reminded me of the Chinese southlands and their fashionable neighbourhoods, of lychees, and even of the famous Wang Zhihe stinky bean curd shop in Peking. We told each other that although there was high-class, middle-class and low-class cuisine, this fish was in a super-class all its own. It not only satisfied the appetite, it had a unique olfactory magic.

Just as the three of us were rhapsodising in this vein, there came a sudden pounding on the door. When I opened up, there was Mrs Jones. The smile was gone from her face. Shaking her finger at me, she said: 'Oh you Chinese! You've ruined me. Have you heard them? Every tenant in the building is protesting. Is there a more awful smell in the world than the one coming out of your room? It's asphyxiating. If you don't move out, they all say they will. And then how's an old lady like me to go on living?'

I would never have imagined such a reaction! But I couldn't harm Mrs Jones, so I agreed to move immediately. The feast was ruined. Hastily we gobbled down our native delicacies, then I settled my account with Mrs Jones, apologising all the while, and that night moved into another lodging house.

SOAS returned to London at the end of July. In August the Battle of Britain began, and then the great London blitz which continued for nine whole months, the lightning war that Hitler hoped would crush the British Isles.

Enemy planes dared not attack during the day, due to the RAF fighter squadrons and London's barrage balloons and the web of wires that tethered them, so the blitz of 1940 took place at night. When day broke again, office staff went to their work as usual, and the labouring men to their factories and docks, while their wives went out to stand in queues for their shopping. At dusk, a thousand and more German bombers could be heard approaching again.

If London hadn't had its underground railway the civilian casualties would have been many times greater. With no block committees to lead the people, with no need for force, the residents would simply take up their bedding at sunset, and go down in good order to the nearest tube station – as Londoners call their subway. The platforms were very long and, since people didn't put down lots of mats to reserve places for aunty this or granny that, you could always find a place. Even though the underground was dug very deep, people sleeping on the platforms felt the earth shake whenever a bomb fell nearby. The next morning they would go up again and see how many homes had been reduced to rubble.

The months of that bombing were my most productive period of work for my paper, the Chungking *Dagongbao*. I sent despatches nearly every week, some of them so long they had to be serialised.

Every morning I, too, would climb up out of the tube and carry my bedding home. Then, stepping on pieces of broken glass and climbing over severed pipes, I would gather material for my report on London after the night's bombing. Firemen aimed their hoses at walls of flame that obscured whole blocks of housing, while civil defence volunteers gingerly rescued victims buried under the rubble who still had a breath of life in them. Milton's tombstone and statue behind St Giles's Church were destroyed and the area round St Paul's was flattened. Not even the insurance companies could protect themselves; one had lost the entire roof of its office.

Occasionally during the day the air raid siren sounded. In those cases, one had to find a place to take cover immediately. I was living at that time in a ground floor flat with a young Tamil lad named Rajarantu. Whenever we were faced with this predicament, we hid under our large dining table. Our flat was in a house that catered especially to Asians; besides us there was a Sinhalese girl who was studying the violin and several Chinese, including a bank teller and a physics student. Only Rajarantu and I were writers – he was studying law but wrote some fiction, too. Later he became a reporter and then, in the 1960s, the first deputy premier and foreign minister of Singapore. But I would see him again only in 1983.

Where individuals are concerned, we like to think that well-bred people remain calm in time of crisis while others become flustered. That goes for nations, too. My news despatches home emphasised the good order maintained by the Londoners during the blitz. Also their gallows humour – the newspapers regularly printed stories about ridiculous events – like a beauty pageant of girls in gas masks.

What left the deepest impression on me were the lunchtime concerts that took place in the heart of London in the National Gallery. Tickets were cheap – only one shilling – but the programmes were devoted to performances by first-rank violinists and pianists like Dame Myra Hess. A table was set up to sell sandwiches. It was an art gallery, so there were no seats, and people ate their sandwiches as they stood and listened to the music. Since Germany was the cradle of European classical music, the programmes tended to include Bach and Beethoven and even Wagner. This, too, showed that England was too wise to take out her anger at Hitler on great German musicians. As I listened to the music, I felt that this was the British people's way of defying the Nazis. Often the sirens sounded outside even as the violins were playing.

Though fortunetellers had promised me a long life, they were nearly proved wrong on several occasions. In those days I spent my nights either down in the tube or with a bridge-playing friend, Gu Xiancheng, who lived in a big reinforced concrete building. (I developed a great fondness for bridge as a result.) When I returned to my lodgings one morning, I discovered that the windows had been blown out and that my bed was overturned and covered with bomb splinters.

Not long after my arrival in England, I had come to know Dr Bluth, a German Jewish refugee who was a poet and a physician. The Bluths lived in the heart of London. Once I went to their house to spend the weekend. On Sunday evening, Dr and Mrs Bluth went to a dinner party at a neighbour's. I stayed at home minding the house. When the air raid alarm sounded at about nine o'clock I was upstairs, reading in bed. I ran downstairs in my pyjamas and hid under the basement staircase. Soon I heard a tremendous explosion. The little two-storey house had taken a direct hit. Fortunately it was just an incendiary bomb. The roof immediately caught fire but the fire brigade soon arrived and the Bluths themselves not long after. The moment she entered the door, Mrs Bluth charged straight upstairs through the smoke and fumes to rescue her suitcases full of valuables. Dr Bluth simply turned his back to the fire and threw up his hands. 'Europe is finished,' he said. 'The future belongs to Asia, to you Chinese!'

At that a volunteer fireman took me by the arm and helped me away to the neighbourhood first aid station. I was still wearing only my pyjamas. They gave me a nice hot cup of cocoa.

As I've already mentioned, in the summer of 1942, I left the School of Oriental and African Studies in London to enroll in King's College, Cambridge. I became a graduate student in cap and gown.

The college took me in and lodged me in its fifteenth-century school building, painting my name on the lintel over the entrance to D-2. The study and bedroom were roomy and comfortable, equipped with bookshelves on either side of the study fireplace, and sofas and easy chairs lining the other three walls, enough to accommodate a dozen or more guests. What excited me most was the view from my window. To the east was the ancient King's College Chapel. Its shadow fell across the lawn with the first rays of morning. At twilight I could hear the pure and melodious sounds of a boys' choir wafting up, complete with organ accompaniment. There were about twenty boys, all ten years old or so in white gowns and red bow ties. They filed past my window in pairs every evening. Out to the north of the window I could look past grazing horses on the meadow to the River Cam.

I was of course already quite familiar with Cambridge. It had been my first home when I came to England in 1939. Though I was only an evacuee from London at the time, many of the university facilities had been open to me. I quickly obtained a library card and was even permitted to attend a few lectures. But guests are still guests. Until 1942 I knew this institution of higher learning only as an outsider.

The organisation of Cambridge and Oxford reminded me a little of our traditional Chinese extended family. There was a general governing body called the Senate House, but the real power, particularly over finances, was divided among the several colleges, which, for reasons of history, varied in their endowments and academic strengths. The Chancellor of the university was a titular officer only; he did not live on campus. The vice-chancellorship rotated among the masters and provosts of the colleges. The pivotal role of the Senate House, a legislative body, was its management of all the students' grades and records. All those accepted for admission to the university had to go to the Senate House to register and enroll. It also conferred degrees at graduation.

To go to the Senate House to enroll was a most solemn ceremony. When the day came, I entered the great hall with my fellows, all of us wearing gowns and mortarboards. On the table lay a thick register with sheepskin covers. Milton, Byron, Darwin – all those who had entered the halls of Cambridge had signed their names in this book and, as was the custom, indicated the professions of their parents and the offices with which their relatives had distinguished themselves. One by one we went up and wrote our names in this book. I was very conscious of the great weight of tradition. To be in the same book with those illustrious men of old was not only a great honour, but a spur to my future efforts.

At that time Cambridge was very particular about niceties of academic dress. I believe my graduate student's robe had one more ribbon than the undergraduates', while those of professors were hemmed in red. For two years, except when I was in bed or at the toilet, my body was covered by that black robe as consistently as a snail is by its shell. This heritage of medieval monastic tradition was something that set Cambridge and Oxford apart from the upstart urban universities. Like discipline in the army, it lent an aura of high seriousness. At night, the college proctor would send out inspectors (called bulldogs by the students) to patrol the streets. If they discovered someone without his gown, they would take out a little book and note down his name and college, for later disciplinary action.

The university had strict rules about the great lawns in the college courtyards too. A college member who did not have his BA must not cross them. Graduate students might walk on the fringes. Only the dons had the right to stride straight across them at will.

Some of the college rules dated from the previous century and stood in evidence of the debauchery of the upper classes. For instance: 'Firecrackers and chorus girls shall not be permitted within the college'.

The front gate of the college closed at 10 pm; all women visitors had to be escorted outside the walls by that time. At my very first meal however, a student I'd never met sat down next to me and told me all sorts of secret ways to climb back in if I was stuck outside late at night when the college gate was closed. He knew about thirty different ways of scaling the wall.

In the dining room we all stood up and said grace in Latin before shuffling down onto our chairs and digging in. The dons sat on a platform, at the high table. They ate exactly what we did, but were permitted port wine at dinner – which was a not inconsiderable privilege in time of war. The wine cellar at King's College was much admired and envied.

On returning to Cambridge in 1984 at the invitation of my old tutor, Dr George Rylands, I discovered that my wife was actually allowed to live with me. Post-war Cambridge had changed a lot. The college had become coeducational, so women were admitted to college residence. Many formalities and regulations had been abolished. And the cap and gown were worn only on special occasions.

Still, Cambridge retained its time-honoured tradition of college pranks. It was said that Thomas Gray (1716–1771), author of 'Elegy in a Country Churchyard', had been deathly afraid of being trapped in the college by a fire. He tied a rope from his window so that he could slide down to safety the moment he heard the fire bell. One night his friends put a large barrel filled with water under his window and then sounded the alarm. To the delight of the students who had gathered to watch, Gray carefully crawled through his window and slid down the rope straight into the water.

Often these pranks demonstrated the students' resourcefulness and, indeed, audacity. One morning not long after I arrived in Cambridge a bicycle and a pair of women's panties in a pastel pink were to be seen suspended from the Senate House flagpole to the right of King's College. It was a real headache for the university administration; only by afternoon was someone found who was able to scale the pole and take down the exhibit. Then there was the notoriously sound sleeper who lived on the ground floor of the college. Conspirators entered his rooms one night and led a horse they found grazing on the common into his bedroom. Only on awakening the next morning did he discover that a horse had been stamping around anxiously in his room all night, leaving massive amounts of manure on the carpet.

At Cambridge, attending class and lectures was secondary to the time spent with one's tutor. Once or twice every week at a set period, usually tea time, student and teacher would find seats on a sofa. The professor did not exactly give the student lessons, but rather inspiration and guidance. The student would then read out loud the essay he'd written that week. He was encouraged to ask questions and put forward his own viewpoint, even if it meant arguing with the tutor at length. It was a teaching method that verged on the over-luxurious, but it certainly opened up the mind and encouraged creative thinking.

George Rylands, my tutor, was a famous scholar. He was not just erudite but also a good actor. I saw him perform in a Greek tragedy and direct *Volpone*. After Lord Keynes's death, Rylands succeeded him as head of the Cambridge Arts Theatre. I was studying British psychological novels at the time. He first encouraged me to read widely, then gradually directed me towards D H Lawrence, Virginia Woolf and E M Forster. I wrote a dozen or more essays under his guidance. It was precisely when I expressed possibly irreverent ideas rooted in my Oriental background that he grew especially interested. In particular, one essay of mine argued that *Finnegan's Wake* could ony be a literary dead-end, like Laurence Sterne's *Tristram Shandy* and Fielding's prefaces to his eighteen books of *Tom Jones*. Each was a unique tour de force, but could never open up a new path for literature – least of all in China.

Now Rylands thought Joyce represented the pinnacle of fiction in the West. My essay, however, began with the social function of literature and proceeded to the exchange of feelings between author and reader – without which literature became no more than a word game in disguise, I argued. Rylands was shocked by this peculiarly Oriental viewpoint. Yet at the same time he was interested in it. We discussed the question for two afternoons in succession. And instead of defending his own views during our talks, he concentrated more on listening to me, the better to understand my foreign perspective.

When he invited me to tea again in 1984, he pointed at the sofa and told my wife that it was there he had 'taught' me. Yes indeed, we had sat at our two ends of the sofa. Puffing vigorously on his pipe and continually rolling his blue eyes, he had listened with patience, concentration and sympathy as I expounded my views. And it was from him that I had learned to listen conscientiously to people with viewpoints different from my own.

Another memory of Cambridge I cherish is of the university's many extracurricular activities. They were an inseparable part of the university education.

First, of course, was the Student Union. It was something like a club (it had a simple dining room and often put on dances) but it was also the cradle of Britain's parliamentary system. It conducted a debate every Saturday night. The setting imitated the House of Commons: the chairman of the proceedings who sat on the dais was like the Speaker of the Commons. Pros and cons sat on either side of him. Each side had its first speaker, second speaker, and advocate. The last was usually not a member of the university, but a celebrity, such as an MP or even a cabinet minister. In one 1939 debate the proposition was, 'England should aid China in resisting Japan'. The side in favour of the motion invited Kingsley Martin, chief editor of the *New Statesman and Nation* and a council member of the China Campaign Committee. The first speaker was a Malayan Chinese, Lin Hua. The camp of the opposition included a Japanese student. The debate was sharply worded, but always orderly. The only thing that grated on my ears was Lin Hua's continual reference to the Japanese student as 'my honourable opponent'. To me such aristocratic civilities rang very false. But, after hearing several more debates, I came to realise that they embodied an important facet of democratic governance: respect for the opposition. Such rules of etiquette eliminated the flying ink boxes and wildly swung walking sticks seen in the Chinese parliament during the early years of the Republic. The extent to which a nation is civilised may be seen in whether it rules its citizens with reason or force. When I participated in political study classes in Peking during the 1950s, I was outraged by the official Communist tactics of questioning people's motives at every turn so as to completely stifle opposition. But now, so many years later, it becomes clear that force makes people submit only for a time.

Cambridge had many study societies; I had to limit myself to those I found particularly beneficial. The film society let me see superb films each week at a rock-bottom price (one shilling), while at the same time providing a systematic overview of the develop-ment of cinematic art. There were famous films from the early period of the Russian Revolution such as *The Road* and *The Watch*, as well as art films that had never officially been released, like the film by Eisenstein depicting Mexican village life. Upton Sinclair, who had provided the money for the film (originally called *Que Viva Mexico!*), had stipulated a maximum length of one hour and forty-five minutes. But Eisenstein, artist that he was, had so fallen in love with the Mexican sky, the clouds and the ten-foot tall desert cacti, that he'd shot two hours of natural scenery before the story even began. Later a mediocre director was called in to finish the piece. Sometimes, sadly, art and ideology cannot be reconciled.

I also joined the drama society.

When I went to spend the weekend with English friends, they often put on an entertainment after dinner: usually a reading of literary works. Among the books I heard read out loud were novels by Dickens, George Eliot and Mrs Gaskell. The readings were minor dramatic performances, lively enough to arouse my interest in the original works.

I'd imagined similarly that experts did the play-readings in the Cambridge drama society and that I could just sit back and enjoy the proceedings. But as I discovered after entering the group, the parts to be read were assigned to us ordinary members by the club secretary in advance; you had to bring more to the meetings than just your ears. I'd never been good at acting and now I had to pretend to be English, maybe even from a century or two earlier. I had a bad time even with the easier servants' roles, stuttering and ruining my lines. Yet it was through the drama society that I learned how important it is that literary works should please the ear when read aloud. I started reading my own writings out loud to see if they sounded dull or had inconsistencies of stylistic tone.

All these Cambridge societies were organised by the students themselves, and most of them met in the student rooms in the evenings.

Tea parties of course had an important place in English social life. During the war, when food was strictly rationed and it was difficult to invite friends to dinner, tea parties became all the more frequent. Each guest brought his own packets of tea and sugar and presented them to the host at the door. In my two years at Cambridge I often went to several tea parties a week. Some were held by the college for students and faculty, some were just for students, and some were held outside. Among the latter, I received invitations to tea from Bertrand Russell of Trinity College and from Joseph Needham, who was studying the history of Chinese science and technology.

Once I received an invitation to tea from a young man who was a former Cambridge student. He'd already been called up and become a bomber pilot, but he rented digs in Cambridge and during his leaves he would take off his uniform and return to his spiritual home. He wrote poetry and venerated T S Eliot. He had many reservations about the war, and felt that the only hope for humankind lay with the East. 'I hope that you can create a civilisation that can combine material force with spiritual values,' he said. He was sent to bomb Italy, and each time he dropped his bombs he felt he was committing a crime. On the afternoon of one of his tea parties I found his door locked and his room empty. He was never heard from again. He'd been gobbled up by the war.

The academic year at Cambridge was divided into three terms, and each had its own major holiday. The first festival came at Christmas. I was invited to a party on Christmas night and was completely overcome by the singing and the liquor. I remember that I made a comparison between Eastern and Western attitudes to drinking in my diary when I returned at midnight. The Chinese took delight in getting the *other* person drunk. Westerners, on the other hand, got themselves drunk, and indeed refused to go home before they *were* drunk. Even so, I must admit that I myself, a Chinese who'd always obeyed Confucius's rule of moderation, usually had to make my way back to my rooms with the help of the nearest wall.

The spring festival of Easter seemed to celebrate young love. I most liked the madrigal concerts on the banks of the River Cam, performed by the boys' choir in their usual white robes and red ties. Mostly they sang English choral music of the sixteenth century, and their clear young voices wafted down the river, in the wake of the hundreds of candles that had been set gently floating downstream. Gazing at the specks of candlelight, one forgot all about the war and one's own cares.

Cambridge had two theatres then. Although the performances were often by first-rank troupes from London, the tickets were much cheaper than in London, and you could book them in advance. There were also classical operas, English operettas, ballets . . . I stuck to plays instead of cinema, knowing that once I got back to China, there would be plenty of Hollywood films to see. Every play I saw was equivalent to an exquisite class in the arts.

During one vacation, Malayan Chinese classmates asked me to teach classes in Mandarin. That was how I got to know Lim Chong-eu (Lin Cangyou), a medical student in Edinburgh. We both availed ourselves of Britain's youth hostel system. You could join for only a shilling. The organisation had set up inexpensive hostels all across Britain. Once registered at a particular hostel you had to help with the cooking and, except on rainy days, you were locked out at 8 am so you had to move on. Chong-eu and I put on our rucksacks and tramped all over the Scottish Trossachs. When my wife and I stayed with him in 1985, he was the chief minister of the state of Penang, Malaysia.

In the summer of 1943, I came down with a strange illness: my whole head began to ache, day and night. None of the Cambridge doctors could cure it, so I went to find a doctor in London. Sulfa had just come on the market then. One doctor took me to be his guinea pig and prescribed twenty tablets a day. The medicine made my whole body go numb, and three days later my symptoms hadn't lessened in the slightest. It was as if someone had put a spell on me that squeezed my head in a vice all day long. It hurt so much that even my memory was affected.

At this point a British fellow student who had heard of my distress asked me if I'd like to learn to play the recorder. His field was chemistry, but he said nothing was better than music for the nerves, and that he was willing to be my teacher. I'd always loved music. Now someone had volunteered to teach me, so I went straight out and bought an instrument and an elementary song book.

I'd met this classmate at the Christmas party. He was tall and thin and very refined in manner. The first day, he played a seventeenth-century madrigal for me. I envied the way his delicate fingers moved so accurately over the key holes.

He often stayed until late at night, patiently listening to my awkward tootling and pointing out my mistakes. In that friendly atmosphere, sooner or later I couldn't help pouring out to him my misfortunes in love – which in fact may well have been the real cause of my headaches. I asked if he hadn't had such upsets in his emotional life, too. He shook his head. I went on: 'Were you never jilted by a girlfriend?' He shook his head again. 'Don't you have a girl?' I asked. His answer stunned me.

'I'm one myself,' he said.

People had told me before I came to King's College that it was a hotbed of homosexuality. Now a homosexual was sitting right in front of me. I was both afraid and curious. Instantly I changed into a psychoanalyst and began interrogating him about his sexual background.

I wondered if perhaps it was living apart from girls all his life that had done this to him. He kept shaking his head, saying that he'd attended coeducational primary and secondary schools. He'd always lived among the opposite sex. He asked me, surely China had homosexuals too? I thought back. When I'd been an apprentice at the Beixin Book Company in 1926, one of my fellow apprentices had seemed sexually rather odd. But he was the only one I'd ever met. I'd also heard that the Shanghai French Concession in the 1930s had an Avenue Albert for male prostitutes. But they were forced into it by the need to make a living, and they catered to foreigners. We Chinese were almost universally heterosexual.

He steadfastly refused to believe this, even saying that I was simply unwilling to admit the truth to him. Looking back on it now, I'm ashamed of my reaction. After our heart-to-heart talk, my interest in learning to play the recorder cooled. Homosexuality was still a crime in England then, and that alone must have been enough to give him feelings of inferiority. Sometimes I felt that he was avoiding me, as if he thought I despised him. I didn't, but in my mind he had indeed changed from a normal person into a freak. Now after all these years, when I better understand homosexuality as a biological phenomenon, I feel guilty about how I treated that man. He confessed a dark secret to me and I not only failed to show sympathy but shunned him.

In truth, when I was about fourteen, I too had once had an undeniable passion for one of my male classmates. I remember naively waiting in front of the school door one Sunday for him to return from a weekend trip. My reluctance to be away from him was a little like the desire I felt later on for the opposite sex. Some other boys were similarly affected. But that was only emotional intimacy, cuddling each other cheek to cheek at most. And we were all soon attracted away from each other by girls.

The Confucius we Chinese respect as the basis of our humane philosophy preaches only the 'three bonds and five relationships' of the customary Chinese patriarchal system. Whenever I study abnormal psychology I ponder the fact that China has no professional psychoanalysts even today. If we had one, he'd go hungry.

Though I can scarcely believe it myself, what finally cured my headaches was a shepherd dog and the hills of north-western Wales, softly carpeted in purple heather.

For that I had the Williams-Ellis family to thank. When I was so ill that I couldn't continue my studies, Susan (the very friend who in 1984 would prod me time and again to complete these memoirs) took me to her home on the Portmeirion Peninsula. After entrusting me to the care of her parents, she returned to London, where she was engaged in secret war work for the government.

It was a region of breathtaking natural beauty. And since 1925 Susan's father, the architect Clough Williams-Ellis, had spent his life savings constructing a fantasy village there. With the determination of a lifetime, this master architect had realised his dream.

The Williams-Ellises were a prominent family of North Wales who counted Welsh kings among their ancestors. Susan's mother, née Amabel Strachey, was an author. They lived in the hill country, their house set in a beautiful flower garden. The furniture, the fireplaces – everything was steeped in history.

I had met Susan in London at a meeting of the PEN Club in 1940. Having studied at the Chelsea Polytechnic under Henry Moore and Graham Sutherland, she now taught painting at Dartington. Her speciality was painting marine life. The day I delivered a luncheon talk at the PEN Club, her mother, Amabel, was ill; Susan, who attended in her place, sat next to me. After that, we often went to concerts and art exhibitions together. I was present at her marriage to the economist Evan Cooper-Willis. When she heard that I couldn't dance, she vowed she'd teach me, and we went several times to the Café Royal. Finally she gave up, saying she'd never met anyone with so little sense of rhythm.

On hearing that I was under the weather with a peculiar complaint, her family opened their doors to me. At first I stayed in the big house, then I moved to a little slate-roofed cottage at the foot of the hill. I boarded there with a simple old Welsh shepherd and his wife who spoke only a few words of English. They owned a spotted black and white sheepdog named Dick. His body was skinny but his eyes were kind and gentle; we quickly became friends. He nestled at my feet in the evenings as I sat before the fire listening to music, often cocking his head and staring up at me. Every afternoon he accompanied me on my walks across the hills. We would climb up to a peak from which we could look out on the Irish Sea, then turn back. As I strolled along, humming some tune or other, I felt a gradual loosening of the vice that held my head. Finally it disappeared.

At Susan's kind invitation I returned with my wife in 1984 and 1986 for a visit to this place that had so miraculously cured me. Susan and Evan had now raised three daughters and a son. Their son Robin and his wife now manage the amazing resort and hotel built by Sir Clough Williams-Ellis at Portmeirion, while their eldest daughter, Anwyl, helps her mother and father design pottery – and they have established a Portmeirion Pottery Works up in Stoke-on-Trent that has over four hundred employees.

Back in the war years I didn't hear much about minority ethnic problems in Britain. But Wales did have a group of nationalists in 1942 who wanted to take advantage of the war to gain independence from English rule. They even set fire to an airfield. It was unthinkable that Wales could become fully independent of England. Even so, when I returned in 1984, I found that notices and road signs were written in both Welsh and English, with the Welsh first. And one television station regularly broadcast programmes in Welsh. Welsh culture also had an important place in the university curriculum. This seems to show that things get better only if a certain amount of determination is shown. For their part, the English were wise enough not to try to suppress regional separatism by force.

Cultural groups continued to ask me to speak during my two years at Cambridge. My most important talk was the lecture I delivered at the Wallace Collection towards the end of 1942. The idea for it came from encounters I had at social occasions in Cambridge.

A favourite topic of conversation among British thinkers at the time was what the post-war world would be like. At his tea parties, Bertrand Russell always said that China ought not to follow in the footsteps of the West. Material civilisation led to a dead end. Post-war China ought to go all-out to preserve and promote its ancient spiritual civilisation. He even accepted my invitation to write a piece in the Chungking *Dagongbao* setting forth his viewpoint.

Finally, however, I couldn't agree with Russell that the two wars in Europe had resulted from an overdevelopment of material civilisation. China, bullied and humiliated by the great powers ever since the nineteenth century, had neglected science, technology and national defence, relying instead precisely on its 'ancient civilisation' to save it. But clearly, in a dog-eat-dog world, without a certain level of material development, a country would only be gobbled up even more enthusiastically by its neighbours.

My lecture, which was a roundabout way of refuting the well-meaning people who were trying to dissuade China from modernising, went something like this:

If I may liken the whole world to a schoolroom, then China entered or, rather, was propelled into this schoolroom some time in the early part of the nineteenth century as a new student, shy yet arrogant, clumsy and outlandish, wearing an old-fashioned pigtail and with fingernails some four inches long. Until then this student had played truant, protected by high mountain ranges and wide oceans, not to mention the Great Wall; but once he entered the classroom he found himself obliged to get his School Certificate, by which I mean his right to a national existence, or perish. Although this boy was much older than the others and had quite a sound classical education, he looked so haughty and behaved so awkwardly that no decent student could help teasing him. One pulled his ear, another tweaked his nose and another twisted his pigtail. He didn't like this, but the person who really upset him was the chap who tried to choke him to death. That student's name, as you will probably have guessed, was Japan. China had never thought the little fellow capable of so much mischief and he didn't know how to cope.

When he grew desperate, he appealed to the schoolmaster.

'Do you know any algebra?' asked the teacher.

'No sir, but I can distinguish eighty varieties of orchid.'

'Are you a mechanical draughtsman? Could you design a drainage system?'

This time the boy decided to have a try. He ground his ink and waved his brush and dashed a few exquisite stokes on to the paper, like wispy dragon-beards seen through cloud.

The teacher snatched away the brush angrily.

'Drainage is a practical thing. You study the dynamics of water and apply them to the needs of an irrigation system. What the devil are you trying to do? Are you dreaming?'

The whole class burst out laughing and the boy felt like crying, but he swallowed his tears.

Then the teacher asked him, 'What about sport? Do you play football? Or tennis? Or squash? Or cricket?'

'I play the bamboo flute and the seven-stringed harp' was all the boy could say.

You see, however superior his accomplishments, they did not qualify him for his School Certificate, and his School Certificate he had to have, if everyone in the place wasn't going to kick him and tease him. In such circumstances, what do you think he did? Do you think he went on drawing dragon-beards? No. You may be sure that he learnt his alegbra by heart, even while he cursed its crudeness; that he kicked his hot-water bottle around the room, pretending it was a football; and that he tried his hand at designing a drainage system, which after all was not as difficult as drawing dragon-beards. Oddly enough, the rest of the school began to take an interest in the dragon-beards after a while, though of course they thought them a spare-time hobby. But when they found the big Chinese boy busily making drainage blueprints, and well on the way to becoming a footballer too, the ones who could no longer tweak his nose began to patronise him.

'What marvellous dragon-beards you used to draw! Why do you waste time with these crude plans which you used to think so meaningless?' they said, or 'I think it's a pity that an elegant person like yourself should have anything to do with a rough game like football. You should have gone on wearing your long gown – and where are your beautiful fingernails? What, no pigtail, either?' And all the time the big boy, being a well-mannered big boy, grinned at them and murmured to himself, 'Don't worry about the dragon- beards. They are in my blood and they are my inheritance. But I'm not going to miss that School Certificate. Just let me get the Certificate and then perhaps I may teach you all to draw dragon- beards. And that wouldn't be a bad thing for you, either!'

As I have said, under Dr Rylands guidance, I mainly explored the works of three English authors: D H Lawrence, Virginia Woolf and E M Forster. As to Lawrence I had only his published works to study, not the man himself. He had died in 1930 and I never had an opportunity to meet his friends or relatives.

I might have met Virginia Woolf for she didn't die until 1941, and indeed I knew many of her acquaintances, but unfortunately she was afraid to live in London in case of enemy bombing. She stayed in a little town in Sussex instead, within five miles of the southern coast and this was off limits to an enemy alien like myself. By the time I had become a member of the grand alliance, she was no longer alive.

I went to Monk's House anyway, and spent a weekend with her husband Leonard. It was autumn and the apples had just ripened. We talked about Virginia in his orchard as we picked the fruit:

about their married life, Virginia's insanity, and how she came to drown herself in a nearby stream. In the evening he brought out a stack of Virginia's diaries and let me copy from them. Early the next morning, we went together with heavy hearts to the little brook where she had taken her life. I stood there on the bank, wanting to rebuke the gurgling waters. Then I felt perhaps I was wrong. The brook was just going endlessly on its way. Maybe it had simply relieved another transparent soul from further torment.

I was far more fortunate in regard to my third subject of research – E M Forster. I have never before written about him, but now, whenever I remember my days at King's College, I cannot help but think of that truly great author whose philosophy was 'only connect' – friendship counted above all else.

We knew each other before I ever entered King's College – indeed it was only at his recommendation (and the sinologist Arthur Waley's) that I was ever admitted.

The English PEN Club held a memorial meeting for Rabin-dranath Tagore in London's Conway Hall on 9 May 1941. The speakers on that occasion included the Soviet ambassador to Britain, Ivan Maisky and E M Forster. Attending as the repre-sentative from China, I was one of the speakers too. Sitting at the head table with us was Kingsley Martin, who knew that I liked Forster's novels and that I had been particularly moved by his censure of British colonialism in *A Passage to India*. He introduced us. I met many British authors through these PEN meetings, such as H G Wells – then head of the organisation – John Lehmann and Stephen Spender. Some kept in touch with me afterwards and some only shook my hand. My one true friendship was with Forster. What will grieve me to the end of my life is the tragic ending I finally made to our once intimate literary friendship.

Our friendship was not really so surprising. Now that I think back on it, we were bound to be attracted to each other. The best friend in Forster's life, and the one who most profoundly influenced him, was Goldsworthy Lowes Dickinson, whose biography Forster wrote. Dickinson journeyed to China in the first year of the Republic (1912). On returning to Britain, he wrote a book *Letters from John Chinaman*, in which he described China as a utopia in order to satirise Britain. It was because of this book, and his friendship with Dickinson, that Forster conceived a passionate interest in the East. I, for my part, had long been interested in the English novel – I admired Woolf up in her ivory tower, but almost worshipped Forster, who welcomed the whole world into his books. Little did I suspect when I first read them that we shared another interest, a love for cats.

Let me begin with them. In the eighty-odd letters Forster wrote to me, which were destroyed in the Cultural Revolution, discussions of literature and other serious matters repeatedly had to yield to the subject of our cats.

Not long after we were introduced, Forster sent me a letter proposing that he come to see me in Hampstead, so that Tinka and Toma (his cats) could send a present to Rhea (my cat). Fish was hard to buy in London at the time and, when he entered my door, Forster undid his big doctor's satchel and pulled out a package swathed in a handkerchief. He opened it up and, holding it out to Rhea, said, 'Tinka and Toma wanted you to have this.' It was synthetic cat food, something that had just been put on the market to meet the needs of us cat-lovers. Raising her head suspiciously, Rhea approached the gift. Then, to my intense embarrassment, she turned disdainfully away and returned to her place by the fire.

I was mortified. I scolded Rhea for her ingratitude, but Forster just smiled and wrapped up his gift in his hankie again, meanwhile telling Rhea how sorry he was that he'd affronted her.

Ever after, our cats figured prominently in our correspondence. For instance, he once confided, 'Tinka is a worms' jungle. He is full of them again, and indifferent to their happy toilings' (9 Feb 1943). In a letter thanking me for some Christmas candy I'd sent, he wrote, 'The sweets will be opened on Christmas Day, and please think of us doing this, four of us; five of us including the maid; and seven of us including the cats, who always approach when they hear any paper crackling' (22 Dec 1941). On hearing that Rhea had had kittens, he quickly sent a greeting thus: 'I hope you have established your kitten safely. I wish I could have invited it down here, and did suggest this to our two cats, Toma and Tinka, but they are very self-centred, and I did not quite like their replies. Toma boxes Tinka's ears, as it is' (31 Dec 1941). In another letter he said 'Toma is sitting in my chair. I am so relieved to hear that you found Rhea well. Toma and Tinka are pleased with her message. I wish they had had the pleasure of seeing her' (11 Jan 1942). When Rhea became ill, he even wrote to console me: 'I am anxious for news of Rhea. Has austerity more charms for her than it is meant to have? Toma mitigates the seriousness of life by asparagus, of which he is passionately fond, while Tinka makes shift with Oxo and milk' (1 May 1942).

In fact Rhea gave up the ghost while trying unsuccessfully to deliver her fourth litter. To help her with her family planning, I would tightly close all the doors and windows every time I went out. But the eight tomcats in the neighbourhood were all of them so in love with Rhea that they mewed all night long. Often on returning home I would see Rhea pressed up against the window glass, while outside a tomcat looked in, sometimes black, sometimes brown. And so it came to pass that Rhea got pregnant again – one of the tomcats, being a Lothario without peer, had managed to slip in under a window I hadn't closed tightly enough.

Rhea's death prompted another letter from Forster: 'I am much upset by the news. That sweetest of cats. Yes, sooner or later, as you say, but it is saddening when life vanishes into the dark before it has received and given all the happiness it might. My mother is also much distressed' (19 July 1943).

At this point I think I should explain how it is that I am able to quote Forster's own words in the present work when his letters to me were destroyed in the 1960s. In 1943 I could scarcely have imagined the Cultural Revolution, but during the winter vacation of 1943 I nevertheless made typed copies of the forty letters he had sent me between 1941 and 1943, arranging them in chronological order and annotating them for later reference. I presented the series to him in a bound folder entitled 'Friendship Gazette', and fortunately I was able to obtain a copy of this from the King's College Library in 1984.

Forster had a flat in the London suburb of Chiswick. It was where he stayed when he was in town. I met him often at the Reform Club, and also at that flat, where I became acquainted with several of his close friends. I also went twice to his home in Abinger, Surrey, where his elderly mother lived. English country houses often have ancient names and that one was called West Hackhurst. What struck me most deeply about this house was that it not only lacked a radio but modern gadgets of any sort. They even used paraffin lamps at night, for they had no electricity. Forster was what we Chinese would call a filial son. In 1942 he was already sixty-three, but in the presence of his mother he was like our legendary Chinese figure Old Laizi, who dressed up in baby clothing at the age of seventy to amuse his parents in their nineties.

At night, as Tinka slept in the old lady's lap and Toma lay at my side, he would recite her the poems Eliot had written about cats. Before breakfast, he played her a Bach concerto on the antique family harpsichord, often turning his head to look affectionately at his old mother and me, his Oriental guest, as he played.

Forster felt special affection for the Orient, particularly China. But when, early in our relationship, I expressed a wish that he might one day write *A Passage to China*, he wrote back that he was not even sure whether 'Hsiao' was my surname or my given name. 'So you see how ill-prepared – alas! – am I to take my Passage to China as yet' (27 Sept 1941). In one letter he enclosed a cheque that called for my signature as endorsement; he wanted me to forward it to the Chinese Red Cross, so that he could 'pay [his] respects to China'. In the summer of 1942, he wanted my help again. His close friend Charles Mauron, a Frenchman, had recommended that he read the book of Tcheung Tseu but these two words of the French transliteration could not be found in an English library. He asked me for the English spelling (Chuang Tzu, today Zhuang Zi) so that he could find the book.

In late 1942, on learning of Forster's interest in China, one British organisation asked him to lecture on that subject. He told me in a letter how much he wanted to accept, but he felt he really didn't know a thing about the country. In the end he declined. However, when I gave my lecture on the dragon-beards versus the blueprints at the Wallace Collection, he not only showed up ahead of time, but wrote to me afterwards: 'Now for your lecture for a minute. I much enjoyed it, thought it amusing and charming. It made me sad, for I felt that I was too old to "take on" China. . . . You must imagine that I have written a novel about China,' he joked, 'the greatest of our age, but that unfortunately its pages have got stuck together during printing, so that it cannot be read.' He concluded: 'The one question I wanted to ask you was: What will the road back from the blueprints to dragon-beards be like? And is there any evidence, in past world history, that any country has ever found the road?' (1 May 1943).

Forster very generously provided materials and support while I was studying his novels at King's College from 1942 to 1944. Through our correspondence I came to know many of his attitudes, opinions and activities that even an English student might not have discovered. He also gave me some of his essays and little booklets that had been published in Egypt and India, but never in Britain. Apart from notes on my reading, I had several volumes of notes on our conversations.

Unfortunately all these perished, along with my diaries from over the years and many bundles of letters, in the great red conflagration of the Ten Lost Years. It was because of that that I never undertook to write about him until now. I hardly knew where to start.

I had, in the early 1940s, met many Englishmen who felt a great sense of superiority on account of the British Empire, but Forster was quite the opposite. Many of his essays in *Abinger Harvest* mock that superiority. Basically he was a liberal – indeed, he was the first president of Britain's National Council for Civil Liberties. He once went so far as to say that 'no political creed except communism offers an intelligent man any hope'. But after the pact between Hitler and Stalin, he changed his mind. When the British Government began purging Communists from the civil service, and the National Council for Civil Liberties passed a resolution condemning the action, he announced his resignation from the council on that account. In 1939 he had printed a little pamphlet called *What I Believe*; it opened with the sentence, 'I do not believe in Belief'. In fact, all his works *do* expound a central belief: in friendship between human beings.

From my perspective as a Chinese reader, Forster's novels continue the honourable tradition of English realism established by Dickens and Fielding, but in technique, (plot construction, depiction of characters, depth and wit of dialogue and layered overtones of language), he surpasses his predecessors; he is truly one of the greats. And, significantly, among all the reigning elder English literati of the Edwardian age, he was also closest in his thinking to that of the young people.

After I handed in any paper on Forster to my tutor, I always mailed a copy to the author. The one that most caught his attention was my essay on *Howards End*. The novel's theme is an attempted reconciliation – or at least compromise – between upper-class intellectuals and the lower-class working people. It is Forster's novel that touches most directly on the difficult problems of social reform. I felt that he was fighting two enemies: human hypocrisy, and the gap between rich and poor. He knew a good deal about the former and so wrote about it very penetratingly, but he was not so familiar with the latter. I said that I found the ending disappointing in view of the expectations raised by the earlier parts.

After reading my little essay, Forster wrote me thus:

'Thank you for your letter, and for *Helen the Dark Trojan Horse* [my essay – H C]. I am afraid that Miss Macaulay is right and that what is wrong is she [I had debated with her by saying that *Howards End* was not a conciliation of the two houses but a tragedy of frustrated social reform]. What I mean is, is that her seduction of Len is a bit of a fake, and its consequences, including Miss Baby [*The Eternal Moment*], falsify the close of the book. There *was* intended to be a Wilcox-Schlegel synthesis at the close, and it was not impossible, in 1910, to locate such a synthesis in the country, which was then emotionally (and it seems economically) distinct from the town. But you are quite right in finding the synthesis unsatisfactory, and I only wish that the Something Else for which you look [the tragedy] was there. I find the fake more harmful than the much more blatant unrealities of *The Longest Journey*, a book which I actually prefer. The critics were shocked, but translated aesthetic into moral condemnation. If the matter interests you, do get hold of the life of Sir Edward Gosse when next you are in the library, and read the strange remarks he made about *Howards End* to Sir Edward Marsh. William Archer, the translator of Ibsen, also reviewed it unfavourably.

'My hopes for Social Reform, such as they were, have certainly been dashed since I wrote the book, and I have now become an Anarchist but one who finds it easier to suffer than to destroy, and who still clings to personal relationships and finds them clinging to him. I see the gradual extinction of taste and distinction between the opposed millstones of War and Public Service. I don't like the world I've lived on in to, but have a feeling that the world I was suited to will come back some day: not in a form which I should recognise no doubt and it won't be an Anglo-Saxon world' (9 Feb 1943; interpolations made by Hsiao Ch'ien in 1943).

Having on an earlier occasion accepted my criticism of the plot of another novel as 'unrealistic', he wrote:

'Sometimes I am for "art", sometimes against it. I am for it now, and feel that the world, not the artist, is in the tower, that the tower is of the cheapest and most hideous materials, and the artist as he wanders towards its base gets now a penny thrown at him, now a brick, and does well to receive them both with cynicism. I have rushed back to the Bohemian nineteenth-century idea of the artist. I feel that the lady from Hampshire was my aunt (they all had aunts). I shall only be too thankful if you could discover that the English were making something artistic, and I want to talk the whole thing over with you' (19 Sept 1941).

Later, I had evidently in another essay found fault with his understanding of the lower classes, and accused him of never having experienced true poverty. He responded:

'I have been considering what you said about poverty and your misery and "crime" in China. Why am I ashamed to hear of such things? Not because I am shocked by them, as you suggest, nor because I feel I ought to have shared them, as Dostoevski might suggest, but because I cannot IMAGINE them, because they emphasise a defect in my mental equipment. For an instant they become real, then they fall back again into words, "Barefoot and without a crust to eat, he . . ." etc. It is an extra barrier too to realise that European poverty is nothing to Oriental' (7 July 1943).

He let me read his novel about homosexuality, *Maurice*, which was locked in a safe and not to be published until a hundred years later, and he often discussed what books he liked and disliked. He worshipped Proust, for instance:

'I have invested in him. Taken much trouble with him, that is to say, as have others with Balzac, and when one has done that one's judgement tends to be too favourable. Still, I am fascinated with this enormous dream – for I think it to be – which keeps to the facts of place but plays the Dickens with time. I wish he hadn't such a monotonous and unfavourable view of human nature. Were he freer, with Miss Austen's freedom even, not to mention Tolstoy's, he would be the greatest novelist who ever flew' (31 Jan 1943).

But he also told me that the books at his bedside were Balzac.

Thus did a young Chinese literature student come to be friends with a distinguished British author. The author deepened the young man's understanding of Western culture, and the youth added to the author's knowledge of China. How then did such a wonderful friendship come to its tragic end?

First of all, being aware of what had happened in Communist Eastern Europe, I wrote to all my overseas friends in September 1949, prior to my departure from Hong Kong for Peking, to ask that they cease communicating with me until I was able to assess the political situation there at first hand – that they were not to send me so much as a Christmas card. Hence my correspondence with Forster came to an end in the early autumn of that year. But when a British Cultural Delegation came to China in 1954, Forster entrusted a member of the delegation who was one of his bosom friends, Jack Sprott, a professor of psychology at the University of Nottingham, with a new book of his for me and a letter – a letter that was now as good as from another world. Surprisingly, since I was already in serious political trouble, I was allowed to go to a reception held by the visiting delegation. When the chance came, as we clinked our glasses in a toast, Sprott whispered 'Morgan has a new book he wants me to give you, and a letter. I'll give them to you once we can meet alone!'

That should have been easy. Both Eastern and Western rules of courtesy demanded that I entertain Sprott: in 1943 he'd invited me to his home at the University of Nottingham and I'd spent the weekend with him. He was a bachelor, with a falcon as his companion. I remember that while we were eating he directed his falcon to sit next to me as a gesture of respect, while he sat on the other side. I trembled secretly as I ate, fearing that the bird might stir to life at any moment and attack me. Apart from that, the weekend was spent most agreeably, and return hospitality was clearly owing.

But in 1954, when I already knew only too well the political difficulties I was in, how could I dare arrange a private meeting with a foreigner? Later I might well have to confess all sorts of shameful things I had supposedly plotted with him in secret.

I'd never been a risk-taker, particularly in the realm of politics. I hesitated for several days, not daring to speak to the leadership in my group, and finally did nothing.

The delegation moved on to another place, left the country at Canton, then flew back to England.

Forster had explained his own philosophy many times: friendship above patriotism. He wrote in *Abinger Harvest*, 'If I had to choose between betraying my country and betraying my friends, I hope I should have the guts to betray my country'. Yet he never lived under a dictatorship; he could not have understood my predicament. I imagine that when Sprott returned to England and returned the book and letter to Forster with the seal unbroken, not only must it have seemed a blow to him personally – perhaps it lessened his very faith in human nature.

The two-volume edition of Forster's letters published in England and America in 1982 contains none of my letters to him. When King's College was kind enough to invite me to stay during my 1984 visit to England, the College archivist Dr Michael Halls further disclosed that not a single letter from me was found among the papers that he left.

Quite so. After attentively listening to Sprott's account, he no doubt cast them into the fireplace as he quivered with grief and anger. I can almost hear him now, calling out to me from the next world: So these are the Chinese – the courteous and conscientious Chinese. Of course this is merely my own conjecture out of a bad conscience.

Over the years I had however always guarded the eighty-odd letters Forster had sent me, keeping them with me always. I took them back to Shanghai with me when I left England in 1946, and from there on to Hong Kong in 1948. Naturally they accompanied me on my return to Peking in 1949.

When I returned to the city in the early 1960's from the labour farm to which I had been sent, still treasuring the letters, I was employed by the People's Literary Publishing House, and was therefore able to read books and periodicals from abroad once more. I read in the *Times Literary Supplement* that Forster was becoming a hot literary topic in England again. The Three Difficult Years following the Great Leap Forward were over, but even so, the campaign against revisionism was moving into higher gear. I began to worry about what might happen to my letters. I was afraid that they'd be seized and used in evidence against me, as had been the private correspondence of Hu Feng and his friends against them. So I casually mentioned to the leader in charge of foreign literature at the publishing house that I owned a bundle of letters that would be considered quite valuable in England, and made a proposal. I was afraid to suggest donating them. Could we not however exchange them with a British library in return for new books?

He was a man who feared being crushed by an avalanche at every leaf that fluttered past him. On hearing such a proposal from a known Rightist element such as myself, he not only did not act upon it, he notified the house library that I was hereafter barred from all foreign books and periodicals.

A few years later, when the Great Calamity [the Cultural

Revolution] swept across the whole scene, those letters were not of course spared. That is the other part of the tragic ending.

At the end of 1943, just as I was starting work on my Master's thesis, the Chungking government sent a goodwill mission to Britain. The delegation included the important politicians Wang Shijie and Wang Yunwu, and also scholars such as Wen Yuanning and my old employer, the newspaper magnate Hu Lin – publisher of the *Dagongbao*. Little did I imagine beforehand that this delegation would confront me with a major decision in my life. Would I become a scholar, or return to being a fulltime reporter again?

The decision was put before me the weekend that Hu Lin and Wen Yuanning came to visit Cambridge. Hu Lin came right to the point. Sitting down and staring at me through his thick spectacles, he said 'I didn't come to Cambridge to see the sights. I came here to get you away, out of that mortarboard and over to the battlefields of Europe, where you can really show your stuff as a reporter.' He threw up his stubby little hands: 'Mussolini is done for and the Red Army has routed the Nazis at Stalingrad. The western front can't remain quiet much longer. The Allies will have to launch their counter-attack, leaving the Nazis caught in the middle.' His eyes were filled with hope. 'Speaking in your own personal interest, I'd say your opportunity has now come. I was the only Chinese reporter in Europe during the First World War. Now it's your turn. Here's the question: Are you content with your degree, and a quiet academic career, or would you rather seize hold of this once-in-a-lifetime chance to do something really big?'

He went on to say that it was time for me to have a new beginning: my estranged wife had at last found someone she loved, so I could consider myself a free man again.

Then he talked more specifically about his plans for me.

'These past three years we've only asked you to be our part-time correspondent in England. You had to teach to make a living, so you ended up as a student. Now I'm asking for your total commitment. Become a full-time correspondent for us and the director of our new London office.'

This was the challenge he had laid before me. He gave me a while to think it over.

When I was a child, I used to pass by a scholar's residence every day on my way to school. (Only later did I learn that it belonged to Professor Tao Menghe of Peking University.) As I looked over the wall and through the French windows into his study, I saw row upon row of bookshelves and sometimes the scholar himself, buried in his reading. How I used to envy the lives of professors and scholars, pursuing their researches wholly detached from the mundane events about them. But my experience in the special Chinese classes at Yanjing University in 1929–30 had taught me something about myself: I was not cut out to be a scholar. For one thing, my work-study programme had left me without a firm foundation in scholarship. For another, I was too restless. I could never be shut up permanently with study. I told myself therefore that Forster, Woolf and Lawrence would still be there in the library when I wanted them. The war, on the other hand, was a great turning point in human events that would wait for no man – if I did not throw myself into the fray now, I would never be able to make up for it afterward.

At the urging of Hu Lin, then, I decided that I would abandon my cap and gown at the end of the term and take up the post as a reporter. That was the end of my academic career.

And Forster? Our correspondence continued until the autumn of 1949. He sent me forty letters more, many of them during my last six months at Cambridge, when we were still corresponding about literary matters. Because I never transcribed them, they are now gone for ever. It was Forster and Waley who had got me into Cambridge in the first place; I suspect that it similarly was Forster who was responsible for the university sending official letters – and even a personal emissary – to me in Hong Kong in 1948–49, asking me to join the Cambridge faculty to teach Chinese. I had to refuse, for that was not to be. Yet even I could scarcely have guessed how final my break with the world of letters would prove to be.

4

To the Western Front
(1944–1948)

I left the serenity of Cambridge to resume my profession as a fully fledged journalist in June of 1944, just as the Allied Armies were landing in Normandy, and I established an office for the *Dagongbao* in the heart of London, in Fleet Street.

In the beginning I was very anxious. Office management was new to me and I was also worried that once the agency was in business, I would be completely tethered to it and lose my freedom to travel. If the *Dagongbao* in Chungking could have sent someone else to manage the office, I would have preferred to be a mere reporter. But that was not possible.

Among my acquaintances was a kindly woman named Kay Murphy, from Sydney, Australia. She was working in England as a manager for the Linguaphone Company, a manufacturer of gramophone records for language instruction. I often spent weekends at her home in Staines, where she lived with the singer Nelson Ellingworth. I told her how worried I was about setting up my office. Not to worry, she said; in London you could find an agent to help you do anything.

Through such an agent, I found a five-room office suite in Fleet Street in the *Manchester Guardian* building. And through another agent, I took on five assistants: my manager, Mrs Gower, and four other women to type, clip newspaper articles, and handle advertising. Within ten days the office was all set up.

When I visited Singapore in 1983 and called on Goh Keng Swee, the first deputy prime minister, we discussed the reasons for his country's impressive development since independence. A major factor, he maintained, was the civil service system Singapore had inherited from Great Britain. From my experience opening up the London office of the *Dagongbao* in 1944, I had to agree, while adding that a major factor in the success of the civil service was the Western institution of the secretary. They (women, mostly) had specialised training, were well-groomed, natural and unaffected in manner, and outstandingly proficient in their work. You had only to make your intentions known and they would accomplish them smoothly, discreetly, and without exceeding instructions.

Thanks to those assistants, particularly Mrs Gower, I was not at all tied down to the office. They lifted the burden of it completely off my shoulders. Whether I was charging around on the other side of the Atlantic or on the European continent, the office remained in smooth working order.

The primary item of business of course was to send despatches to Chungking. I went out to gather news every morning. When I returned in the afternoon, the day's newspaper clippings of interest would already be laid out on my desk. Then Mrs Gower whirled into my room at about four o'clock, to take my dictation. I didn't even have to bother with the subsequent cables or letters.

The office also began taking advertisements and I opened a reading room where my fellow-countrymen could peruse the *Dagongbao*. To get our advertisements we again relied on an agent, and since British industrialists expected great things from the post-war Chinese market, the man had no trouble filling and surpassing his pledged quota of advertising space in our Chungking edition. In my two years at the office it handled a great deal of money, thanks to the advertising income. Not only did it cover our operating expenses, it was enough to buy several little Austin motor cars for the *Dagongbao*, as well as a colour printing press. When I finally got back to China, the boss praised me for my initiative. In fact, without those secretaries, agents, and the whole set of capitalist management institutions, I could have done very little.

In order officially to become a war correspondent, I had to file a form with the British Ministry of Information (MOI), enclosing my identification papers from the Chungking *Dagongbao*. Since I'd served part-time as the paper's reporter in England ever since my arrival in 1939, the ministry had already seen a good many of my despatches, so my official credentials were sent to me immediately. They came in the form of a little passbook. On one side was my photograph, with the name of the newspaper. The other side read:

'If captured, the bearer should be treated as a captain in accordance with the provisions of the League of Nations.'

When I read those provisions, a forbidding scene came before my eyes: of myself, clutching a bowl of gruel behind barbed wire. I couldn't help shuddering.

During the war Britain rationed clothing very strictly, for it was in pathetically short supply. But I was given a stack of ration cards sufficient to buy army-style uniforms for all seasons and went off to the designated shop. I got a khaki summer outfit, a winter-weight one, and even an officer's army overcoat. There was a great big pocket on one leg of the trousers. In a small voice I asked the shopkeeper what it was for. He said, 'Sir! It is for your map'. I detected a note of sarcasm in that *Sir*! What sort of officer was I, without even that beginner's knowledge?

I hurried over to the full-length mirror for a look. Certainly, I was snappier now than in my civvies. I wore a peaked cap on my head, and my epaulet had the words 'Chinese War Correspondent' embroidered on it in gold. With another ration card I bought a pair of riding boots and strode off clicking like a general.

Next I went to the Bank of England to acquire French, Belgian, and German currency. I sensed new respectful looks and all because of that epaulet. I even felt myself to be a new person.

I was informed that I had been assigned to accompany the American Seventh Army as it left for the front. The night before my departure I wrote out my will. I can't now remember what it said. I was alone in the world, without anyone to worry about, and I had nothing to pass on anyway. Perhaps I simply asked my executor to notify my closest friends in China and bid them all farewell.

I arrived at the appointed time on Platform 14 of London's Victoria Station, the platform that before the war had exclusively served trains headed towards France. I was leaving on a special military train. Officers went first class, where the compartments were spacious and comfortable. At eight o'clock sharp the whistle blew and we started rolling. I felt that I was off on an adventure. Having never enlisted, much less gone to war, I was naturally filled with excitement. All the scenery outside the window seemed captivating, but what thrilled me most was my unknown future. All sorts of images flashed before my mind: now I was soaring in the sky over Berlin; now I was burrowing into the trenches.

At eleven o'clock the train arrived at Newhaven, the port directly across the English Channel from Dieppe. From the train station we could see the ship at anchor in the port. However, a lanky lieutenant with a stentorian voice informed us: 'Nazi U-boats are particularly active in the Channel. You cannot cross at the moment. You'll be notified when the time comes. Assemble in the waiting room for now, officers to the right, men to the left. Your bags will be seen to.'

How disappointing. There was nothing to do but board a coach bound for nearby barracks where I and the other officers were to spend the night. We were there five days, while a battle took place in the Channel. The British Channel fleet had surrounded a pack of several German subs.

During those five days I killed time with a dozen or so army officers. The district had been a famous English summer resort. Now, because of the war, the hotels were boarded up and the beaches were overgrown with weeds. Each officer had had his own trade before the war. Frank was assistant manager in an insurance company. Tom ran a bookshop. Peter was a lecturer at Birmingham University. Then there were two American women Red Cross workers, on their way to Belgium.

Every day we pestered the lieutenant, asking when we could cross the Channel. Eventually, while we were eating supper on the fourth day, he told us that an air force rescue boat would be making the crossing the next morning. It could accommodate only twenty-five of us. And since it was just a small boat with no covering over the deck, only men would be permitted.

I tried to be first in line. At daybreak the next morning, a coach took us back to Newhaven, where we boarded the boat. It was the dead of winter and the wind was piercing. After I'd found myself a sheltered spot to sit, I discovered that I was close up against a depth charge. And just then the young captain of the boat warned us through a megaphone that a lot of enemy mines were floating around in the Channel. He hoped we'd all be on the lookout and immediately report any object we happened to notice on the surface of the water.

With that, he weighed anchor and we left the safety of the English shore. A violent gale was blowing. When a Swedish reporter took out his food ration cards to show me, a gust immediately sent them flying off, far out across the sea.

Suddenly there came another warning from the captain over the megaphone: 'Everyone look out, there's something on the water straight ahead'. I clung to the railing and looked. Sure enough, something black was bobbing up and down. The seamen hastened to untie the life rafts.

We slowed and then the motor switched completely off. Slowly and gently our little boat neared the black object. It appeared to be cone-shaped, with a little flag on top. It was only a navigation buoy, blown here by the wind. The captain ordered it to be sunk by our ack-ack gun.

Finally we reached Dieppe. Only the previous year a regiment of Canadians had nearly been annihilated during a night attack on the port. Now the French tricolore flag flew above the customs house.

When we went ashore, a captain in the US Army saluted us. 'Welcome to Dieppe', he said. 'The major in charge here wants me to inform you that there's nothing here for you to eat, nowhere for you to sleep, and above all no jeeps to transport you on to Paris. Good luck.'

After disposing of my rucksack, I went to the town hall to negotiate with that American 'major'. All along the road I saw French women and children dressed in rags. In the town square, some wrinkled old ladies had laid out mats and were selling lace. Since the Nazi occupation, most of the local able-bodied males had been dragged off by the Germans to work in their factories. The only men I saw in town were well-fed American GIs. Clutches of haggard-looking children followed after them, yelling out in broken English, 'Thank you. Any *chocolat*?'

With its 30,000 inhabitants, Dieppe could be considered a middle-sized port on France's Channel coast. But now it was in the hands of an American major in his thirties. Sitting cross-legged in his chair with a cigar in his mouth, he listened as I explained why I was so anxious to catch up with those on their way to the front. Hundreds of millions of Chinese readers were awaiting my report. The Seventh Army was driving forward from eastern France towards Germany, with the Rhine as its first objective. Should Chinese readers be left in the dark about all this? I pleaded with him to find some way for me to go.

But he simply threw up his hands. Apart from allowing me to eat a meal, he couldn't come up with any way of helping me. Finally I found out for myself, after striking up a conversation with a colonel in the mess hall, that a truck would be leaving for Paris. The driver agreed to take me.

The countryside along that four-hour trip was devastated as far as the eye could see. There were blown-up bridges and villages reduced to rubble. And, from time to time, the platforms on tracks from which the V2 flying bombs had been launched on London.

Paris was tragically demoralised. By the majestic Arc de Triomphe, pedlars were trading Chanel perfume and nylon stockings for Camel cigarettes. In the resplendent Opera House, jazz was played on stage, while GIs in the boxes put their feet up on the railings and puffed at their cigars. The French, always so arrogant about their mother tongue, had hung out signs in all their shops: 'English spoken here'.

I was assigned to stay at the Hotel Scribe. Here I met the American critic Edmund Wilson, author of *Axel's Castle*. He was representing *The New Yorker*. Frequently seen at the bar were Ernest Hemingway, a big strapping fellow; the energetic William Saroyan; and George Orwell, who had been sent by the BBC. All these writers were in uniform. One day as I passed through the hotel corridor, I suddenly heard someone shout out my name. I turned around and saw Edgar Snow.

An old friend is all the more welcome in the midst of strangers. We went into the bar and talked away the whole afternoon. He was one of only six Americans permitted by the Soviet Union to cover the Eastern Front, and he had been all over Eastern Europe. When I mentioned his wife Helen, he frowned. I sensed that a rift had come between them. He told me he'd bought an old house in Connecticut with the royalties from his book *Red Star over China*. He longed to return to Peking, feeling that so long as China did not throttle her intellectuals, she had high hopes.

There was plenty to see in Paris, but I felt I must catch up with the Seventh Army. The Nazis were war-weary and retreating, and the information officer at Supreme Allied Headquarters told me that two days earlier Seventh Army headquarters had been established at Nancy. He guessed that by now the army might already be approaching the German frontier. I boarded the night train from Paris to Nancy. The carriages were not illuminated and the berths were very hard. Still, it was a lot more comfortable than the carriages the refugees rode in. I was able to spread out my overcoat and get some sleep.

At Nancy I learned that the offices there had already become a rear headquarters. The chief of staff told me that the enemy had made a last-ditch stand in the Saar region and then retreated towards the Rhineland. He said if I hurried, I might still catch the Allies as they fought their way across the Rhine. The Public Relations Office that took care of the press was now on the Franco-German border. Once I caught up with the PRO all my problems of food and lodging would be solved.

However, he had no means of transportation; he wanted me to find my own. So I picked up my rucksack and set off. Soon I'd hitched a ride on a jeep, but they had to dump me when they took a turning towards the south.

I entered a village. I saw no people, only ruined buildings and scrawny dogs scrounging for food. My stomach was empty, too. But a uniform is worth a lot in wartime – sentries saluted me and I could use it to eat anywhere. I strolled into the kitchen of a nearby army camp. Without a word, the cook in his tall, white cap laid out two pieces of bread on my plate and ladled a big spoonful of corned beef hash on them. Then he grinned and saluted.

I strode off down the road to Germany, turning around every time I heard a motor, and sticking up my thumb. Whenever a jeep slowed down, I would yell, 'Going to Sarregemines?' After a while a procession of trucks came up, loaded with TNT for blowing up bridges. Every man in them was a black man. I jumped up into the cab of one truck and sat down next to the driver. He kept on chewing his gum and humming his little tune as he gave me a friendly nod.

I was in luck. I located the PRO at Sarregemines by dusk. And in the morning my convoy was setting out for Germany.

At the first glimmering of dawn, I jumped back up into my truck. Once over the bridge I would be in Germany.

It was like crossing an unmanned frontier. On either side of Hitler's broad, smooth autobahn, we saw red hills that reached all the way to the horizon, and then lush green pine forests. No one was on the roads but refugees. One ruined village followed on another. Battered tanks littered the fields, with the corpses of men and horses piled around them. When our truck convoy entered the relatively intact little town of Homburg, white flags were hanging from the doors of each of the houses. Prisoners released from their camps had their country of origin written in chalk on their back: Greece, Belgium, Poland . . . They looked haggard, but they smiled at us, rejoicing to have lived to see the Nazi defeat. The Germans, by comparison, kept their heads down in silence.

That evening we reached Grünstadt. By then headquarters of the Seventh Army was already in Worms. The trucks along the way were mostly carrying parts for pontoon bridges. It looked as if the Allies might charge across the Rhine that very night.

The next day we set out in a jeep for Mannheim. This district was not so devastated, for at this point the Nazi armies had been so exhausted that they had fled without much of a resistance. But there was a vast unbroken stream of refugees along the road, bearing up their young and their old, in search of woods where they could find shelter. As we turned towards the village where we were to be stationed, we could see smoke billowing up before us down in the valley. That must be where the Americans planned to cross the river.

I had imagined that being a correspondent at the front would mean digging trenches and braving a hail of bullets. As it happened, this place was both quieter and safer than London had been under attack from the V2s.

We were quartered in a deserted publishing house. Paper was stacked up on the ground floor. The shelves of the library were filled with sets of the works of Goethe, Heine, and Schiller, all in rare editions. In the office someone even turned up the owner's Nazi party membership card and evidence that he had paid his party dues the week before. He could not have realised that the fires of war would encircle his house so quickly.

The wines of the Rhine valley are famous. There were two wine cellars in the village and the Public Relations Officer, a colonel, announced that we could open two dozen bottles – whereupon an American reporter from Louisiana sat down at a piano and began playing popular tunes. We drank and sang along with him, hearing the thunder of artillery only around midnight, when we sobered up. The Nazis were at the Rhine, putting up their last struggle.

My companions were mostly correspondents for the major British, American and Swedish press services. I realised that I could never scoop them on combat news from the war zone. With one cable they could send their news directly to their home news agency for transmission all over the world. Mine had to go through London, so that Mrs Gower could retransmit my despatch to Chungking; there colleagues had to translate it into Chinese. The transmission time also put me at an absolute disadvantage, so I decided instead to cover the military government the US Army had temporarily set up. I asked the Public Relations Officer for a jeep; he even sent along a colonel to be my guide.

I dashed up and down the banks of the Rhine, investigating the towns and villages. The vineyards were overrun with weeds. Bombed-out tanks stood in the fields, corpses in steel helmets around them. When the military government entered a village, finding Nazi party headquarters was their first objective. Some of the local leaders fled in such panic that they forgot to put in their false teeth.

Suddenly someone arrived from headquarters with a telegram for me. I was wanted back in London post haste.

When I got there I learned that there was to be a meeting of the United Nations in San Francisco. The newspaper office in Chungking had decided to pull me out from the Western Front and send me immediately to America. The cable added that our general manager, Hu Lin, was going there, too – as a delegate for the Republic of China.

First I had to ready my passport and visa. When in 1939 I came to London from Hong Kong, the newspaper had arranged for my visa. Entering America was much more difficult. I had to arrange things myself and fill out a long form with all kinds of questions, from 'Are you an atheist?' to 'Do you intend to overthrow the United States government?' Carefully I wrote a big 'No' after every question. At the end, I had to be fingerprinted, for the first time in my life. I looked over and saw a Polish reporter at my side being given the same treatment. I found this quite upsetting. However great it might be, America needn't treat its allied reporters like animals.

Within thirty-six hours I found myself in Glasgow, on board the *Neo Hellas* with some journalists from England and other Allied countries. The fifty-odd ships that were to form our convoy assembled at sea outside Glasgow. Nazi submarines were active, so we were surrounded by warships on all sides. We had to cross the ocean in zigzags, with the result that a voyage which ordinarily took four and a half days ended up requiring eleven.

Apart from our reporters' delegation, this *Neo Hellas* was carrying over eight hundred British war brides of Canadian soldiers, plus their five hundred children. Seeing these little foreign babies, I began to consider Asian babies rather dull by comparison. I couldn't even count their different hair colours. And there were eyes of blue, green, brown . . . an exhibition of variegated European babies every day.

We twenty-two reporters on our way to America to cover the founding meeting of the United Nations Organisation were also of all colours, and we represented diametrically opposed political philosophies. To cite only the British, there was Iverach McDonald from *The Times* of London, and Frank Pitcairn, reporting on foreign affairs for the Labour Party. They happily played chess every day with the reporter from *L'Humanité*, the organ of the French Communist Party, but when they got to talking about the post-war world, they were poles apart.

One of the English reporters had a birthday on 12 April, on which day the naval officers arranged a wonderful party. There were wines and liquors galore, and a big birthday cake with forty-six candles. There was a heavy sea that night; the sound of crashing plates was heard a lot. Being half drunk to begin with, we swayed more than ever as we sang and toasted each other. Suddenly the first mate entered, sought out the head of our delegation, and whispered in his ear.

Everyone stopped talking and looked on with curiosity.

Someone asked, 'Are we under attack?'

'It's worse than that,' answered the first mate. He raised his voice and announced, 'Gentlemen, we've just received a signal from the flagship. President Roosevelt is dead.'

The party came to a close after that and we returned dejectedly to our cabins, leaving the cake uncut on the table.

The next day our flag flew at half mast.

Eventually our convoy reached Nova Scotia and entered the port of Halifax. It was five hours until the train for San Francisco, so we strolled through the city.

After five years of living in an England under siege, I felt as if I had just entered paradise. No bombers droned above my head. Sausages, hams and entire chickens were hanging in the shop windows. Restaurant menus were a foot long, and you could buy a steak as thick as a brick. There were oranges from California piled up like mountains, South American bananas, pineapples, and mangoes. We put aside our manners and ate on the street, praising the natural bounties of Canada as we went.

Today people usually make such journeys by plane, but I have the fondest memories of that five-day train trip from Halifax to San Francisco. We rode in a roomy Pullman sleeper. Along the way we stopped for an hour or two in Quebec, Montreal, Chicago, and Salt Lake City. While the train was taking on coal and water, we explored the streets and back alleys. In one Canadian museum I even saw an exhibition of Chinese musical instruments. In Chicago, I mounted a skyscraper. After going through the Rocky Mountains, I saw the Mormon Temple in Salt Lake City.

When we got to Chicago, we heard that tickets to San Francisco were being sold only to participants in the founding ceremony of the United Nations Organisation. The city of San Francisco was singlemindedly gearing up for this unprecedentedly large international conference. All the shops had hung out signs saying 'Welcome Delegates of All Countries'. In our hotels, free newspapers were slid under our doors every morning. The Post Office gave each of us a postal album with stamps bearing portraits of all the American presidents, while the wineries sent over basket after basket of Californian wines. The hundreds of pigeons that inhabited St Francis Square had all been caught and caged. Many local women and girls volunteered their time to act as chauffeurs and guides for the visiting delegations.

I soon came to realise the true purpose of my newspaper in sending me to San Francisco. I was not only to serve as a reporter, but as the assistant to the general manager, Hu Lin. Unless there was a press conference, we always met for lunch and dinner at the Apricot Blossoms Restaurant in Chinatown. Hu Lin was closer to Dong Biwu – the only Communist member of the Chinese delegation – than were the other delegates, so I got to eat with this Chinese Communist almost every day. He usually talked only about conference sidelights though, seldom about domestic politics. I sat at the end of the table and said little.

The conference establishing the United Nations Organisation officially opened at the San Francisco Opera House at 9 o'clock on the morning of 25 April 1945. Flags of all the nations fluttered throughout the city. The main opening ceremony was to begin at

4.30 pm and the Opera House was full an hour and a half earlier, the spectators having entered by three different doors according to status. There were delegates, experts and journalists from the world over. The great domed building was crammed with people, tier upon tier. US Marines checked passes at every stairwell and landing, while girl scouts in short skirts patrolled the aisles, distributing programmes. An orchestra behind the stage played light music. The atmosphere was both solemn and joyous, as befitted a festive celebration for humankind.

The stage backdrop was sky-blue and set with apricot-coloured pillars, decorated with the flags of the forty-seven participating nations. The heavy stage curtain was dark grey and the tables on stage were light blue, with yellow chairs. Representatives from the major press agencies sat in the balcony, while ordinary reporters were scattered in seats on the floor.

At 4.30 precisely the music abruptly ceased and uniformed young men and women representing combat units from the three American armed services marched out on stage from either side to form a straight line. Next, US Secretary of State Edward Stettinius came up to the dais, with the governor of California, mayor of San Francisco, and secretary of the conference. The Secretary of State banged the gavel three times and thus began a second experiment in global collective security – after the failure of the League of Nations.

Once delegations from all the nations had sung their individual praises to world peace, they began the next day by arguing themselves silly about who would be chairman of the conference. After that, various great powers lobbied for delegate status for their respective client states. Three weeks before, Washington had reviled Argentina, even forcing Britain to sever relations with the country. Now, though, in order to demonstrate the strength of its pan-American bloc, it was the United States which pressed for the admission of Argentina. Small wonder then that the Soviet Union argued for the admission of the Ukraine and Byelorussia.

On 2 May, as I was listening to a speech, news suddenly arrived that Nazi armies had started surrendering to the Allied Armies in northern Italy. Peace was dawning. Then came news of the suicides of Himmler, Goebbels and other Nazi leaders in succession – and word that Goebbels had shot his own wife and children before going to the grave. Finally we heard that Hitler himself and his woman, Eva Braun, had been cremated in an underground bunker. That night Churchill announced that the war in Europe was over. It was the day they called VE Day.

That day, as I stood in a Pacific Ocean port, my celebrating was tempered by certain feelings of uneasiness. On the Asian battle-fields China, the ally that had been invaded first and struggled on the longest, was still fighting with her blood. In Chungking, the bombs were still dropping and Kuomintang secret agents were still terrorising their fellow countrymen. What would China be like when the war was over? That was still a big question.

I had my own private worries about the nature of the post-war world.

My ten days at the United Nations conference had given me my first lesson in international politics: they taught me that whereas such a thing as altruism might occasionally appear in relations between individuals, there was only the most naked self-interest in relations between nations. Even the Soviet Union, which boasted that 'workers belong to no fatherland', was no exception. On the dais of the Opera House I saw all taking and no giving. And struggling not for equality but for supremacy. War had depleted the great British Empire; now America was undisguisedly trying to reshape the post-war world into a big alliance with America at the top. Nor would the Soviet Union be outdone in its desire for power.

As an Asian I was naturally anxious that the post-war world loosen the fetters of all enslaved people, but when South Africa passed sixty laws discriminating against black people, the American representative on the UN Human Rights Commission (Eleanor Roosevelt) said that it was 'a legal question, not a matter of human rights'! The question of 'trusteeship' made one even more depressed. The mandate of this commission was to guide pre-war colonies towards national self-determination under inter-national supervision. But there were exceptions and loopholes. If territories given to the United Nations to supervise were deemed to have strategic value to the big powers and were designated 'defence zones', then the United Nations could not concern itself with them. By that mechanism, the people in them could be deprived of self-determination virtually for ever.

I was not the only Chinese reporter in San Francisco, of course. The Kuomintang's Central News Agency had sent a dozen or so reporters from its English-language department, the cream of the crop. Not only did they have the advantage of numbers, they had direct access to the Chinese delegation, led by T V Soong (Song Ziwen). They had a teletype machine and news photographers. I was all alone, so I had no way of scooping them on anything.

And yet on one occasion, the *Dagongbao* did scoop them on a fairly important item, thanks to the shrewdness and alertness of that old veteran newsman, Hu Lin.

That day we had lunched as usual in the Apricot Blossoms Restaurant. Hu Lin had told me that the Soviet delegation (led by Molotov) would be fêting the Chinese delegation that evening, so I could have the night off. In the evening a BBC reporter had invited me to go to a drag show, but I had declined both that and an invitation from a Canadian newsman to go with him to a nightclub. I was used to the nearly rustic life of Cambridge and had no hankering after the big-city bright lights. My plan for my night off was to take a shower and crawl into bed for a good night's sleep. And so it was that I was in my hotel room and half asleep when the telephone rang.

It was the boss, Hu Lin. He said, 'You must come at once to the Mark Hopkins Hotel. I'll explain when you get here.'

After throwing on some clothes I rushed downstairs and called a taxi to the hotel where the Soong-Molotov banquet was taking place. No sooner had I got out of the cab than I saw Mr Hu at the entrance to the lobby, already nervously waiting for me. He said, panting, 'I just managed to overhear what Molotov said to T V Soong as he toasted him. It was, in translation: "We will welcome the Chinese delegation soon in Moscow, to sign the Sino-Russian Mutual Non-Aggression Pact."' Pleased with himself, Mr Hu continued, 'I hurriedly excused myself, pretending I had to go to the lavatory, so I could give you that telephone call'.

Having finished his message, he headed back towards the banquet. I rushed out onto the sidewalk and called another taxi to make a dash for the Great Western Undersea Cable Company. I sent the Chungking *Dagongbao* a special priority telegram. Printed in a special box, this became the first item on the front page of the next morning's *Dagongbao*.

If I'd thought I could have discovered something at the United

Nations conference really worth reporting, I would have been willing to stay at my post for however long it might have taken, like the farmer in our Chinese story who gave up hunting and watched a stump all day long because he once saw a rabbit accidentally knock himself unconscious on it and hoped another rabbit would do the same thing. But the longer the conference went on, the more discouraged I grew. In the little meetings as well as the big ones, the nations simply argued procedural matters back and forth. So I suggested to Mr Hu that rather than hang around at the conference all day, I should go see more of America. Then I could return to Britain to cover the general election there. Britain was, after all, my original posting.

I am grateful that he approved. I put forward a plan to the US Office of War Information. They quickly made my arrangements. Saying farewell to the boss and to San Francisco, I boarded a night train called the 'Nightingale' for Los Angeles.

The first movie I ever saw was in 1921 – I remember that it was Charlie Chaplin's *Gold Rush*. From 1930 to 1939 I saw practically every Hollywood film that came to China, so it was as a pilgrim that I visited Hollywood and watched pictures being made at the Warner Brothers studio. I ate lunch that day in the Studio City canteen. As I watched stars come in one after another, my idol Bette Davis sat down at the next table. She was arguing with her male lunch partner, who seemed to be a director, so though I wanted very much to shake her hand, I didn't feel I could interrupt.

From Los Angeles I travelled east across the vast mountainous stretches of Arizona and New Mexico, through Texas, and then to New Orleans, an old city rich with the charm of eighteenth-century France, unhurried and refined. Palm trees lined the plazas. In their shade people loitered over cold drinks, while others in Panama hats fished along the shore of Lake Pontchartrain. I ate supper in a crab house. Just when dessert was set before me, the light above me went out. In the gloom I could only make out a thread of green smoke approaching. When the lights went on again, a cup of coffee flaming with brandy had been set before me.

From there I went north, up the Appalachians, to the head-quarters of the renowned Tennessee Valley Authority. In three days I visited two of the nine dams; the great river that had once been this region's sorrow was now tamed and produced cheap electricity, turning poverty into wealth.

After that I took a bus through the Smoky Mountains – where there were said to be bears though unfortunately I saw none – to Washington, DC, the capital. In London and Paris, every corner is filled with history and tradition. The greatest impression this New World capital gave me was of youth and idealism. Next I went to New York. Particularly unforgettable was a play on Broadway that friends took me to see: *Othello*, with Paul Robeson.

On 6 June I took a bus to Baltimore and that evening boarded a seaplane. After a brief stop in Newfoundland, I found myself back in England, where Churchill of the Conservative Party and Attlee of the Labour Party were battling it out.

Having gone to America from ancient Britain, I couldn't help comparing the two countries, so similar in language and ancestry. England attached importance to tradition, and so was more particular than America about class and status. Once a San Francisco business magnate who owned a chain of department stores on the west coast invited me to dinner. Dessert came, and then coffee, still without a sign of the hostess. Only at the meal's end did I learn that the servant in her white apron who had been running back and forth to serve us our food and pour our wine was the hostess herself. I doubt if the English in 1947 would have found that very funny.

At nightclubs in New York, I saw American senior executives dancing, singing, drinking, and having a very expensive good time. At the Tennessee dams, on the other hand, even the most important chief engineer would roll up his sleeves and do manual labour. Any nation that imitates how Americans enjoy themselves, without also learning how hard they work, is in for trouble.

I was profoundly moved by the British general election of 26 July 1945 and the loss of Churchill. I could never have anticipated that a leader who had made such a contribution to his nation might be recalled by the people and replaced with another. The comparison with the dictatorial government in my own country at the time made me yearn all the more for the coming of Western style democratic government. That power ultimately should rest in the hands of the voters was something quite beyond my experience. This lesson may well have predestined me towards my sorry fate in 1957.

In our Asian terminology, Churchill was a great saviour. How could he be driven out of Downing Street? Yet he was. And so he obediently packed his bags and turned over the prime ministership to the quite unremarkable Mr Attlee. It was 'the will of the people'.

And yet I was not so intoxicated with Western democracy that I had no reservations about it. In flipping through old issues of the Chungking *Dagongbao* as I was writing this section of my memoirs, I came across this despatch of mine, printed on 6 July 1945:

> Election campaigning appears to be a combination of modern advertising and auctioneering. He who has money has access to publicity, and he who has the publicity can control the thoughts of the electorate. Many campaign speeches neither present a political platform nor debate the issues; they are simply tools of mesmerism.

While the Conservative and Labour parties were campaigning against each other, I kept my ears open for any unusual stories. A farmer from Northampton named Hancock came forward to run against Churchill as an independent. He said that if elected prime minister he would nationalise all necessities and he threatened to enact a one-hour workday. Then again, while campaigning in Scotland Churchill wanted to make a speech in Glasgow's George Square. But Glasgow was a stronghold of the Labour Party, and a woman who worked for the city council refused Churchill's request, on the grounds of protecting the grass.

On election day, I went with an English friend to observe the polls. Each party delivered last-minute appeals to the voters: 'If so-and-so is elected, he will build better housing for you!' 'If so-and-so is elected, he will increase bereavement, disability and old-age pensions five shillings.' These were small promises, but they did indicate that the election would revolve around social welfare for the voters.

When Japan surrendered on 15 August, many important British politicians wrote or cabled our office, asking the *Dagongbao* to convey their congratulations to the Chinese people, whose war had lasted eight long years. I was happy and excited, but at the same time anxious about China's political situation after the war. If the Nationalists and Communists did not truly cooperate, China would sooner or later become the Poland of the East.

There really was no respite for me in those days. As soon as the

British general election was over, I had to go to Berlin to cover the Potsdam Conference.

I boarded a C-46 transport plane in Paris. French towns and villages that had been bombed into rubble came into view below. Then the Marne and the Moselle, meandering through the green fields. Finally we saw the Saale River out of the window and knew we were over the Soviet zone of occupation.

The plane landed at Tempelhof Airport in Berlin. This airport, which had seen so many Axis puppet leaders come and go, now had the flags of the Soviet Union, United States, Great Britain, and France fluttering from its control tower. The German-language signs and posters covering the main airport building had been plastered over with new ones written in Russian.

A US Army liaison officer was already standing outside waiting for me at the entrance to the airport. Picking out the sole Oriental in the crowd was easy for him. We boarded a waiting jeep.

From the Brandenburg Gate, where the Soviet, British and American zones came together, past the zoo to Adolfstrasse, headquarters of the British army, the streets of Berlin were broad and long, the more so since everything on both sides had been pounded to the ground. Everything was oversized, like the stone blocks of which most of the houses were built. In fact the city seemed excessively grandiose, lacking both the charm of London and Paris and the spectacle of Washington. And yet I kept seeing women and children walking the streets carrying baskets or with bags on their backs, searching for food.

My press pass was immediately good for rations: ten packages of chocolate bars, one dozen razor blades, a pint of gin, a pint of whiskey, and one carton of Camel cigarettes.

It was obligatory for visitors to Berlin to see Hitler's supreme headquarters, the Chancery of the German government on Wilhelmstrasse in the Soviet zone. We reporters set off together in jeeps to tour it. The Red Army sentry at the gate looked at our passes and let us in. The great reception hall downstairs was cavernously empty. The chandeliers had been shaken down during the bombing and many of their little light bulbs had already been carried off by visitors as souvenirs. Upstairs was Hitler's office. When we visited, the furniture was stacked as if ready to be auctioned off. When a Red Army soldier posted there saw the word 'China' on my shoulder patch, he snapped me a friendly salute and gave me a bunch of Nazi decorations as mementoes. (When my house was raided in 1966 during the Cultural Revolution, my Nazi medals would become one more 'proof' of my 'guilt'.)

The liaison officer addressed us reporters in a group: 'Gentlemen, tonight you'll be put up in an idyllic spot, the one place in Berlin that escaped bombing: Zehlendorf.' It turned out to be an ideal residential neighbourhood in a quiet tract far from the city centre, like Hampstead in London or the Bois de Boulogne in Paris. We lodged in a requisitioned hotel, and when I went to the lavatory I met a middle-aged German man, possibly the landlord, in the corridor. With shame on his face, he begged a cigarette from me. I gave him one. He turned it over and sniffed at it, completely lost in the aroma, gratitude and delight beaming from his face. Then he asked if he could have another cigarette for his wife. I gave him one immediately.

Back in my room, as I was packing my bags, a golden-haired little girl not much more than ten popped her head inside my door. She hesitated, then quietly walked up to me. She was clutching a watercolour painting to her breast.

'This is the Wannsee,' she said, pointing to a lake in the picture, 'My mama painted it. How many cigarettes is it worth to you – Camels?'

The painting was pretty good. It had an azure sky and rooftops were visible amid the trees in the distance. She pointed to them and said, 'That is the Sans Souci Palace in Potsdam.'

It would have made a very good souvenir. But I rememberd the Allied Army regulation prohibiting fraternisation with the Germans. I gave her a pack of Camels and sent her back to her mother with the message, 'No quantity of cigarettes is enough to buy a work of art, even if they're Camels.'

Post-war Berlin reminded me of Tianjin. When I had been there in early 1935, you could be in the Japanese concession one minute and the French concession the next. Now Berlin was much the same. You could walk a mile and come to a white billboard reading 'You are leaving the American zone.' The American MPs in their white helmets disappeared; instead there were Soviet traffic police-women standing on boxes at the intersections. All of them were about twenty years old, wearing khaki uniforms with green ties, and brandishing two flags, one red and one green, to direct the traffic.

Going from Berlin to Potsdam was simply leaving one set of ruins for another. Once upon a time, Voltaire had visited the Sans Souci Palace for talks with Frederick the Great. But we were kept far outside the gate, our passage blocked by military guards. Our press passes only got us into the environs. The next day, the whole area was sealed off for three miles around.

The life of a reporter often requires superhuman patience. It would have been wishful thinking to imagine that Potsdam would yield me any information at all about the meeting of the three great leaders. Far from helping us fifty-odd reporters cover the conference, the Russian press liaison officer seemed to be throwing us off the track. The first press conference consisted of this: 'Yesterday evening President Truman and Marshal Stalin dined together. The menu consisted of cold cuts, turtle soup, fried steak.' It was as if the three leaders had come to Potsdam simply to spend the weekend together.

I came to feel that hanging around outside the walls of the San Souci was as futile as waiting for news to break in San Francisco. Even if they threw us a few crumbs, with all those big press agencies around I would get little. So I began to think about what my readers in Chungking would want to know most.

I figured that there must be quite a few Chinese foreign students in Berlin. If I could interview them, I could better understand the current state of the city, and also report the students' condition to the people back home. After six years of war – which was to say, six years of the bombing of Berlin – who wouldn't be curious about the fate of their fellow-countrymen?

Back in Berlin I went immediately to the embassy of the Japanese puppet state of Manchukuo. There I found students who had been stranded in Berlin for six or seven years. When they heard that I represented the Chungking *Dagongbao* and not the puppet government, they warmly embraced me and we began to talk excitedly.

'You can't say Hitler was incompetent. He kept the Berlin subways running right up until the last day.'

'Hah, the subways here weren't put deep enough into the ground, so they were damaged by the bombs. When we construct our own, we'll build them deeper down.'

'The Nazis are evil, but the German common folk are all right, particularly the middle and lower classes who rented us rooms. Although I haven't paid rent for several years, they not only didn't evict me, they kept on feeding me. Now we're hanging our Chinese flag over their doors in gratitude, since the American gendarmes won't search the house of an ally.'

'China ought to think of some way of repatriating us as soon as possible. I studied medicine and he studied engineering. They'll need us back home. Here all we do is eat scarce food.'

'Will the Nationalists and Communists make peace? How wonderful that would be.'

We had coffee, or so they called it – it was made from sawdust, really. First eighteen of them, then thirty, then the door would open, and in would come one more. We talked about the future development of Taiwan and Hainan, and about how Hong Kong ought to be given back to China. Then a young man changed the subject back to the Nazi regime. 'The Germans were once a very upstanding people. The problem is that instead of enjoying their good lives in peace, they had to establish secret police and concentration camps. What we need is the planned economy, but *without* the Hitler-like secret police.'

In my subsequent cable despatch to Chungking, I pointedly quoted that last remark: 'We must never choose the Hitler way!'

When I was a child, on the way to school I sometimes encountered the cart that pulled criminals to the Bridge of Heaven execution grounds, outside the Temple of Heaven. Crowds would gather to watch them, but I lacked that kind of curiosity. Personally, therefore, I was not too keen on covering the Nazi war crimes trials that were to be convened in Nuremberg in October. But, since I was a reporter sent to the battlegrounds of Europe, I couldn't pretend that the trials weren't happening. And in fact they showed first of all how differently the democracies operated from the Axis governments. Furthermore the trials themselves were a process of exposure. They were very educational.

I stayed in the city of Wiesbaden, at the Grünwald Hotel. It was not a big city, but its hot springs had made it a popular summer resort for monarchs and sons and daughters of the nobility from all over Europe. There was a fine opera house and concert hall. General Eisenhower had continually spared the city from bombing, intending to make it the post-war headquarters of the Allied armies.

Outside my hotel was the square in the centre of town, and straight ahead was a Gothic church. Little boys in steel American army helmets gnawed on their black bread while playing hide and seek. In the streets, men were chopping firewood. Housewives waited nearby with baskets and sacks to buy it. There were long queues in front of the bakeries. And barbed wire surrounded the prison that held the accused war criminals. When a vehicle with prisoners stopped, people on the street would immediately surround it to get a look, to see what Nazi officers might be inside. Old men who had seen their country defeated in two wars loitered listlessly along the prison walls.

A whistle blew abruptly at 10 pm. It was curfew. Germans without a pass could not leave their homes.

Early in the morning I went for a stroll down the wet cobbled roads. Suddenly the deep and solemn sounds of an organ wafted over, coming from the church; a boy was practising there. Along the wall of the church a white arrow pointed down towards the basement. It had been an air raid shelter.

On the way back I saw another yellow face on the street. I hailed him in Chinese with a *Ni hao*. Indeed he was Chinese, a merchant named Xu from Qingtian, Zhejiang. We always thought of people from poor and stony Qingtian as our Chinese gypsies. The merchant class there had begun by selling the very stones under their feet, for seal carving; some had gone to Europe on foot, across Siberia. And now this man of Qingtian took me to the UNRRA refugee camp where he lived.

He pointed to a white barracks where he said Poles were housed. Next to it was a building for Greeks. The refugees had all hung their laundry out the window to dry. As many languages were being spoken as at the Tower of Babel. Some people were clearly arguing; some may have talked of love. It was, in short, a world in miniature.

Mr Xu led me to the building where he lived. Most of the residents were East Europeans. The entrance halls were pitch black, with a smell strong enough to choke you. We saw a wizened old woman spreading cold hash she had just been issued on a piece of bread. Some boys were arguing as they boiled water. The rooms were terribly messy. The odour of the lavatories reminded me of China.

'Are you for General Tito or Mikhailovitch?' I asked a young Yugoslav man while he sliced bread.

He stuck up his thumb and said, 'Tito, of course.'

At this point a young English-speaking Belgian woman entered. She said that the Nazis had brought her older brother here in 1940 to labour for them. Unable to rest easy, she had insisted on coming with him. Now he was dead and she had married an American soldier. Soon there would be a boat to take her to Ohio, she said, beaming.

I attended a trial of Nazis in Wiesbaden.

During the trial the Nazi war criminals were allowed lawyers in court to defend them, an idea quite beyond the comprehension of many people besides us Asians, whose concept of rule by law is admittedly weak. On this occasion the accused were five men and one woman, all of them administrators of the Hadamar Mental Hospital: the director, a physician, a male nurse, a female nurse, a registrar and a man in charge of burials. They were accused of murdering 4,400 Russians and Poles with lethal injections.

The trial was held in the town hall. Six chairs had already been laid out on the stage in front, with a big American flag hanging in the background. On chairs in the front row sat the defence for the accused, of whom four were German lawyers in long robes and three were American lawyers in military uniform, with pistols at their sides. Behind them sat the six defendants, and behind them again were the German reporters. On stage, at the left of the front row, sat the chief and associate judge and the prosecution. In the middle of the hall, near the stage, were two court stenographers. There were also two court interpreters. In the front row of the public seats sat senior officers from the American, British, French, and Soviet armies of occupation, the chief justice of the British Supreme Court and the chairman of the United Nations War Crimes Investigation Commission. Behind them were American soldiers and officers and personnel from the Red Cross and UNRRA. There were many Germans in the audience as well as refugees just released from concentration camps.

As the lawyers for the defence quietly conferred with the accused, broadcasters tested their equipment, shouting 'New York! Calling New York!' into the microphones. GIs snapped their chewing gum while staring at the defendants.

At 9.30, the chief judge and five colonels serving as associate judges entered the courtroom. When all were in their seats, the tall chief judge, who wore a pistol at his side, announced that the court was in session. The defendants were identified one by one by their lawyers. The chief judge asked the lawyers to raise their right hands to take their oath. Then came the interpreters. Finally the judges got up and raised their right hands: 'I swear before God to be just and impartial; I shall remain silent about the proceedings until the final verdict is announced.'

With that the proceedings began. The prosecutor read a list of charges, accusing the defendants of murder. Their lawyers then rose to defend them as not guilty. This was a feature of English and American jurisprudence: until guilt was proven, the accused were presumed not guilty. The defendants listened attentively to the crimes with which they were charged, cupping their ears with their hands.

When the prosecutor stood up to begin his case, one defence lawyer jumped to his feet to object that the whole proceedings were contrary to law: The defendants were not accused of murdering Americans and the court only had jurisdiction over cases involving Americans. Secondly, the Soviet Union was not signatory to the Geneva Conventions and therefore had no grounds to seek protection under its provisions.

The chief judge rose to speak. If international law had nothing to say in a case of premeditated murder of 4,400 people, humankind was in a sorry state! The United States was signatory to military regulations as well as international treaties. Those regulations explicitly prohibited the killing of prisoners of war through abuse. The Soviet Union might not have signed the Geneva Conventions, but Germany and Russia had both signed the Treaty of the Hague in 1907. According to Article 46 of the latter, the lives and safety of prisoners of war were to be protected. As a force of occupation in Germany, the United States naturally had jurisdiction there over the premeditated murder of citizens of nations who were allied with her.

The defence rose to object again, saying that because the accused were civilians, under the law they could not bear responsibility for the maltreatment of prisoners of war. Then he cited an opinion from the *New Yorker* which seemed of no particular relevance.

The chief judge responded that although he had brought no magazines to court, he would think it beneath the dignity of the proceedings to quote from them even if he had.

Then the prosecutor charged that the accused had, up until 1 July

1944, injected poison into war prisoners, several at a time. All had died a few hours later. The corpses had been taken down to the basement and buried. He also asserted that the prisoners of war sent to the hospital had had no trace of mental illness, nor had the hospital any equipment for the treatment of mental illness. Also medical records had been falsified by the registrar to show, among other things, that the prisoners had been housed in the hospital for ten days or two weeks, when in fact they had been brought in only on the night of their murder.

The charges were recorded by the court stenographers and repeated sentence by sentence in German by the translators. Then the first witness came on the stand. It was a woman, about fifty years old, with brown hair and a haggard face. Trembling, she said that her name was Minna Saukel. She had worked in the mental hospital from 1940 until the time that the US Army attacked. Her job was to make the beds. During cross examination, she admitted that she had also administered medicine to the patients, though she flatly denied any knowledge of what was in it.

'How did you know that new patients were arriving?'
'The nurse ordered me to prepare new beds.'
'When was that?'
'About eleven o'clock at night.'
'Who came to check the patients afterwards?'
'Nurse Huffner.'
The prosecutor stood up and asked the witness to identify her.
Seven or eight cameramen took pictures of the accused Frau Huffner from every angle – a brutal-looking woman with an ugly and ferocious face.
'Were the patients naked or wearing night clothes?'
'They were in night clothes.'
'And then?'
'Henri Gollob entered.'
'What for?'
'To give the injections.'
'What happened after that?'
'They all died.'
'How long did it take?'
'One or two hours.'
'And what happened after they were dead?'
'They were carried down to the basement.'

'Who carried them?'

'Hans Blum.'

The focus of attention then shifted to Blum.

Finally a lawyer in a colonel's uniform stood up and asked Fraülein Saukel, 'Just how many people did the hospital murder?'

She looked at the chief judge and answered, listlessly, 'I don't remember – '

Interrupting, the lawyer said, 'Ten thousand?'

'Not that many,' she said.

'Then five thousand?'

She was still shaking her head.

'Dreiundvierzigtausend!' [forty-three thousand] shouted a young German man in the audience.

He was out of order. The military police acting as bailiffs quickly escorted him out. That made another good picture for the photographers.

Those on trial in Wiesbaden were just Nazi small fry. The big war criminals were locked up three hundred kilometres away, in Nuremberg. The next morning I went directly there by jeep.

My driver, a corporal, told me that he had to return that night to meet a blonde Fraülein on the steps of the post office, so we sped off through the Black Forest like the wind. On the way we came across Germans going home after their release from Allied POW camps. They walked along in twos and threes, with knapsacks on their backs. Shortly after noon, we arrived in the suburbs of Nuremberg.

This ancient city reminded me of my home, Peking, from its zigzagging city wall to the weeping willows beside the moat. But it was here that the Nazis had gathered, year after year, and where the SS had goose-stepped and saluted Hitler before going out to massacre the Jews. Now this famous city housed twenty-three Nazi leaders who had failed to commit suicide before capture.

Accommodation for the press was much more extensive than at Potsdam. Rooms for three to four thousand reporters had been prepared just outside the city, in the village of Stein, at the splendid Schloss of the world-famous pencil magnate Faber. It had three acres of flower gardens, woods with secluded paths, fountains, and marble sculptures. The oldest parts of the mansion dated back to the middle of the seventeenth century. The war crimes trials had not started and most of the reporters had yet to arrive, so I had half a castle all to myself. At night I twisted the electric light switch and on came a thousand little bulbs in the chandelier. It made me uneasy, after all those years of living in wartime England and being encouraged to save electricity.

After dinner I got to talking with the cook. It turned out that he had been a lookout in a Panzer division of the German army. His ability to speak English and good cooking had led to his release from his POW camp after the war. He was originally from Saxony, which was now in the Soviet zone, so he still had no idea if his wife and children were alive or dead.

For convenience, the twenty-three Nazi war criminals were housed in a jail next door to the court. I presented my identification papers. Only after the colonel in charge had telephoned the press corps and confirmed them did he sign my visitor's pass.

There were many more prison doors and checkpoints inside. I walked along wooden galleries above the prison courtyard. Through cracks in the boards I could see three Nazi prisoners taking a walk, their hands clasped behind their backs. An armed guard paced along behind each one of them.

The colonel who was my guide told me that all the criminals here, regardless of rank, were imprisoned in individual cells six feet wide and twelve feet long. Each cell had a bed with a straw mattress, a small table with a straight-backed chair, and a flush toilet. The prisoners were shaved once a week by the prison barber. The colonel said his men's most important duty was to prevent the war criminals from committing suicide.

As we mounted the stairs, he said I could look inside the main building. The prison was three storeys high. All the landings were covered over with barbed wire to prevent prisoners from jumping from them. Each floor was divided up into cells; each cell door had the prisoner's name and number on the glass nameplate.

Time was needed to prepare for the trial and this batch of war criminals would not go to trial until November, so I decided meanwhile to visit Munich, the capital of Bavaria.

While on the train to Munich I met a German dressmaker. She was about thirty-five with a gaunt face and pale blue eyes, and she told me her story.

'Herr Chinese, my fiancé is a major in the American army. I own a dress shop in Nuremberg and it employs ten workers. I used to live with my mother in a big house, but not any more, for it has practically been flattened by the bombs. Poor Germany! I'm going to America.

'Why am I going to Munich? Now don't make fun of me, but I'm going to see a lady who reads faces. In 1938 I was living very well in a good neighbourhood of Nuremberg, but she told me that I'd have to move within five years. She was right. The English and American bombers came and my house was bombed. We had to move to the town square. She also predicted that I would marry someone who spoke a foreign language. She's really good! I want to find her again and ask her, "Does Major Sam have another wife? Am I really destined to be a citizen of Oklahoma?"

'I don't know anything at all about Major Sam's family. I don't even know what town he lives in. Is Oklahoma big? If I write to "Major Sam, care of the Postmaster General of Oklahoma," do you think he'll get it? I've never loved anyone since 1939, I've just kept my nose to my work. I was disillusioned with men. Then Major Sam came along. If *he* has taken advantage of me I'll never love again. I'll wait for him to the end of my days. Herr Chinese, do you think he lied? He was so good to me. He swore he'd marry me, and he promised, "If the US government doesn't let you immigrate, I'll sign up with UNRRA and come back to Germany to wait until I can take you back with me." He belongs to the winning army, so he didn't have to make these promises. Whatever he wants, I'll give him. Yes I will. Heavens knows why he loves me so much. He said that before me he had had a nineteen-year-old Polish girl. She was always at him to buy things for her. Now that he had me, he didn't want anybody else.

'But last Friday Major Sam suddenly came to my shop to say that he had to return to America right away. He even had to send for his baggage later. He hugged me and kissed me, then jumped into the jeep waiting for him outside the door. He was gone in a flash. When I borrowed a bike and rode to his barracks, they said he'd already gone to the airfield. I asked the sentry on duty if he knew whether or not Major Sam was married. He didn't know. I asked an officer for Major Sam's home address, but he said, "We can't give a German the address of an American without authorisation."

'Herr Chinese, do you think Major Sam will come back for me? Could he be the kind of person who already has a wife? I hope that that lady who reads faces is still in Munich. But what if she says that Major Sam is married? What will I do then?'

★   ★   ★

Thomas Mann once called Munich a beacon of European civilisation, and Thomas Wolfe compared it to paradise. But it was
heavily bombed during the Second World War, with the loss of
30,000 people and half its architectural masterpieces. Statuary from
ancient Greece still lay shattered in the streets, while the citizens of
Munich kept their heads down and walked close to the wall,
picking up cigarette butts discarded by American soldiers while
searching for food to fill their bellies.

Ironically, the beer hall where Nazi leaders used to assemble still
stood, only slightly damaged. But its rusty iron gate was closed
and looking through cracks in the metalwork I saw about fifteen
prisoners of war sawing up tree branches in the yard. A little shed
to the right had been hit by an incendiary bomb. Several hundred
iron chairs stacked there had curled up in the fire like Chinese
noodles.

The leader of the group I was with summoned a POW to open
the gate. First we entered the former secretariat of the National
Socialist Party, where we found some German women making
cakes for the American Red Cross. They invited us to have some
with cups of coffee. Next door was the great assembly hall of the
National Socialist Party. Now it was an American-style gym-
nasium fitted out for indoor volleyball. It was in the adjoining
dining hall that the Nazi party had convened its founding meeting.
The floor was a complete wreck, so we made our way around it to
the cellar where the beer was stored. We had to ride down in a
hand-operated lift.

Munich's other chief historical site was the Brown House, where
Chamberlain, Daladier and Hitler had signed the Munich Pact in
1938. The building was mostly destroyed by bombing. An old
man was sleeping on the steps. He said that originally it had been a
sculpture museum built by Ludwig I. A picture gallery was across
from it. Pointing to the air-raid shelter in the basement, the old
man said that if he'd gone there for shelter five minutes later that
day, he'd have been smashed to smithereens along with all the bas-
reliefs.

We drove to the concentration camp at Dachau. It was the first
human killing factory Hitler devised, built in March 1933. Two
hundred and eighty thousand men, women and children died
there. The French premiers Léon Blum and Edouard Daladier had
been imprisoned there, as well as the Austrian premier, Kurt von

Schuschnigg, and Martin Niemöller, the German theologian who dared openly to defy Hitler. Now, five thousand SS troops were locked up in the camp. The American army of occupation was just then constructing a church within the perimeter fence.

The sign pointing to the gas chambers said 'To the Showers.' But what sprayed out from the ceiling spigots was a poisonous gas. From the bloody fingernail scratches on the walls you could imagine how desperately the victims must have struggled during their final moments. There were four crematoria, each capable of burning six prisoners at a time.

The jeep passed through forests and Alpine villages on the way back. I remained silent the whole way. When we reached the banks of the Tegernsee, I got off and went quietly to the press camp of the Third Army. Dinner was in the Austrian style, wienerschnitzel and sauerkraut laid out colourfully on the plate just as if on an artist's palette, but I couldn't taste it. I kept staring blankly out the window at the lake water. That night I was visited by one nightmare after another.

At Dachau I had lost a good part of my faith in humanity.

There was still more than a month before the trials of the major war criminals, and I knew there would be exhaustive reports of the proceedings from all the major wire services. Just as I was wondering if it was worth waiting, I met at the dinner table a naval lieutenant from California. He had a jeep and he wanted to see the Alps, then pass through the American and French zones on his way to Paris. He had rations, petrol, and a tent in his trailer, and he was looking for a travelling companion. In a place like that Chinese and Californians were almost fellow countrymen so I notified the press camp and joined up with him.

The Germans are an artistic people. However poor they might be, the women in the Bavarian villages wore beautifully embroidered clothing. The doors and windows of their log chalets were ornately carved, and walls facing the street were painted with scenes from the Bible or rustic landscapes.

The day we left we breakfasted in a dining room with French windows on three sides. The Alps, blanketed in snow the year round, were framed as if in a picture. Thin clouds wound around the mountains like white gauze, as the bright gold of autumn touched the treetops.

Apart from a rusting tank or two lying in the fields, there were hardly any signs of the war here. Strings of cured meat hung from the eaves of the peasant homes and firewood was stacked up in their backyards. Shopkeepers in Munich had accepted only marks issued by the army, but here they still used their own currency. Everybody – men and women, young and old – wore a green felt cap and stuck a goosefeather in the white hatband.

We were on our way to supreme headquarters of the US Third Army, but not to visit General Patton – we needed to arrange for passage into the French zone with the French liaison officer stationed there.

As our jeep climbed the mountains, we passed an oxcart loaded with straw. Sitting on the straw were village girls in embroidered kerchiefs whose loud clear singing echoed through the sky. Nearby, black and white goats chewed quietly while chickens and ducks pecked away between their feet. Other young women walked by with milking pails, fresh flowers bouncing in their hair. Children in leather pants laughed and played. A nun went by in her solemn white habit. Later, peering down from the mountain, we could see a silvery lake, inlaid with ash-brown reeds at the sides. Looking up, we saw the rocky barrier of the Alps.

As we approached the Austrian frontier, the landscape changed. Gothic steeples were replaced by onion domes (they were more like garlic bulbs, it seemed to me) while wooden statues of the saints lined the roads every few paces. Young women here wore their hair in braids wrapped around their heads. The road twisted up the brown crags of the mountains, as Waldchensee now glimmered below. A transparent green brook gurgled on its way towards the lake. Above, a cascade fell a thousand feet over a precipice. In the valley cattle bent their heads to the grass, the bells on their necks sweetly breaking the silence.

Weaving our way down the mountain, we came to a famous town on the German-Austrian border, Garmisch-Partenkirchen, site of the 1936 winter Olympics, and checked in at an inn. A Hungarian woman, a refugee, was in charge. Her husband had been an officer in the Hungarian army, but she had heard no word of him since the war ended. This inn had been a fashionable place before the war. On the walls hung wood carvings and antlered stags' heads. Copper tools were displayed on the shelves, and in the middle of the room was a big porcelain stove. We drank Austrian wine as if we were in Vienna and then, in high spirits, went for a stroll.

The village was ringed with mountains and stood at the foot of Zugspitze, the tallest peak in the Bavarian Alps. A bright moon was slowly rising, reflecting a silvery gleam from the snowy summits. Cows just down from the mountains were on the streets and we followed the tinkling cow-bells into the centre of town.

There was a coffeehouse run by the Red Cross especially for military officers. The proprietress was a gaunt-faced German woman. The waitress was seductively made up, but when she started talking she sounded very depressed. Her home was in Saxony, in the Soviet zone, and there was no news about the men in her family.

At the next table was a tall but slightly pudgy British colonel, wearing black-rimmed spectacles. He and his companions began to talk with my California friend about photographic equipment, and then to display what they'd managed to liberate.

The colonel said, 'From D-Day to the time of the German surrender, I "liberated" fifty Contax cameras for myself and, for my wife, five hundred yards of silk fabric and three hundred yards of woollen cloth'.

When he got on to how many bottles of wine he'd liberated I said, 'I bought a bottle of whiskey at the PX, but I had to pay tax while going through British customs just the same'.

The colonel smiled. 'You journalists don't have your own private airplanes to go back in,' he said.

Then he started telling us all about how to get through customs, to the point that his companions became embarrassed and made an excuse to leave.

The next day we rode the electric tram up the Zugspitze. After two hours we were at the top, communing with the clouds. The tram had passed over the Garmisch valley, crawled up over the Chinese-lute-shaped Eibsee, and then an engine was added at the back, so that we were pushed from the rear at the same time as we were pulled from the front. As the tram went up the incline, my ears began to pop. Then we passed through a tunnel in the mountain. On the other side was the inn at the summit. Several husky Germans in blue and red sweaters paced around with their arms crossed in front of them, as if waiting to be called. Their blue arm badges read 'Ski Instructor'.

This was the highest point in all of Germany. Standing at the lookout I was told that on a clear day you could see all the way north to the plains of Bavaria, and get a panoramic view of Austria to the south. Unfortunately the weather was not so good. At the lookout point I struck up a conversation with a German woman. Her father, a submarine commander, was now imprisoned in Japan. On the way down I had a very different encounter. A young German woman brought me up short with the words '*Shi Zhongguoren ma?* – Are you Chinese?' pronounced in a perfect Tianjin accent. It happened that she had been born and raised in Tianjin, where her father ran an import-export business. She had come to Germany with her father for the first time just before the war, and had married a Nazi. Her husband ran a paper-making factory, and if he hadn't joined the party he would have had a hard time keeping his factory, she explained. Now he was in a POW camp. She, with a child to raise, was the chauffeur for an American lieutenant colonel.

She invited me to her house in Garmisch-Partenkirchen that evening for a glass of wine and to meet the colonel. We talked through the night about Tianjin, the Little White Building district in the British Concession, the steamed meat dumplings made at the Goubuli shop, and a lot of other things.

We began by drinking German schwarzwasser, then graduated to champagne. The colonel drank with wild abandon. Leaning on the woman's breast, he kept murmuring, 'The Contax factory is already back in operation, exclusively supplying demobilised American soldiers with cameras at thirty dollars apiece . . . Me? I've already got at least a hundred fuckin' points towards retirement, and seventy-five is all you need. But Germany is my paradise. *Bavaria* is my paradise. I know the hair colour and eye colour of every woman in Garmisch. . . . I know them all by heart.'

The curfew hour was long past. I tottered back to my inn. When I awakened the next morning, I discovered that I'd worn my hat to bed.

When we got back to Bad Tölz, we knew we were about to exchange the materially well-supplied American sector for the austerities of the French zone, so we stopped for petrol and bought several jerry cans besides filling the tank.

We gave our itinerary to the liaison officer from the French zone. After leaving Germany we would go to Innsbruck, visit Liechtenstein, thread through northen Italy, sticking close to the Swiss border, then pass through Strasbourg on our way to Paris.

All sorts of vehicles were on the roads in the American zone. Once in the French zone, you could sometimes drive an hour without meeting anything. Some of the French sentries were not even armed, and the only planes at the Innsbruck airport were four light fighter planes. The victorious Tricolore, however, was everywhere: on the roofs, the fuselages of the planes, fluttering from the airport buildings.

No one was out on the streets, except for an old lady with trembling hands who was setting up a stall to peddle black bread.

We were only twenty miles from the Brenner Pass, where Hitler had often met with his fellow dictator, Mussolini. We drove on through the Alps. White poplars lined the road on either side. At the foot of the mountains was a branch of the Danube, with upside-down reflections of red leaves. Then the highway followed the course of the Innsbruck River the whole way.

When we came to a tricolore barrier gate a French sentry shouted rudely, 'Hand over all travel papers!' My companion yelled back at him, 'United States of America!' I began to feel uncomfortable, but the sentry hastily saluted and let us through.

At the blast of a bugle, our jeep was blocked by police once again. It was getting dark; we could make out a plaza ahead, with a group of local Germans of all ages standing to attention and looking dispiritedly towards the centre of the plaza. The French flag, flapping in the breeze, was being lowered. I wondered what feeling this nationalistic exercise by the French occupation authorities would arouse in the next generation of Germans. Would it be humiliation, or a desire for revenge?

The proprietor at the inn where we stayed had formerly driven a trolley in Berlin. Asked about how the French occupation army was behaving, he shrugged his shoulders: 'We lost, so what more is there to say?'

In the bar, a short, fat Frenchman approached us to exchange francs for US dollars. We didn't do a deal, but got to talking about politics instead. Marshal Pétain was being tried at the time. The Frenchman asked us our opinions about the trial, but started right in with his own without waiting: 'When a flood comes, you ought not to blame those who try to stop it and fail. You ought to investigate the guys who didn't build good dykes in the first place, like Blum, and Daladier.'

When he went to the garage in the morning to get his jeep, my travelling companion discovered that his beloved pistol was missing. He checked again and found that two cases of army rations were gone, too. We went to the police station at once. 'An American military officer demands to see the chief of police to report a theft,' he roared at the man on the desk. 'If you don't help me, I'll telephone Washington.'

The chief of police was eating breakfast. Through the window he appeared to be a fat, red-faced, middle-aged man with three gold bars on his shoulders. He sipped a big cup of coffee, completely unmoved. My companion never got in to see him.

We went west, skirting Lake Constance. Twice we found ourselves at the Swiss border after misreading the map. How severe were the faces of those neutrals! Without an entry visa, no other document on earth could get you in. While my partner went to negotiate, I found myself surrounded by seven or eight small children. They were well fed and their faces were ruddy as apples. These children had never tasted the bitterness of war. They approached me only out of curiosity (perhaps I was the first Asian they'd ever seen), not with their hands outstretched for cigarettes or chewing gum like the children of Germany. Having never experienced the calamity of war, they were much too proud to beg.

At this period there were still almost two million US soldiers stationed in Europe, most of whom had been there for two years or more. Transport facilities were insufficient to get them all back home at once, so headquarters made other use of their time, organising groups of men to go sightseeing and running many vocational colleges for soldiers on active duty to prepare them for demobilisation.

They had divided Switzerland into four sightseeing districts; you could choose one and tour it for two weeks. Headquarters took care of all border procedures, transportation and lodging; the soldiers only had to pay $40 apiece. It was a 'reward' to the soldiers for their service, and was also intended to be educational.

I got permission to go and see one of these centres, at Mulhouse. It was located in an old French army barracks which had been a concentration camp under the Nazis with a capacity of eight thousand people. The buildings were divided with wooden partitions into a uniform mending shop, manicurist, barber, beer hall and the like, all of which offered services free of charge. The service staff all wore green uniforms with three big letters on the back: POW. There was a notice on the wall: 'You are being served by prisoners of war. Do not tip them, give them gifts, or thank them!'

Thus, German military officers who yesterday flew airplanes and drove tanks to invade the territory of other nations now bowed their heads and wore thimbles to mend the trousers of draftees from Chicago and New York. At breakfast, five of us had a dozen young Germans waiting on us. When we put the jeep in for repairs and a fill-up, a half-dozen POWs who had been military engineers rushed up with their tools at the ready.

Not far from Mulhouse, we saw the now much-ridiculed Maginot Line. Route 19 from Paris had been torn up by the heavy tanks passing over it, almost to the point of impassability, but we saw truckload after truckload of German POWs lurching along it on their way to repatriation. I remembered something I'd read in the American armed forces newspaper, *The Stars and Stripes*:

> Due to the labor shortage, French authorities have continually requested prisoners of war from the American zone, beginning with an initial contingent of 1,500,000. When they arrived, France was unable to feed them. America has sent more grain under the Lend Lease Act, but French authorities are not distributing all of it to the prisoners. Casualties in the prisoner of war camps are mounting daily.

The American Red Cross filed a protest with the French authorities over this, since the prisoners had been sent from the American sector.

As we crossed the Marne, we saw a family of gypsies cooking dinner over a campfire outside their tents. These roving folk without a land and without a country paradoxically seemed now to be the most carefree and fortunate people in all of Europe. It was beginning to grow dark, and crows were flocking out of the fields where white grave stones formed a ragged skyline that stretched as far as the eye could see. Haze covered the woods in the distance. Behind them, a crescent moon was rising, its clear light shining down as much on the tombs of American soldiers as on the trees.

We spent the night in the ancient city of Troyes, by the Seine. The next morning, needing to wash, we went to the fire station and used the water in vats set aside for fighting fires. Fourteen months after its liberation, this provincial French capital could provide even non–drinking water for only a few hours a day.

War! A little band of power-hungry opportunists had brought untold suffering to millions.

At the end of 1945 I received a letter from Hu Lin. It began with a commendation for the work I had been doing but added that parts of the many despatches I had sent had been censored for fear of offending the Chinese authorities. Some pieces that had been printed had led to difficulties as it was. For instance, the Polish ambassador in Chungking had filed a protest against a report I sent about the situation in his country. But Mr Hu felt that a newsman must report the facts, so he did not say this as criticism. At the end of the letter he suggested transferring me back to the main editorial offices in Shanghai early in 1946. He wondered what I thought of taking over the *Dagongbao* Literature Supplement again.

As I think back on it now, it seems to me that if I had delayed for another two or three years, until the dust had settled in China, my circumstances would be very different today. I was a traveller without a map, yet possibly able to see things a bit more clearly because of that. There was still a lot of post–war Eastern and Western Europe to be covered, and such information might be of use to China in figuring out where *her* future lay. And if I stayed, perhaps my own future would be brighter too.

Still, after seven years abroad, I was very homesick. I wished I could sprout wings and fly back. I wrote to my boss, telling him exactly how I felt and agreeing to prepare the way for my successor.

Then came another letter. Before I left Europe for good, Hu Lin wanted me to tour Switzerland. So did I. During my eighteen-day trip out of Munich, I had twice gone knocking at the door of Switzerland, but had been denied admission. I wanted to get the feel of a country that had never been bombed, never known rations or wartime prohibitions, that had stayed out of the fight.

The trip to Switzerland was my farewell to Europe and one last lesson in Western democracy.

I stayed a few days each in Berne, Basel, Geneva on Lake Léman and Lucerne, the setting for one of Tolstoy's novels. I revelled in the beautiful Swiss scenery. In the regions crossed by the majestic Alps, lakes nestled at the foot of the mountains. Glaciers often filled the higher mountain valleys. Sunlight reflected off the snow revealed layer upon layer of glacial scars.

I also visited Locarno, near the Italian border, and ascended the Jungfrau, one of the three great Alpine peaks.

As I did my sightseeing, a question kept going around in my mind: Why was Switzerland, with its three completely different peoples, four languages and two religions, so completely at peace with itself – and indeed so unified, so well-ordered? In a hundred years it had suffered from no external threat or internal trouble. The country was as poor in natural resources as the Sahara Desert. It had heavy industry, yet it produced neither steel nor petroleum and little coal. Transportation? It was far from the Atlantic and the Mediterranean, a landlocked country that could be sealed off by its neighbours at any time. Yet it was highly developed. The electrified trains that ran in north London were made in Zürich, and the building of atom-smashers at Cambridge and Paris was contracted out to Switzerland, too. Its light industry, led by watchmaking, was world-renowned. Certainly the Swiss were diligent and careful in their work – but that couldn't be the only explanation for their success.

During my two-week visit I constantly searched for other reasons.

I discovered that nearly every Swiss household owned a rifle and all males served in the military, but that the number of professional soldiers was hardly worth mentioning. This lessened their countrymen's financial burden and prevented the establishment of a military class.

I also discovered that the Swiss president lacked the powers of a Roosevelt, Churchill or Chiang Kai-shek. He was completely subordinate to the legislature, which was in turn made up from the assemblies of the twenty-five cantons. Elections to the latter were still held in the open air, just as in the Middle Ages.

This little country was home to many international peace organisations, and the International Red Cross in Geneva had, during the past six years of war forwarded fifty million letters between POWs on both sides and their families, and distributed almost a hundred million gift packages. Their registry office maintained a file of fifty million cards with histories of prisoners' transfers or deaths on them. Several hundred female workers (some paid, some volunteers) compiled them and kept them up to

date. I flipped through a box. Each card had just a few lines on it,
but they all told stories of distress:

> Plane shot down over Hamburg. Died in the military
> hospital.
> Contracted tuberculosis at Bergen-Belsen. Later died.

You saw few policemen on patrol in Switzerland. This had to be
due to the good state of their educational system. They had seven
universities and four hundred newspapers. Switzerland was the
ancestral land of the great philosopher Rousseau and the psychoanalyst Jung. It had attracted scholars from all across Europe. The
German philosopher Nietzsche and the French critic Sainte-Beuve
had taught there. Yet Swiss education stressed the primary and
secondary grades, and had more thoroughly wiped out illiteracy
than any other nation.

I chatted with a middle-aged man in my second-class train
compartment while travelling from Zürich to Geneva. He had all
sorts of statistics immediately available – so much so that I was
amazed at his knowledge of the Swiss economy. Only when he got
up to leave the train at Berne did I learn that he was the minister of
grains and foodstuffs. There was a story about an American soldier
on vacation in Switzerland who held forth to a trolley passenger
about how democratic America was, and how people could go into
the White House at any time and see the president. The Swiss on
the trolley told him that in Switzerland there was no distinction
between the president and ordinary people to begin with.

'Have you seen your president?' the GI asked, unconvinced.

'I *am* the president.'

I didn't really believe this story, but a friend in the Chinese
embassy in Switzerland told me that the Swiss president did indeed
ride the trolley to work.

I would have returned to China by any means of transportation at
all, so anxious was I to get back. When I found there were no planes
available, I enquired about steamers. Many passenger liners had been
converted into cargo ships during the war. So a cargo ship it was.

Today you can fly from London to Shanghai in a matter of hours;
my 1939 boat trip from Kowloon to Marseilles had taken a month.
Yet on the cargo ship *Glenogle* it took us a hundred days to reach
Shanghai in 1946, for the port facilities along the way had sustained
heavy damage and many mines were still waiting to be swept.

You could still call it a satisfying trip. All of my travelling companions were on urgent business and entitled to preferential treatment or they would not have been able to board even such a ship as this. We sailed across the peaceful Mediterranean. Once in Egypt, I wondered if perhaps the Suez Canal, crossroads of the world, would be able to tell me what the new post-war world order would be like. I stood for a long time on the bridge, staring down at the confusion. Brown-skinned Egyptians did the loading and unloading in their long, tattered gowns, while yellow-skinned Chinese sailors from Ningbo in greasy caps operated the machinery and an English sea captain, in a snow-white uniform adorned with gleaming golden epaulettes, directed them.

Passing through the great, misty expanses of the Red Sea and Indian Ocean, we reached Singapore, gateway to the Far East. The ship stayed there for more than thirty days, and I was able to make a news tour of seething Malaya. A national independence movement was fermenting in this British colony.

What I scarcely realised was how divided against herself China had become during my absence. Still less could I have guessed the effect this would have on my life – particularly my married life, since I had met Gwen, a beautiful half-Chinese, half-English young woman in Europe and we were now married.

When I arrived in Shanghai, however, my first difficulty was quite a practical one. My newspaper had not arranged lodging for us, and to rent rooms in Shanghai during those days of hyper-inflation you had to pay in gold bars. Finally I had to take a position at Fudan University, simply to solve my housing problem. Fudan settled us in a single-storey Japanese-style house in Xuhui Village. I received a huge wad of banknotes for my first month's professor's salary. My friend Jin Yi urged me to exchange them for hard goods as soon as possible – to buy anything I could find, since tomorrow my money would be worth less than half of what it was today.

Fortunately I was only nominally in charge of the *Dagongbao* Literature Supplement. My real work was writing editorials about international affairs, continental Europe and the British Isles; I did not even have to go in to the office. In 1946 I was also writing some special columns and a series of satires entitled *Hongmao Changtan (The Platitudes of a Red-Haired Barbarian)*, under the foreign-sounding pen name Tatamulin. Pretending to be a Latvian businessman, I wrote with an odd foreign-sounding Chinese syntax, exposing the abuses of Kuomintang rule and particularly criticising the impending civil war.

After the war, the domestic struggle forced you politically to 'lean to one side' or the other – the KMT side or the Communist – you couldn't blaze your own trail. Swords were drawn and bows were bent, even as the economy neared collapse. Internationally, too, you had to belong to one camp or the other. Stalin and Truman didn't believe that their two peoples could coexist on this earth. America in particular, which thought it had a monopoly on atomic weapons, seemed to be itching to start the Third World War.

The *Dagongbao*, which advertised itself as 'impartial' (its other name was *L'Impartial*, in French because the paper had been founded and was registered in the French concession) was itself in trouble. Those on the left accused it of helping the KMT more than criticising it, while the bureaucrats in Nanking gave the paper several warnings about its pro-Communist stance. Once I was attending a meeting on Minguo Road when the office was surrounded by a band of right-wing thugs. They pounded loudly on the door and cursed at the newspaper for 'speaking for the Communists'.

It was in this period, during the small hours of the morning as we lay asleep in my new faculty housing at Xuhui Village, that there suddenly came a violent knocking. I crawled out of bed and opened the front door. My wife Gwen was frightened that it was robbers, but instead soldiers armed with rifles strode into our bungalow and rushed to the bedroom. After turning all the bookshelves upside down and ripping the stuffing out of our mattress and pillows, and finding nothing treasonable, they rammed my tatami mats with the butts of their rifles, mad as hornets at having to go away empty-handed. The students at Fudan were holding demonstrations against the KMT at the time, and evidently the authorities thought that some of us professors were behind the students.

I'd never been actively involved in politics, but ever since I'd started writing editorials, I'd been obliged to take certain stands. I detested capitalist bigotry, particularly the McCarthyism that was raging in America, but during my seven years in England I'd also heard about the purges in the Soviet Union in the 1930s. From my youth I had detested the outrages of imperialism on Chinese soil. I made my first political speech at the age of fifteen from a soapbox at the Dongsi Arch, and had gone on to join the Communist Youth without really understanding anything about Marxism, simply feeling that communism meant patriotism. My heart had still been with the Communists in the thirties, so I printed nothing from the KMT writers in the Literature Supplement of the *Dagongbao*, though I included much material from Yan'an and the Communist liberated areas when I resumed my work for the paper in Hong Kong during the war. Thus in the end I retained tender feelings for Communists at home, even as I grew ever more suspicious of Soviet Communists from what I had read about them in England. Little did I or most other Chinese intellectuals realise that Yan'an had had its own purge of intellectuals in 1942. After all, in the late 1940s, it was the Communists who were dead set against civil war, and that completely coincided with my own thinking. It was inconceivable to me that just after its eight-year war against Japan, China would choose to plunge into another war, spilling the blood of its own people. Why was America staunchly supporting the Kuomintang's evil rule? I was perplexed and in pain. In foreign matters, my editorials blamed the Americans more than the Russians, and on the home front I blamed the KMT entirely for the great suffering. I sincerely hoped that post-war China could go its own way, apart from both the Soviet Union and America. This put me in agreement with the basically neutralist viewpoint of the *Dagongbao*.

But the responsibility for editorials in the *Dagongbao* could not in all fairness rest only with the author, for editorials had to be discussed first in a committee meeting. Ultimately it was the chief editor who made the decisions. I remember that once, when a co-worker wrote an editorial fully supporting the [anti-KMT] student movement, his viewpoint was turned completely around in the article finally printed.

Home after seven years' absence, I found myself once more taking up the most dangerous profession of all: writing. I had edited the literary page for several years before I left, without offending anybody, yet in 1937, when the newspaper was reduced in size and the Literature Supplement had to be sacrificed, I was among the first to be discharged. I had decided then that if I ever worked for a newspaper again, I'd better have another strong suit to fall back on. So I now got to work studying international politics and from 1946 to 1949, I was both literary editor for the paper and a lead writer on foreign affairs.

I might not have got myself into real trouble if I'd just written a few editorials about international affairs. But the Communists insisted on allegiance in all matters cultural as well. A single line in one of my editorials sealed my fate.

In May of 1947, the editorial committee wanted me to write a cultural piece to commemorate the May Fourth movement of 1919, which had become a national festival day for literature and the arts. I wrote that whereas George Bernard Shaw was still writing in his nineties, we honorifically called our authors 'Venerable Mr So-and-so' when they were barely fifty and gave them big birthday banquets. Had I known more about recent domestic cultural affairs, including the fact that a certain Great Authority, Guo Moruo, had already been appointed as the Communists' supreme commander in literature and the arts, I would never have made this gaffe. People had begun calling him 'Venerable Mr Guo'.

Difficulties began coming to me linked together like a chain. In 1947 a family problem inserted itself into the picture. That made it a link in still another chain, of my long history of misfortunes in love.

I was first married in 1936 to a girl of nineteen. She had lost her mother at a very early age; when her father remarried, she found herself with a stepmother not much older than she. Her childhood was lonely and unhappy. After our wedding, my wife confessed to me that she had married in order to escape her miserable home life and get into the world. Being in love, I pretended I had no objection to that, and soon after we were married, she went off on her own to Tokyo, where she found work in a school.

I did not realise until then, when it was too late, that I had wanted to get married for the opposite reason: to have a home as a refuge from the world. I was tired of the single life. Yet marriage had not afforded me a home. In those days I lived in the White Russian quarter of Shanghai where I rented a single room from a White Russian landlady and took my meals in a restaurant downstairs. My sole companion was a lame cat that I had rescued from beneath a motor car.

Then in July 1937 came war with Japan. My wife sailed back from Japan just at the moment I was being discharged from the

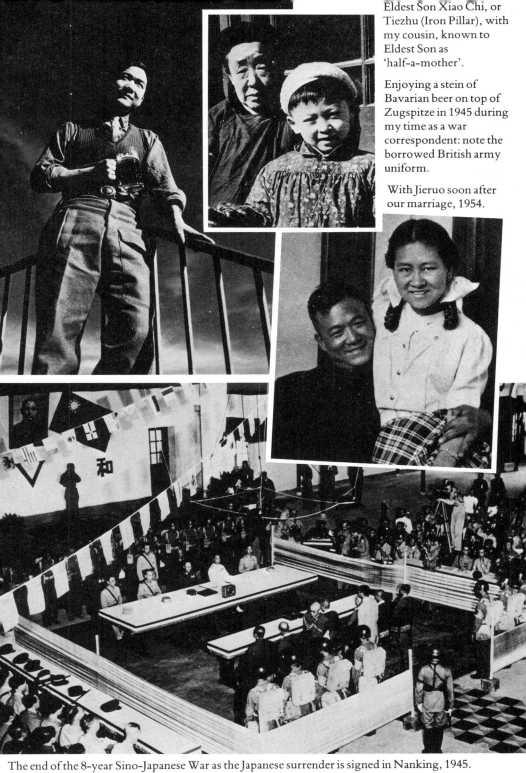

Eldest Son Xiao Chi, or Tiezhu (Iron Pillar), with my cousin, known to Eldest Son as 'half-a-mother'.

Enjoying a stein of Bavarian beer on top of Zugspitze in 1945 during my time as a war correspondent: note the borrowed British army uniform.

With Jieruo soon after our marriage, 1954.

The end of the 8-year Sino-Japanese War as the Japanese surrender is signed in Nanking, 1945.

Teachers and students parading in Tian'anmen Square in August 1966 during the Cultural Revolution. Their banners read 'Hold Aloft the Great Banner of Mao Zedong's Thought'.

The frightened faces of my family and me in Hubei at the May Seventh Cadre School in 1971. Mao badges are pinned to our jackets.

Children singing at a training school in East Jiangxi Province.

Edgar Snow with Mao Zedong, February 1972.

In company with writers from North and South America, Africa and the Far East at the International Writing Program in Iowa, 1979.

With Jieruo at Portmeirion in August 1986. It was here that Susan Williams-Ellis kindly brought me in 1942 to recover from my mental breakdown.

In the company of some much-loved books.

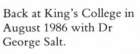

Back at King's College in August 1986 with Dr George Salt.

After my lecture at New York University in October 1986, with Jieruo and the University President, Dr John Brademas.

Dagongbao. I welcomed her and we left Shanghai as refugees, looking for work first in Canton and then in Hankou. There were no jobs to be found. Finally, in 1938, I was summoned again by the *Dagongbao*, this time to go to Hong Kong, where a new edition of the paper was to be started. I was again appointed its literary editor.

Soon after my arrival, wishing to brush up on my French, I discovered a Swiss professor from Peking University living in Kowloon who was just then looking for a native of Peking to help him study the syntax of the Peking dialect who was willing to come to an exchange arrangement with me.

On the first day of our meeting, a most charming girl appeared at intervals from another room of his flat. She wore a blue outfit and I was immediately attracted to her. After sitting down with us to serve tea, she told me that she had long heard of me and read a number of my stories in the *Dagongbao*. At the request of the Swiss professor, whom she addressed as 'Daddy', she played the piano for us.

That day I returned to our dormitory feeling completely enchanted. Before I realised it, I was deeply in love with her. But I also felt immensely guilty towards my wife. Admittedly, soon after our marriage she had told me more than once that although we were formally wedded, she did not want me to feel bound by the law. 'If ever you fall in love with someone else, just let me know and I will set you free.' But although I did now confess to her what had happened, I felt ashamed and told her also that I would do all I could not to see the girl again. In fact I ceased to go to the professor's flat and before long I joined a Communist friend from North China in a trip to east Guangdong, where I did a series of articles for my paper, and then on to cover the construction of the Burma Road. All the while I tried to forget the girl in blue, but I could not.

In July of that year, I returned to Hong Kong. My wife rejoined me there and, after a month-long discussion, she decided to grant me the divorce and then to go and live in Kunming. It was very simple. All we needed to do was put an advertisement in the paper announcing it. At the last moment, it was I who faltered. Although she and I did not enjoy intimacy as husband and wife, we never quarrelled. Because our relations were so peaceful and I was then busy with my arrangements to go to England, I proposed that she give me her final word only after she had gone to Kunming. So she left in an undecided state.

On her arrival in Kunming, she cabled me: 'No divorce'.

I left for Hong Kong and England with my heart completely anguished. The girl in blue and the Swiss professor soon departed for Geneva and I was left with an undivorced but alienated wife in Kunming.

The girl in Geneva and I wrote to each other regularly, until the fall of France. Then our postal liaison was cut off by the Nazi invasion. It was then that I had my worst mental breakdown.

In the winter of 1943, Hu Lin, my boss at the *Dagongbao*, came to England. From him I learned that my wife, though having refused to grant me a divorce, was now the mother of two children by a Communist in Chungking. I divorced her, therefore. But the following year, when I went to Paris soon after its liberation, I discovered that the girl in Switzerland was married and also had a child.

Then it was that I met a young woman in London called Gwen. Her father was Chinese and her mother English, but they had divorced during her infancy. She had been raised since early childhood in England by her mother – brought up to be a little upper-middle-class English girl. Indeed she had graduated from Oxford. She didn't know a word of Chinese, yet, because of her Eurasian origin, people in England regarded her as a Chinese and that was how she felt herself. So did I, even though, with her lovely chestnut hair, she bore little resemblance to one.

Gwen was glamorously beautiful. We fell in love soon after meeting and decided to marry. That was not long before I sailed for Shanghai in March 1946. She had left for America beforehand, to visit her father in Minneapolis, and we arranged to meet in Shanghai, her birthplace, where we were to marry. We never suspected that the city would be in such chaos.

In spite of everything, we went ahead with our wedding. It was quite a grand affair, attended by colleagues of the press and my fellow writers. Because of the scarcity of housing, we had to spend our wedding night in the home of a poet friend. Later we moved to a hotel where bedbugs crawled out over the sheets in the middle of the night. It was the first time Gwen had ever been bitten by one and she began to have misgivings about her life ahead. I moved her to five new places in the space of three months, but until I found the job at Fudan, her nightly refrain was 'This is not my country! I want to return to England!'

Our Japanese-style home on the campus at Xuhui Village was tiny but all in all we were quite pleased. To help Gwen's cultural adjustment, I managed to get some grass seed and we planted a small stretch of turf in front of our bungalow. Knowing that she was fond of pets, I even managed to get a dog, a mongrel called Ah Fu, meaning 'Happiness'. In a word, I tried to make our life as English as possible.

Nevertheless, people on campus regarded Gwen as a foreigner, and children often whispered behind her back, 'Here comes the foreign devil', a term which she got to know and found upsetting. Every time this happened she would feel depressed for a long while after.

Then came the ransacking of our house by the KMT soldiers. Gwen was at her wit's end, and just then she became pregnant. A poet friend recommended an obstetrician to us. It seems to me now that my wife had a psychological leaning towards older men. She was brought up by her stepfather and there was not much affection between them. The doctor was very fatherly to her. He was about fifty and my wife was then twenty-six. He often called her his daughter.

I began to suspect something. Being an honest woman, Gwen confessed the whole affair to me. Still worse, she had decided to marry the doctor.

That was the heaviest blow I had suffered yet. I felt the ground collapse under my feet. The doctor came to our bungalow to confirm their decision. I tried to dissuade them and pleaded for the sake of the newly-born baby, but to no avail. She persisted in her decision, even letting me have the baby. Our home was finally broken up in November 1947, when we advertised our divorce. I was a disillusioned man with a baby; Gwen went back to England. I was anxious to leave Shanghai, but not my country.

Just at the time when Gwen was shouting that China was not her country, the boss had called me into his office. He said the government in Nanking had told him they wanted me to go to London as the Cultural Councillor for the Chinese [KMT] Embassy. He wondered how I felt about the idea. I resolutely refused, saying 'I'm not a member of the Kuomintang and have always been averse to entering the bureaucracy. Besides, it took me a long time to get back to China and I don't want to leave'. My refusal led to another uproar at home. If we had gone back to England then, it might in fact have saved our marriage.

The situation grew more bizarre. One day a Shanghai financier invited me to lunch. The president of a university in Anhui was also present. The purpose of the meeting was to invite me to tutor [KMT] General Chen Cheng on the European political situation. I refused.

Subsequently the university president came calling for me at Fudan University three times. If I wouldn't tutor Marshal Chen personally, would I be willing to teach him as one member of a class? I was still dead set against it.

It was this incident which finally made me decide to leave Shanghai for Hong Kong in June 1948 to join the staff of the *Dagongbao* there.

5

Moving House
(1949–1985)

As I think back on my life now, I realise that I have always felt out of place. No doubt I never really made much of an effort to find out what my place was. When the political storms finally reached me, I was swept into total chaos. Only after decades of being tossed about – that is, not until 1983 – did I muddle my way through to a way of life in which I could feel at peace and be myself – one which, by the look of things now, I won't have to leave.

After I moved into this flat, some of my friends were actually dissatisfied for me. My home is right across the street from two apartment blocks fitted out for high-placed intellectuals, they complained, yet I have no washtub, no wooden flooring above the cement. In fact, I was originally given three places to choose from. I didn't even look at the other two. I said, this is it, from now on I'm not moving ever again. For I knew how many Chinese families still lived in the same little hole where they'd always been, three generations in one room, and how many were sleeping in bunk beds. How could I have the face to pick and choose when so many citizens still had to queue up to go to public toilets?

The day I moved in here, I heaved a sigh. Life is short: how can so much of it be spent in moving – above all in hustling and haggling, putting one's very life in jeopardy, simply to be allowed to move?

If I didn't now have my home, or if I had it but were still dissatisfied, wanting to move up one more rung, I wouldn't be writing this. I'd be setting other plans into operation. To avoid suspicion, I'd be shunning this subject.

I've only turned to this subject now because I've decided to live out the rest of my days in this place. Now, my own story of moving, however complicated, is by itself insignificant, not worth wasting ink on. But my particular journey reflects that of society. Unofficial histories are useful supplements to the official ones. Maybe the history of my moves can present the changes in our country and our society from a different enlightening point of view.

A homing pigeon on its journey will encounter storms and even lightning, but when it gets home, it can settle down in peace. But once I'd flown back to mine, I had to move a dozen times more. Often those relocations were bound up with my political fortunes – which in turn were part and parcel of the times.

Pigeons, homing pigeons in particular, have fascinated me all my life. What attracted me – what held me enthralled – was their attachment to 'home'. It's a stubborn instinct that no river or mountain can obstruct.

That home of theirs is nothing more than a tiny nest laid out in rice straw. There are no fancy furnishings in it, but this nest holds those pigeons, body and soul. And it's that stubborn attachment to home that people make use of to train them.

Then again, rats. Some years ago, during spring planting, I dug out a nest of rats with my spade. I don't recall if it was the Four Pests or the Five Pests we were exterminating at the time, but rats were on the list. They raided our grain supply and that was undeniably a crime. Now, I'd never shrunk before from acting against our natural enemies, but when I dug out that nest, I simply couldn't lift my spade to destroy it. I was attracted by the neatness of the layout. Everything was in its place.

The soil there was the same as in other places, yellow with a touch of blackness. No one would have guessed that less than a metre down such a home lay in it. Those meticulous rats had divided it into compartments, like a doll's house. Our stolen property was not strewn about; the corn was piled separately from the beans and there seemed to be a nursery too. (Either the adult rats had been frightened away by then, or they were outside foraging for food.) I say nursery because seven or eight new-born rats were curled up asleep inside. They were smooth from head to tail, light pink and only an inch long. Dropping my spade, I knelt and studied the scene, amazed at the rats' grasp of household management.

Home is the rudder that keeps one's life on course. Certainly I never wrote anything presentable during my seven years abroad.

Even when strolling on the shores of Loch Lomond, or gazing up at the snow-covered Alps, my mind was never at rest. The more beautiful the scenery around me, the heavier I was at heart. On other people's holidays, come Easter, come Christmas, coloured lights would glisten among the branches of the fir trees, and everyone would dress up and go dancing. But I found it hard to join in the merriment. To the exile, it only fanned the flames of homesickness.

At the beginning of 1949 I stood at another great crossroads in my life. Now living in Hong Kong and remarried, I was about to decide the fate of myself and my little family. Since the political upheavals seemed to be over I had just decided to return to Peking, my home, when Professor Gustav Haloun, head of the new Chinese department established at Cambridge, invited me to go and teach modern Chinese literature there. He not only made his request by mail; in March he came in person to Hong Kong. After enquiring about my address with the *Dagongbao* he came panting and wheezing over to my flat on Flower Market Street in Kowloon to plead with me to accept the university's invitation. Professor Haloun was a Czech who in the mid-1930s, seeing the storm clouds Hitler was gathering, had later become a British subject. He told me he had made his trip for two purposes: to purchase books for the new department, and to persuade me to return to Cambridge. This time, unlike 1939, the university was offering travelling expenses for my whole family and an appointment with tenure. Two days later, the old professor, who could hardly climb the stairs to my flat, came again. This time he told me he was making his entreaties as an old friend, not just on behalf of the university. He said that Jan Masaryk had died mysteriously after the war and spoke of the many innocent people who had come to grief in Hungary after Cardinal Mindszenty was tried. Pointing his forefinger at me, he said: 'Don't go to Peking. Any honeymoon between intellectuals and a Communist Party can't last. It simply can't last.'

As he was getting ready to leave, he said he would come again for my answer early the next morning. Tickling my little son Tiezhu, who was sucking at a milk bottle in his pram, Haloun added: 'You've got to think about what's best for him, too.'

When they got wind of my plans to go to Peking, several Chinese friends had come over to discourage me, too. Some said,

'It doesn't matter that they're all smiles towards you now. That can change at any time. The Communist Party tolerates only yes-men. Disputatious people like you are sure to get into trouble.' Others suggested two alternatives. 'The best thing would be for you to accept the invitation from Cambridge. Second best? Ask to be allowed to continue working in Hong Kong temporarily. That way you can retain your present job and at the same time keep an eye on how things are going back home. In any case it would be rash to just up and go. Once you enter China, it's not easy to get out again! Of course the big party bosses are making welcoming noises now, but just see what it's like once you're there. Particularly a Yanjing graduate like you, who's been abroad for several years. They'll call you a slave of the foreigners, maybe a foreign agent. Unfair, you say? I tell you there won't be any Emile Zola to come forward to arouse the public if you become a Dreyfus. . . .'

Sometimes sleep is a reluctant bedfellow. That night the worries on my mind were like a door bolt; once they were in place, it was useless to try to escape. Even closing my eyes was like sitting in the middle of the front row of a cinema; the pictures flickered by without cease. I seemed to see myself as the White Russian beggar who had died in the street when I was little. I had become a homeless White Chinese, a man without a country.

It grew light. Shafts of sunlight spread across the green mountains outside my window. My baby son in his cradle seemed to be having his own nightmares, for he was sobbing without any reason.

I sat up. When my head had cleared a bit, I wrote a letter for Professor Haloun:

> Forgive me, but I have urgent business at the newspaper office that does not allow me to wait for our appointment. I'm sorrier still that I made you call on me three times. But it is precisely because of my child that I must not change my mind.

One day at the end of August, my wife and I and little Tiezhu boarded the S.S. *China Peace* and sailed to Qingdao en route to Peking. We arrived on the eve of the founding of the People's Republic. Thinking back on it now, I believe it was the idea of returning home that persuaded me. My homeland was a magnet. Like a homing pigeon drawn to its nest, I hastened back to my birthplace.

It could of course be countered that I had never had a home. My mother died when I was young. After that I moved into a school dormitory, and at fourteen I was shifted again. But the city of Peking was my home. Even during the London blitz, while lying on an underground platform through the night, my thoughts would fondly return to the ancient city, its protective walls and moats, its weeping willows. I had often kissed the city gates of Peking in my dreams. It was as if my heart had long been buried deep beneath a corner of the Peking city wall. So, however many misgivings I had – however indecisive I may have seemed – my return home was really predetermined. When a man gets to thirty-nine he becomes less interested in travelling abroad. In Peking I would build the very first home of my own, a stable and reliable one. There I would make my contribution, as best I could.

I heaved a long sigh as my foot touched the platform at the Eastern Railway Station. Back at last. Ready to play my part in the revolution. The things that ought to be overthrown had now been overthrown. From now on I would be helping to rebuild my homeland with everybody else, following the flag of revolution.

I know now how naive I was in 1949 to have thought that a stable and reliable home was such an easy thing. But as I entered middle age, the future looked bright.

Until 1949 of course, I'd never lived under the hammer and sickle. In London I'd attended meetings of the British Communist Party as a journalist. After the liberation of Berlin, admittedly I stayed in areas occupied by the Soviet Red Army. But when it came to actually living under a communist political regime, I had no idea what to expect. So, from the first day I went ashore at Qingdao in 1949, I was filled with curiosity and cautious excitement.

In my memory, communism existed in two completely different contexts. I'd read a great many pamphlets in my youth, principally anti-imperialist, attacking the way strong countries bullied and humiliated weak ones, and exposing the gunboat diplomacy adopted towards China by the West since the nineteenth century. They had aroused my indignation and from then until 1939, communism meant to me a society run according to reason and mercy, an ideal system under which all iniquities would be swept away and everybody would be equal.

Although in the thirties I no longer dreamed of becoming a

professional revolutionary, I was still basically in favour of revolution, of the Soviet Union, and of communism.

But when I went to England in 1939, just after Stalin had concluded his pact with Hitler, England was passionately anti-Soviet. In the mid-1930s most British intellectuals, particularly in literature and the arts, had been on the left. W H Auden, Stephen Spender, Christopher Isherwood, even Orwell, all had leaned that way, whether they came from the hereditary aristocracy or the middle classes. But, after the Moscow Trials and then the pact with Germany, they did an about-face. Newspapers, magazines, radio and film were unanimous in depicting communism as evil, and they inevitably influenced me. Many of the terrors that Khrushchev revealed in 1956 at the 22nd Soviet Communist Party Congress had already been exposed back then in the West, and although I myself was not much interested in the internal power struggles of the Soviet Communist Party, however cruel, I was deeply concerned about the fate of Soviet intellectuals. For a while, of course, the Soviets became our allies and such matters were tactfully overlooked, but after the Second World War, I had become very concerned again about the situation in Eastern Europe. And so it was that my two views of communism came into conflict. And so it was, also, that I first approached post-Liberation Peking with a hopeful but cautious attitude.

Several families had made the journey together with us from Hong Kong. After getting off the train, we checked into the Asia Hotel in Xiheyan, outside the Front City Gate. That was my first lodging after returning to the ancient city. A lot of so-called 'Democratic Personages' were already housed there, left-wing but non-communist individuals who had returned from Hong Kong before me. Although we editors had been moved to Peking, our magazine, the *Zhongguo wenzhai (China Digest)* was still being published in Hong Kong. As soon as we had unpacked our baggage, we rolled up our sleeves and set to work.

By then people who'd just taken up residence in the surrounding Guest Houses were already anxiously weighing up our relative ranks and perquisites. Those at the highest level went to the Peking Hotel. Next came the Green Moon Estate. Some people complained about this sort of stratification, but I didn't resent it myself.

I did long, however, to eat with the young Party members who'd come up with us from Hong Kong, but even that was impossible. The Asia Hotel wasn't big, yet it had two kitchens, and the young cadres had arranged for me to eat at a special table, while they went off to their ordinary table, to chew on their *wotou* (coarse cornmeal dumplings). This made me feel very uncomfortable. At the same time, such distinctions communicated to me an encouraging attitude: these Party members were a new breed, especially solicitous of educated people. And although they showed me respect and took me seriously, they always called me comrade and made me feel as if I were one of them. That made me reproach myself for having been so untrusting.

Great Front Gate Street was bustling with capitalist activity. This puzzled me. Shops selling traditional funerary clothing, incense, devotional objects and so forth were still in business. Close by the Asia Hotel was Bada Lane, a quarter where the brothels were concentrated, and even they were still open. Church bells still rang and the smoke of incense still curled up from the temples and lamaseries.

I was puzzled. Revolution was supposed to entail massive destruction and stripping down – so why were these things still intact? A Party organiser quickly set me straight: Relax, everything will change. Our Chairman Mao understands above all else that haste makes waste. He's never acted rashly, and it's because he goes about things surely and steadily that our country's communist government is in power today.

My department, the forerunner of the Foreign Languages Publishing Department, which they tell me now has several thousand Chinese and foreign employees, had in those days only the seven of us. Early every morning we friends who had come from Hong Kong would ride our bikes together from the hotel in Xiheyan to our office in a little family-style compound with a courtyard in Nanheyan. Late at night we returned to the hotel to sleep. On Sundays, for recreation, we would sit down together for community singing, songs like 'The Sky Over the Liberated Areas Is Bright', or twist our way through the rice-sprout dance, a peasant amusement the words of which had been adapted to promote socialism. Our lives were monotonous, but we got along with each other very well. We non-Party members were made to feel like prodigal sons, and the Party members reiterated that 'In the revolution there's no distinction between those who joined early and those who joined late', a promise they made with apparent eagerness and absolute sincerity.

I began to feel that Chinese intellectuals were, generally speaking, pretty fortunate. Our leaders had learned from the bloody lessons of the Soviet Union in the thirties and from the tense relationship between the Party and intellectuals in Eastern European countries. And maybe our Oriental ways of thinking had had an influence, too. In particular *The Selected Works of Mao Zedong* told me that the New Democracy could continue for a number of years before we underwent the transition to full socialism. My generation of intellectuals, half in the old society and half in New China, would have a transitional period. If the Party gave us leeway and we worked hard at it ourselves, adapting might not be such a strain.

Not long after, we were moved to a neighbourhood called Silver Thread Creek. It was a narrow alley and was separated from East Everlasting Peace Street only by a red-painted wall. In front of our gate was a little stream which probably came down from the Golden Water Bridge in front of the Gate of Heavenly Peace. It was a little two-storey building and I and my wife and son lived upstairs.

After the new government was officially established, the magazines we published, which had now been moved up from Hong Kong, came under the Foreign News Department of the Information Administration. We worked off the courtyard of the New China News Agency, in a compound on Parliament Street, where the national assembly of the early Chinese Republic had met. It used to be a dirty and disreputable place. Many plots had been hatched there, from Yuan Shikai's attempt to make himself the Great Constitutional Emperor to Cao Kun's expensive plot to get himself elected president. Now, however, it had become the centre of New China's propaganda-making for domestic and foreign consumption.

At this time, our living accommodation was moved yet again, from Silver Thread Creek to the Great Street of the Imperial Son-in-Law Shi, in a mansion with three interconnecting courtyard quadrangles running back into it, probably the official residence of some senior administrator in the early Republic. It was presumably out of regard for my work that I was put in the courtyard at the very end, where it was extremely quiet and secluded.

Bada Lane, meanwhile, had been dealt with. One afternoon, several dozen trucks arrived and surrounded it. The prostitutes of each and every grade, the madames, the waiters, the servant boys – the whole lot of them were chased into the trucks in one smooth operation. It was done as dextrously as a post office sorts letters, so that in only a few days each person on the truck was in his or her proper place. The prostitutes were in their study classes and pimps and procuresses were in jail.

Covering the story of the prostitutes' reformation was very instructive. It made me understand why there must be a revolution and why revolution was liberation. I often thought of Chekhov's *The Cherry Orchard*. Tree roots, once rotten, must be dug up. And unless it was cut out ruthlessly, would it have been possible in one stroke to destroy a system of prostitution that was more than a thousand years old, and a market in human flesh that had existed for millennia? How else could these women, abducted and sold into their living hells, be returned to the world of humanity?

At one of the regular Meetings for Speaking of the Bitter Past, I listened appalled as those women (some of them already in their forties or fifties) reminisced about how their slave masters had used whips and starvation to force them to sell their bodies. They denounced the men who took out their animal lusts on them, hardly caring whether they were alive or dead. And they told many stories of the brutal circumstances in which they lived. When the pustules of disease showed on them, for example, the women were not cured, but were simply forced to burn them off with flat-irons. And when they died, they were just thrown out and incinerated on piles of hay at the abandoned lot by the Happy Pavilion.

When I got home, I stayed at my typewriter all night long. In one sitting I wrote 'They Came to Daylight', a passionate celebration of these women's new freedom, for the English edition of *People's China*.

Later, at the mass trials convened at the Temple of Heaven and in the suburbs, I heard judgement given on the former vice boss of the Southern District. That was really a day to make people smile. The sky over the liberated areas was in fact bright. A few months later, those hurt and humiliated women had passed through the government's basic literacy programme and had learned useful skills.

Some became tellers for savings associations, others child–care workers at nurseries.

In September 1950, I was suddenly informed that I was wanted for a delegation to England, to be its secretary. In those days to be sent abroad was very significant, a sign that one was trusted. Just before our departure, Premier Zhou Enlai met the entire delegation in the Purple Light Pavilion in Zhongnanhai [headquarters of the Chinese government]. In a sentimental moment the premier told me that he had known a general in the Red Army whose name was exactly the same as mine; that Hsiao Ch'ien had died in battle. Every time he had read my articles in the Wuhan papers of 1938, it reminded him of his old war comrade. But then, late at night the day before we were to depart, I got a call from the head of my unit, Qiao Guanhua. He informed me that the delegation would be leaving as planned, but that I wouldn't be going. 'People like you,' he said, 'are better remaining in the country and not travelling abroad.' He meant that I wan't trusted to leave. A shadow fell across my heart as I realised that being called comrade didn't mean you were one of them. (Ironically there would come a time in the Cultural Revolution when so many people who had gone with delegations abroad were accused of being 'enemy agents' that I would be very glad that I had been forced to stay at home.)

Soon after September 1950 I was assigned duties in the field of foreign propaganda and went to Hunan to report on the land reforms there. This was an even more profoundly significant act of revolution than the closing of Bada Lane. From Hunan's Meetings for Speaking of the Bitter Past, I learned the evil connotations of the word 'feudal' and saw with my own eyes the joy of peasants as they cast off the shackles of millennia. The day they burned the old land title deeds, I took the best photograph of my life. It was shown at national photographic exhibitions and was used on the cover of America's *Life* magazine. Nothing could better demonstrate China's need for a land reform movement than the happiness in those peasants' faces as they watched the historic property deeds go up in smoke.

While we were living in the mansion on the Great Street of the Imperial Son-in-Law Shi, I reported also on the rehabilitation of beggars and of the men who had been policemen under the old regime. I saw that the Chinese revolution, after eliminating the truly evil people, focused wisely on turning the merely idle or foolish into useful citizens. These reformations were undertaken lovingly, like a surgeon wielding a scalpel, not like a woodcutter swinging an axe.

Since I was working in the field of foreign propaganda (as deputy chief editor of *People's China*, an English-language publication) I also had the opportunity to see, on a daily basis, readers' letters from every corner of the globe. In those days many black-skinned, brown-skinned and white-skinned peoples took heart from the Chinese revolution. For the Third World, it meant that there was hope. Workers on rubber plantations in Africa, fishermen in Latin America, Japanese steel workers, even small shopowners along the Mediterranean, all were heartened and inspired. It seemed that revolution might still retain some humanity; besides food and clothing, there might still be room for art and literature; and disputatious intellectuals might still speak out as they pleased, without being dragged off to labour camps. In sum, everything that could with reason be enjoyed under the capitalist system could be enjoyed here too, with the glorious difference that the poor in China were no longer exploited on the land or in the factories.

It wouldn't be truthful to say that I had no political doubts at all during that period. Apart from my own personal problems, I had the greatest trouble accepting the thirty-year Sino-Soviet Treaty of Friendship, Alliance and Mutual Assistance that was signed in 1950.

In fact, for some time I had felt uneasy paying my monthly dues to the Sino-Soviet Friendship Association; one was supposed to pay them without question, like union dues. After all, paying them was a political privilege – there were some in our department who didn't qualify. But when the treaty of 'friendship and alliance' was announced, I couldn't help remembering the previous treaty of friendship and alliance agreed to by Stalin and Chiang Kai-shek in 1945. Of course the new treaty brought a massive loan with it, but it also stipulated that for a time Port Arthur and Darien were to be under Russian control, that the Chinese Eastern Railroad in Manchuria would be operated jointly, and that Sinkiang was to be jointly developed by the two countries indefinitely. Was that any way to treat a brother country?

At a study meeting, luckily before I could utter a word, someone else spoke out about the treaty. He only spoke lightly, but immediately he was in serious trouble. And so we all came to understand from this episode that whereas we could speak out freely on minor matters, we were not supposed to comment on major political policies. I felt knotted up in my heart: I remembered the serious 1948 Communist criticism in Hong Kong of Xiao Jun's condemnation of Russia's atrocities in Manchuria, and realised that such questions must not be raised. But clearly this meant that proletarian countries used the techniques of capitalist power politics on each other.

When a film about the life of the educator Wu Xun was criticised in 1951 for its unrevolutionary attitudes, it was clear that we intellectuals with foreign training were in fact the target. I and some friends whose experiences were comparable to mine 'marched in with the guilty', as the current phrase went.

We criticised our own moderate reformism time and again at meetings large and small. I who had studied in England, the headquarters of Fabian socialism, had to humble myself with particular thoroughness.

At the end of the Three Antis campaign we had to make a clean breast of our faults again, even though we weren't targets of the campaign.

When the campaign developed into an attack on financial corruption, I was made deputy head of a tiger-hunting team. 'Tigers' were those who'd made up to one million yuan through graft. For the first time I saw the abuses that were encouraged by such campaigns: for one thing, all organisations that had handled a given amount of money had to offer up a certain quota of tigers. And for another, it was temptingly easy to 'bite' people. In one day, a single tiger bit more than twenty other people, each of whom was then immediately 'isolated' – held in custody incommunicado – without any corroborative evidence whatsoever.

I saw that, during such campaigns, once a person was sandbagged, people continued hitting him while he was down and no one at all would speak on his behalf. Anyone who did would fall into the same pit, from guilt by association. Those in authority would never call off their witch hunt until they'd met their quota, while those below clearly took pleasure in the misfortunes of others. Seeing others brought down presumably gave them a feeling of personal security. The fabricators of evidence and those fabricated against seemed to have a tacit understanding; everybody was doing it for the revolution.

When I saw this side of the revolution, I began to be afraid.

Not long after the anti-corruption campaign, we were moved to the Great Street of the Sheep Market. Never in my life had I visited, much less lived in, such a luxurious mansion. It had originally belonged to the head of the Chamber of Commerce under the Japanese occupation. Within the red front gate, which was big enough to admit a horse and carriage, there was a courtyard surrounded with magnificent living accommodation. Then, beyond a further gate, there were painted verandas leading to wings both left and right, and in the centre was a ballroom big enough to hold a hundred. The rooms assigned to my family, complete with private toilet facilities, were in the right wing. Back in the third and deepest courtyard were the bedrooms and reception rooms of the original owner, set around a big flower garden with a cellar in one corner, perhaps for protection from air raids. It made a good place for children to play hide-and-seek.

The best thing about the place was that the staff apartments and offices were all under one roof. By now the Foreign News Department had become the Foreign Languages Press and the staff had increased from a few dozen to over a hundred. There were many different languages in use, but English was the one in most demand. As well as our own regular work, we were continually getting extra rush jobs: translating Foreign Ministry speeches, going to the central government offices to do simultaneous interpretation for the Australasian Congress of Workers, and translating into English the speeches made by Wu Xiuquan and Qiao Guanhua at the United Nations in 1950. It often kept us pecking away on our typewriters into the small hours.

Did I feel at ease during those first four or five years? I can't answer that in one sentence. I knew a foreign language and to be put to use and taken seriously kept me satisfied. Basically these were years of getting acclimatised. Of the people who lived and worked with me, a small minority were from the old Communist areas; the majority were, like me, reasonably cosmopolitan. Although it was already clear that I wasn't completely trusted, at least I didn't feel that I was seriously out of step, so I was mostly happy.

Yet I did have one profound regret: since I'd begun writing, in the early Thirties, literature had been my real calling. In July 1949 I'd been given a membership card for the Chinese Writers'

Association, but since I'd lost official trust I felt as if I'd been tacitly expelled from the ranks of the writers. I wasn't satisfied with being a mere translator: secretly I longed to write again.

One afternoon in the autumn of 1952 therefore, when Feng Xuefeng, deputy chairman of the Chinese Writers' Association, suddenly came to visit and said he was thinking of transferring me to a literary unit under his aegis, I was so excited I didn't sleep a wink that night.

I was going back to where I belonged, to my real profession. I could take up my pen again and write. How could I not be excited?

But after the summer of 1957, how many times would I regret not having been satisfied as a mere translator? Having taken up a writing instrument that burned the hand that held it, I would learn to envy those who carried loads on shoulder poles, sold goods from blankets on the pavement, peddled potatoes from little carts. I would often say to myself: In this society, any vocation is safer than that of the writer.

After some thirty-odd years' experience and observation, I had already acquired a wary attitude towards the workings of fate. In particular I had learned that it was wise not to be too quick to judge the personal significance of events. You should not let things get you down, but neither should you let your head be turned by apparent good fortune.

From 1951, when I entered the literary unit, until the time when personal staff histories were opened up and examined in 1956, my life was fairly trouble-free. That was because I had gone to work for the *Dagongbao* directly after leaving college: I had not gone near Chiang Kai-shek in Chungking and I had passed through Wuhan, where Communists had been asked to collaborate with Nationalists, only in transit. Hence I got through most tests reasonably smoothly. On the other hand, a friend whose record was quite as spotless as mine became an 'element put under surveillance' as early as 1951 simply because, as a high school principal (in pre-Liberation times), he had been forced to take out membership in the Kuomintang.

At first I thought my return to the ranks of literary workers was good luck. I moved out of the enormous mansion on Great Sheep Market Street and put up in the corridor of a good friend while I waited to be allocated rooms from my new unit. Sadly, I was already divorced again by then. My son Tiezhu, not yet six years old, boarded at a kindergarten.

Not long afterwards, my new unit bought a giant home for itself, a former soy-sauce brewery and pickling house, complete with salesroom and a huge bean-milling works. The road frontage was not wide, but the place extended far back enough to accommodate three courtyards. The main structure in the middle, which faced south, had probably been the residence of the factory owner. The dozen or so rooms out in the wings must have housed his assistants and apprentices in their various ranks. The company had failed, or else simply ceased operations. Anyway, with the brewery came more than three hundred earthenware jars for pickling and marinating.

My happy marriage with Wen Jieruo began as a literary friendship. We met when she sought me out to polish a translation, and we quickly fell in love. We began our life as husband and wife in a little three-room lean-to on the west side of this big pickling factory off the rear courtyard.

It could not have been done any more simply. We went together to the Civil Administration Office to get the license. There was no ceremony. On the afternoon of 30 April 1954, a pedicab brought her to me from the Eighth Lane of the Dongsi Pavilion. One old suitcase rode with her, beneath her feet, and I, the groom, pedalled my bike behind her. When we got to the gate of the pickling factory, I carried the suitcase and showed her the way in.

Even on our wedding night Jieruo worked late, reading galley proofs on their way to the printer. Early the next morning, she took part in a May Day parade. After the holiday, we went to work as usual.

I deeply regretted my move into the big pickling factory. I hadn't felt out of place in my previous job because everybody – or almost everybody – was a returned expatriate. In the pickling factory however, although many of them were old acquaintances who'd been writing with me in old Beiping or along the Shanghai Bund in the thirties, they had all then gone to the sacred revolutionary capital at Yan'an and undergone revolutionary tempering at the Lu Xun Academy of Arts or Resist-Japan University. Now, they had inevitably become engineers of the revolutionary soul. Some were members of the National People's Congress. Some lived in Peking, to be able to go on writing, while concurrently serving on the Party committee of some steel mill far away. And some, even after having taken off their army uniforms, still had the air of generals about them. Their famous red works had been printed in the People's Series. Some had even won Stalin Prizes in Literature, like Liu Baiyu, the head man at the Writers' Association. As for me, I could only tie my own pitiful literary contributions up like poisonous weeds in a bundle with rope and hang them from the ceiling to keep them safe from the rats until the time came for them to be criticised.

The first day I moved in, when the housekeeping man came to fill our thermos with hot water, he instantly tried to find out, in a roundabout way, what Communist base area I'd worked in. When he discovered that I hadn't been to either of the revolutionary meccas of Shijiazhuang or Zhangjiakou, he put on an expression of utter disdain. Small wonder. Even he had 'participated in work' in the Communist centre of Zhengding. He quickly ferreted out the fact that I was the only one in the whole pickling factory who wasn't paying dues to the Party.

In those days men from the old liberated areas liked to drop in the phrase 'after we entered the cities'; it showed that they had come from the rural Communist bases, while those already in the cities were probably employees kept on from the old Nationalist regime. If I'd still been working for the *Dagongbao*, I'd probably have been thought of as from the old regime, too. Even so, after going to live in the big pickling factory I quickly became conscious of the chasm that had opened up between me and my acquaintances from the thirties.

And this was even though I had deliberately cut myself off from outside influences. Before leaving Hong Kong in August 1949, I moved decisively to end all contact with 'overseas connections', as I have already described. I sent a letter to all my friends abroad, Chinese and non-Chinese alike, asking them never to write to me again. They were not even to send Christmas or New Year cards. After marrying Jieruo, I learned that her elder sister in America corresponded regularly with family members in China and often sent money. At my urging, this relationship was broken off, too. Overseas connections could be one's greatest liability. Invariably one was suspected of being a spy.

I studied Mao Zedong's article 'Combat Liberalism'. Gradually I realised that the people in our courtyard were right to be cold and detached towards me. Class lines were not to be blurred! But fortunately for me not everyone was so doctrinaire. An old acquaintance in the front courtyard by the name of Yan Wenjing remained friends with me, though he'd lived in revolutionary caves and drunk from the revolutionary river. We'd both written articles in Peking and Tianjin in the thirties, and he didn't seem disgusted with me, encrusted with bourgeois dirt though I was. We liked the same things too, from Beethoven to clever little household gadgets. In the whole big pickling factory, he was about the only person who had social intercourse with me. Whenever I wrote something, I would always give it to him first to criticise. Perhaps it was on that account that he would face particular tribulations in the days to come.

It would be dishonest of me to say that I was completely reconciled to my lot. When a more important man in the courtyard built a high wall in front of my lean-to, closing off his southern-exposure suite, I did a little grumbling at first. Every time I passed by his gate – which was invariably shut tight – I'd be reminded of the Forbidden City and its out-dated secret inner sanctum. Yet I quickly got used to that, too. Every day I told myself: In the old days, when the revolutionaries were eating millet out in the fields, I was eating bread in bourgeois comfort. Whenever I remembered that, it seemed to me that everything was as it should be.

We kept a cat with a mottled coat; we called him Spotty. My son loved him dearly. But that cat didn't understand where our household stopped and others began. What trouble that caused! Today one family would come to complain that our Spotty had run off with their most precious chicken in his mouth; tomorrow someone else would claim that he'd swallowed their fish. Spotty was the prized possession in our house, but he was everybody else's favourite hate.

I'd always been a cat lover. In those years when I was abroad, I'd depended on a cat for my sanity. Spotty seemed conscious of my weakness for him; he was especially affectionate towards me. As soon as I got home from work, he'd look for me. Then, flicking his tail and mewing, he'd rub back and forth against my legs.

But I was constantly worried about the trouble this cat might bring down on us. I thought of giving him away, so I asked around, but nobody wanted him. Then, one afternoon, gritting my teeth, I stuffed Spotty into a burlap sack and put him in the front basket of my bicycle. The cat made a terrible racket, protesting that he was so good to me, never did a thing to offend, so why was I so cruelly abducting him? In my heart I begged his forgiveness: 'Spotty, try to understand what straits we're in. I can't afford to offend anyone in this courtyard. And you, you're so greedy and so stupid, all you do is get me into trouble. If I don't evict you, I'll have no way of staying on myself.'

In those days the city walls still stood. I pedalled to the foot of the East Wall. There I got off my bike, opened up the bundle, and brought Spotty out. He just glared at me. Finally I gave him a pat and offered up a silent prayer: 'May some person of good will who lives alone take dear Spotty in and feed him.'

Then I fled away on my bicycle as fast as I could. But as I pedalled I still heard his grieved mewing.

More difficult still was my confrontation with my son. As soon as he came home from school he asked me where Spotty had gone. I'm afraid I told him I'd taken him to an old lady in Tianjin who loved cats even more than we did. She'd be able to feed him his favourite pork liver every day. The child cross-examined me as to why I'd ever give poor Spotty away. I told him Spotty was always eating things belonging to other people and that if that went on, we not only would we not be able to keep the cat, we ourselves would have to leave.

He cried and argued all evening long. And when we finally coaxed him to sleep, he still called for Spotty in his dreams.

With a cat, at least you can get rid of it and be done with it, but a nursemaid can be a lot more troublesome. My son was already seven years old when Jieruo and I got married. We both worked and our first maid, an older woman, said the boy was too lively and she couldn't control him. Fortunately, a friend came up with a countrified young woman fresh from Northern Jiangsu. She was only eighteen, and having come to Peking in search of an opening in a factory, she was willing to help us out for the time being. She was simple, honest and kind, quick and hard-working. Her biggest asset was that she had nothing of the professional nanny about her. She'd take my son with her to buy baked sweet potatoes and she treated him like her little brother.

Then, at about eleven o'clock one night when I was fast asleep, Chen Baichen, a renowned dramatist and general secretary of our organisation, who lived next door, suddenly arrived under my window. He woke me with his shouting: 'Hsiao, you rogue, our nursemaid wants to quit and yours has put her up to it!'

This time I really lost my temper. I was mad not only at the accusation, but at this business of yelling at me from beneath my window. And early the next morning, still flushed with anger, I fired the wretched peasant girl. She kept saying how she was being wronged, that it had nothing at all to do with her, but I took no notice.

All these years, I've blamed myself for my cowardices. Not only did I fail to stand up to a slanderer, I sacrificed an innocent because of my own weakness.

When I got a new nursemaid, a widow with bound feet, she complained all day long that the houseboy would light the stove for the house on the left and draw boiled water for the house on the right (there was a boiler in the courtyard) – it was only our house he wouldn't lift a finger to help. So I asked him what was wrong, whereupon he laid his cards on the table: 'The others gave me a big padded jacket, or money, or theatre tickets, but what have you ever given me?'

Clearly this houseboy, regardless of the monthly wage he got from our unit, served each household in accordance with the extra income he got from them. But our peasant girl hadn't tried to get him to help her, so up to now we had had no trouble with him. In a fit of anger I said: 'This is sheer extortion. Let's go to the head office and let them sort it out.' People are dangerous when they're cornered, and my handling of this matter was really foolish. I might well be right, but I was also threatening his rice bowl. He fidgeted, then ran off to launch his own preemptive strike by filing an accusation with my superior that I was a 'bad element'.

Today the five black categories are landlords, rich peasants, counter-revolutionaries, bad elements and Rightists. In those days before there was an Anti-Rightist movement, the label didn't exist, and you couldn't be called a landlord or rich peasant if you didn't own land or hire labourers, and neither could you be named a counter-revolutionary without proof of guilt. The label 'bad element' was looser. It included just about anything from petty thief to murderer and rapist.

That evening at dusk, the North Jiangsu girl whom I had discharged suddenly rushed over to my place panting with rage (she'd already found work in a factory). She said the personnel section of my unit had come to her factory to have a talk with her. They were investigating her 'after-hours relationship' with me.

Fortunately, the time of the tryst they'd invented made no sense, as I was still at work then. What infuriated me was that the houseboy hadn't been content just to settle scores with me, he implicated an innocent girl into the bargain.

Naively I then went to the Eastern District People's Court to accuse him of slander. I should have realised that the court, the work unit, and the Party were one and the same. Naturally it all led to absolutely nothing.

This, of course, was just a small mishap in our lives. But I mention it because later, on the eve of the Anti-Rightist movement, when I was being encouraged from several sides at once to admit my resentments, what finally trapped me into revealing the truth was that particular injustice.

I mistakenly thought that by being moved to a literary unit, I was returning to my old profession as a creative writer. In reality I'd been transferred so I could do preparatory work on a magazine that would publish translations of foreign literature. At first it was exciting anyway, for it was aimed at readers here at home, and I didn't have to sit in front of a typewriter trying to figure out the psychology of foreign readers. But I wasn't there long before the difficulties started. The magazine's editor was a famous advocate and practitioner of verbatim translation. Now I had translated few books myself, but I'd always felt that a translation of a foreign work for the Chinese reader must at the very least read like genuine Chinese, so I tended to stress the fluency of any translation. And inevitably these two theories of translation soon came into conflict in the course of my daily work.

One afternoon I read a translation of a Bulgarian short story, a great favourite of mine. The original was witty and irreverent, but the translation was completely serious. Perhaps because I was so fond of the story, I took it home with me. Working through the night, I revised the translation rather more than was my custom. What I had foolishly failed to notice was that the translator was the boss's wife. When the boss sent it back after his final review, his comments severely reprimanded me for the changes I'd made. I remained unconvinced and at the next editorial meeting I complained, arguing that I hadn't distorted the meaning at all, I'd only made the translation more fluent. But of course the boss, who was seething with rage, couldn't allow a subordinate from outside the Party to contradict him. When people lose their temper, they lose control of what they say, and although the matter was in fact resolved fairly, it made me want to stay no longer than I had to.

Fortunately – or so it seemed at the time – early in 1955 I learned that the Party Central had formulated a new policy towards intellectuals. One day the major poet Guo Xiaochuan (a general secretary) came to my home to see me. Seemingly aware that I was unhappy, he asked me if I had any requests. I blurted out my desire to be a creative writer. And so wonderful was the new policy that it was able instantly to grant me my wish.

Jieruo knew that I was envious of the authors I saw in the courtyard working by lamplight, absorbed in their writing, when I got home from an evening meeting or went out late at night. So when I returned home from work that day I was able to tell her, excitedly, 'I've got great news!'

Before long I was relieved of my editorial responsibilities and formally notified that I was a creative writer with an official writer's subsidy. I'd never before been a 'creative' anything. I'd gone directly from college into the *Dagongbao*, where the few things I'd written were generally derivatives from my journalism. This was going to be the first time in my life when I could spend all my energy on genuinely creative writing. I was wildly happy. Being by then already nearly half a century old, I resolved not to waste a moment of this opportunity.

With the greatest earnestness I called on several friends to ask for their advice. You can write if the spirit moves you, they told me, and if it doesn't, you can read or go off travelling – you don't really have to produce anything. There were some who'd received their writer's subsidy every month since 1949 without writing a thing. But that wasn't for me. In the thirties I'd had plans to write a novel, but the war had snuffed them out. Now that I had both the time and the means, I wanted to make the most of them.

I quickly made a report to my superiors, taking into account both the objective social needs and my personal strengths: I wanted to experience life in a coal mine for three years so that I could write a novel about the workers' movement of the twenties. Thinking back on it now, it was really pretty silly. Not only was I foolishly putting theme ahead of character and technique, but whatever I might have written would almost certainly have been considered ideologically unsound. My friends' advice about taking the lazy man's way out had in fact been shrewd and farsighted. But in those days my confidence was running high. I was itching to put on my miner's lamp and get started. Anyway, a few days later the political weather changed. The campaign against Hu Feng had begun.

In my youth I used to play with a kind of firecracker at New Year that was called 'mouse droppings'. After you lit it and threw it on the ground, it would dart about unpredictably first this way and that, until finally it went out. The political campaigns of the 1950s often reminded me of those fireworks, except that they were no fun.

In October 1954, the failure of the *Wenyibao* (*Literature and Art Gazette*) to print two young persons' articles criticising a respected old scholar had set off a movement in which the entire literary and arts establishment criticised the journal. A big meeting was convened in the Young People's Art Theatre, at which the famous poet and critic Hu Feng, who had many disagreements with the Party's literary policy and had even written a 300,000-word statement on the subject, couldn't restrain himself. So the 'mouse droppings' were tossed in his direction. In just a few days Hu Feng, who had hitherto been treated respectfully, went to jail and took a big group of his friends with him. His letters to them became proof of his counter-revolutionary crimes. Immediately the bitternesses of a class struggle spread across the whole country. It became a terrible ordeal for the intellectuals.

Quickly people responded to the Party's call by unanimously condemning Hu Feng whether or not they'd read his works or understood his literary advocacies. Now, although I'd met Hu Feng in Shanghai during the thirties, I'd had only a nodding acquaintance with the man. I'd never really understood his poetry, still less his criticism. Even so, I never wrote a word against him. But it would be ridiculous of me to cite this now, with hindsight, as evidence that I was wise or clairvoyant. At the big meeting only the bookish translator Lü Ying was willing to take the podium to give Hu Feng his proper due. He was of course driven from the stage and put into prison. I had no particular objections to such carryings-on. At the time I was more concerned that my own precious plan for writing not be sacrificed and continually worrying that the storm might next come down on me.

I learned two lessons from the campaign against Hu Feng. First, write as few letters as possible and do not keep letters from friends, in case they be implicated too. If you absolutely have to write, stick to routine business. Every word should be crystal clear, not open to later re-interpretation. That means reading a letter over several times before mailing it, making sure that people with noses particularly sensitive to the smell of class struggle won't be able to distort your words. Writing diaries and memos that might provoke a dispute is particularly taboo. Second, do not express an opinion of any kind, even if solicited, not even as a Party member criticising a Party-run journal.

Two years later it would be clear that I had not taken the second lesson to heart. There were always times when I was unable to restrain myself; it was at the root of many of my calamities.

In fact at that time my plan for a mining novel was not rejected, it was only postponed following the imprisonment of Hu Feng and his friends, while the investigation of backgrounds began. For the moment however, not only could I not go down into the mines, I had to ask for leave from the personnel department just to go and see friends on a Sunday.

So Hu Feng went to jail and we went back to our courtyard to be investigated.

You saw people on the streets who were clearly fact-gathering. They sidled past on priority business, black portfolios under their arms.

I'd known ever since the cancellation of my 1950 opportunity to go to England that I was regarded as having a suspicious past. So I enthusiastically participated in the background check on me. I bared myself from head to toe – gave them my blood and urine for testing, too. I wrote a self-critical autobiography of nearly 50,000 characters. In the appendices I gave them every letter I had on me and a copy of everything I'd ever written. I wanted to make myself completely transparent.

It was not in vain. One day the deputy secretary called me to the office and let me see the official political verdict on me. Apparently I had pursued revolution in my early years, taken a dangerously neutral stand during the war of Liberation, but then had fallen suitably in line after Liberation (1949). In sum, my history was spotless. I was particularly gratified by what the verdict had to say about my involvement in the controversial magazine *New Road*. I can still roughtly recite it from memory: '*New Road* was a periodical established in 1948 by high-level Democratic Personages in Peking and closed down by the Kuomintang. Hsiao Ch'ien ceased participating in its editorial work on the advice of underground Communist Party members.'

After the investigation of staff backgrounds, my living conditions improved to match my new political status. We were moved into a four-room suite in the west wing of the middle courtyard. I was given a study of approximately ten square metres where I met with editors from all quarters who were soliciting contributions. This one invited me to be a consultant, that one begged me to be a special correspondent. All of a sudden I had joined a group visiting Inner Mongolia; then I was escorting authors from foreign countries on a sightseeing tour across half of China. The sky above my head seemed always to be sunny. Now that my value had risen, when I looked in the mirror the wrinkles on my face had completely disappeared. I stood straight as a ramrod. My mind, which had grown decidedly rusted, seemed suddenly to run on well-oiled bearings.

Up till then we'd burned low grade charcoal in my house, but in the winter of 1956, three tons of the very best Yangquan coal suddenly turned up on my doorstep. I thought it was a mistake. Only when I looked and saw 'Author Hsiao' written on the invoice did I realise that this was part of the special treatment my respectability had brought me. The coal burned briskly and with little smoke.

When it arrived we thought the Yangquan coal a piece of good fortune, but it was to become Jieruo's calamity. More of that later.

The climax in my re-evaluation came when I was visited at home by Zhang Guangnian, the chief editor of the *Literarature and Art Gazette* – China's leading cultural journal, which had already brought about the downfall of several writers. He insisted that I become one of his three deputy editors. I graciously declined, saying that I wasn't equal to it. But in the end, afraid to appear insubordinate, I gritted my teeth and agreed.

Since I already received a stipend as a creative writer, I was only to go in to the office one afternoon a week. And my work load, even then, was very light. I was met by kind and affable people who treated me with flattering deference as if I was an old hand in the business of magazine editing. The general editor also agreed to let me go into the coal mines as originally planned once the office was running smoothly.

Since I sometimes had an official limousine sent for me when I was going off to report to important government departments, Jieruo went out and bought me a blue woollen Mao jacket and trousers. She was planning to buy me a briefcase too. 'No,' I said, 'it's best not to put on airs.'

'You mean you've been to London and New York,' she said, 'and been a professor at Fudan, and you still don't dare to carry a briefcase?'

'That was then and this is now,' I said. 'Now I have to remember to keep my head down.'

In the spring of 1957, I wore my brand-new tailored uniform to the famous conference on national propaganda work at which Mao Zedong urged non-Party members to make criticisms in order to hasten reform. Judging the effect of that extraordinary conference is a task for the historian. Certainly it encouraged cautious people, long used to speaking with discretion, to forget themselves. And certainly at the time I myself felt that great confidence had been placed in me and that there was no higher honour than to be allowed to attend. But these many years since, having lived through the aftermath of that conference, I have come to realise that, under the dictatorship of the proletariat, the safest thing for me would have been to stay out of the fray and remain a humble common citizen.

Back in 1940, some friends and I had gone mountain climbing in England's Lake District. There I encountered the only avalanche I have ever experienced. It was both sudden and violent. We were happily striding out across the splendid landscape, each with his rucksack on his back, when a whirlwind blew in seemingly from nowhere, and in a moment the ground just ahead of us crumbled away and we lost our bearings. Sweltering heat changed into bitter cold. Our trail map was useless, for the path had disappeared. For a short while I feared that the mountainside might be my grave.

The Chinese political avalanche of 1957 caused me to lose my sense of balance once again. I was more confused and dispirited even than at that time in the Lake District. I wanted to end my life, but now I had three small children and there was another on the way. I became completely paralysed.

I can't say for certain whether or not I could have avoided that storm. Though my label was that of an inveterate Rightist, for many years I believed that I could survive it. I was very apologetic. During meetings and afterwards I'd bow my head. I'd suffered before. I'd seen how truth bowed to expediency, and how the official technique was to destroy a man's reputation first and ask questions later. In fact, as early as 1950 I'd known that I was not trusted. So why didn't I hold my tongue? I only had myself to blame.

That summer and for a long time afterwards, I was filled with just that kind of remorse. I blamed myself for having moved back to China in the first place and particularly for having accepted the job at the magazine – one I wasn't in the least equipped for – on the very eve of the storm. After all, I'd declined the honour repeatedly at the start. If I'd really thought about where I stood, I'd never have agreed to take it on. As it was, I had been in my new unit less than six months, thinking I'd stepped into a flower garden, before it turned out to be an abyss.

Besides being full of regrets, though, I did have grounds for gratitude.

One trend at the time was that if a man or woman became a target for attack, his or her spouse was dragged in too. This was a common occurrence among my friends. And of course if both members of a working couple went under, then the children were left in a tragic fix. That possibility worried me most. Thank heavens I managed to avoid it. At the time I told myself I'd admit to anything to keep it from happening.

Even when things were at their worst, Jieruo seemed absolutely calm. We'd been married just three years and the children were still so small – how did she manage to be so composed when disaster stared her in the face? Only much later did I learn that she was secretly frantic.

One day early in August she told me that the foetus inside her was no longer kicking, though things had seemed normal at her regular six-month check-up. We went back to the Longfu Hospital. The gynaecologist there listened for what seemed forever without hearing a heartbeat. She prescribed two weeks' rest and said that if there was no improvement after the next examination, it meant there would be a miscarriage.

Jieruo stayed at home, showing her physician's sick-leave certificate. The first official meeting for ideological struggle against me and my beliefs just happened to fall within her absence from work, so she didn't join in. This immediately caught the attention of the activists, who said she was deliberately avoiding it. Her unit sent someone to our home to tell her she must return to work immediately. And she must be present at all the ideological struggle meetings against me, with no excuses. Moreover, someone was appointed to check up on her at the entrance before every meeting. These campaigns were not noted for their mercy.

Ordinarily she would have gone to the meetings directly from work, not only because it was closer and more convenient, but also to demonstrate that her status was not as high as mine. But for once my Guizhou-born wife, who was ordinarily gentle and submissive, became very stubborn. She insisted on coming home from work early, so that she could walk with me to the meeting.

Among the many accusations thrown at me was one claiming that I had plotted to usurp the leadership of the literary journal that employed me. Now, the *Literature and Art Gazette* was run by a committee of three Party members plus me, the only non-Party person, and I was only a deputy editor. Some who live abroad have asked me why, then, did the entire blame for the magazine's policy fall on my head?

One day in late May 1957, the man who was editor-in-chief (Zhang Guangnian) invited me into his study, which was elegantly furnished in the classical style. Beaming with satisfaction, he told me that he knew I'd joined the journal only with the greatest reluctance. Respecting my wishes, they had therefore asked me to attend only two or three hours of meetings weekly. But now one of the deputy editors sent by the Party (Hou Jinjing) was ailing and would have to stay at home for a spell, while another (Chen Xiaoyu) was busy on assignments across the country. Also the executive editor wanted to take a vacation. So would I be executive deputy editor just for a short time? I could deliver manuscripts directly to the printers without even consulting him. Reluctantly I agreed.

As things turned out, I never published a single piece that hadn't passed his inspection first. And indeed at that very same time Zhang Guangnian was approving manuscripts I'd never seen.

No amount of foresight on my part could have seen such a cunning trap. Only when reading a Red Guard publication years later, during the Cultural Revolution, did I finally learn that he'd chosen me as his scapegoat after learning in advance from an inner-Party document that an Anti-Rightist campaign was in the offing. At the big meeting arranged to criticise me he then boasted, without shame, that he'd 'smoked a snake out of his cave'. Thereupon he became an Anti-Rightist hero.

But this was not the only factor leading up to my Anti-Rightist humiliation. For one thing, in that memorable spring of 1957, Zhang Bojun, representing the Democratic League, asked me three times to edit a magazine for Democratic Personages called *Zhengming* (*Contending*). I refused each time. Then he pressed his request on me once more, at dinner. Still I declined. Every time I returned to my unit I gave an on-the-spot report of the matter to Kang Zhuo, a Party member who acted then as my head. And yet the first poster attacking me said 'Hsiao Ch'ien is an agent planted in our organisation by the Democratic League of Zhang Bojun and Luo Longji'. [Zhang and Luo had just been named leading Rightists.] After much hesitation, but feeling that I must clear myself, I finally wrote a poster myself. In it I briefly explained that in fact I had declined Zhang Bojun's offer four times and reported it each time to Kang Zhuo. If he had hesitated for a few hours before pasting up his own counterattack, that at least would have been something. It would have shown that his conscience was not wholly dead – that he'd suffered internal conflict at least temporarily. But that was not to be. His refutation of my rumours came out immediately and confirmed my crime. Only then did I realise that the class struggle was simply a matter of winning – that downright lies could be spoken without shame or hesitation.

Some weeks before I had also sent the *People's Daily* an article urging the Party not to mistrust intellectuals and to tolerate well-meaning dissent. But when the 8 June *People's Daily* published an article kicking off the Anti-Rightist movement I immediately regretted having sent anything and insisted that the editors return my article to me. The general editor of *People's Daily*, Deng Tuo, called me on the telephone. For half an hour he kept reassuring me: 'Your article clearly shows that you love and support the Party. Why do you want it back?'

They printed it anyway.

For many years after that, I always considered Deng Tuo to have been like my magazine's chief editor – out to frame me. Having now read his uncensored works, however, I am convinced that he acted sincerely. His fate was more tragic than mine. He was so persecuted that he committed suicide.

Clearly each of the meetings to criticise me was artfully organised. At one of them, the participants were those who had once worked with me at the *Dagongbao* and Foreign Languages Press. Another was attended by my old friends from the thirties. I analysed the charges as I listened. There was well-intentioned advice, malicious slander. Some of the criticisms came from genuine indignation and some were obviously delivered under duress. I listened intently and, I hope, open-mindedly to all my critics, no matter how far-fetched their charges. Neither then nor later did I argue with them. It was only my flaying by the children's literature author Ye Junjian [translator of Hans Christian Andersen's fairy stories] that really made me lose faith in human nature.

At the beginning of his speech, he held up a photograph of a Siamese cat for all to see. Then he explained that an English publisher, Mr Kingsley Martin, had asked him to bring the photograph to me seven years earlier, when he was returning from England to China. 'I didn't pass it on to Hsiao Ch'ien.' He meant that he'd confiscated it on his own authority. He went on to say that I'd obviously bought the cat at some shop in London and then pretended to have brought it from China as a gift for this major publisher. It was because of this gift that I'd been allowed to publish a book in London and thus enter the British world of letters. (At this point there was tittering from the audience.) Two days later, the *Guangming Daily* published an article by Mr Ye based on this fairy story. His point was that men of letters behave to others according to the standards they set for themselves.

Of course to have confiscated something that he should have given me seven years before suggested that Ye Junjian had planned some sort of attack on me long before the Anti-Rightist campaign. It was a ridiculous story anyway which simply played on his listeners' ignorance of a foreign country, simultaneously insulting me and making fools of them. But what really distressed me was that he went on to peddle the improbable story on the international market: a version of it appears in *Birdless Summer*, the autobiography of Mr Ye's friend Han Suyin.

Fortunately, when Kingsley Martin himself (he was a columnist not a publisher) published his memoirs, they contained a passage to the effect that 'a Chinese friend, named Hsiao Ch'ien, who lived in Hampstead, had to change his lodgings to an address where he was unable to keep a cat to which he was much attached. We kept it for him.' The photograph even appeared as the frontispiece to the book (*Editor*). Hence the article I published some years later, after I regained my rights as a citizen, 'The Case of the Cat: The True Story.'

Of course, the vindication of me by Kingsley Martin was of no help at the time of Ye and Han's vicious accusations. Indeed, Han is a respected intellectual in China today, and her unjust version of the incident is still widely believed. A small libel, perhaps, but one that has caused me much suffering and unhappiness down the years.

That autumn my friends, who had learned since Liberation to keep in step with the Party, wrote one newspaper article after another criticising me.

Unfortunately our rooms were next to the main gateway of the complex, in the shade of which the motor-pool drivers often conducted their study classes, loudly reading out the criticism of me in the paper. Never in my life had I been so slandered. Those who knew me turned away from me as we passed. Once, I remember, an author had come to visit a while before and had brought along his younger sister. After the Anti-Rightist movement, on the single occasion when we met, I asked him 'How is your sister?' He glared at me and said 'I don't have a sister.'

At 9 pm on 29 September 1957 our second daughter was stillborn. Jieruo gave a name to this daughter, who'd been long dead in her womb. Violet. She was unable to bring herself to look at her.

Jieruo went to work as usual. In the past, when something came up, she often telephoned my office and asked the person on duty at the message centre to call me to the phone. After the Anti-Rightist campaign began, she called as seldom as possible. Once she had to, because of something urgent, but she wasn't sure how to refer to me. Remembering that someone had called me 'mister' at a criticism meeting, as opposed to 'comrade', she said 'Please fetch Mr Hsiao Ch'ien.' The orderly flew into a rage. 'We have no *misters* here!' he said, and slammed down the phone.

Towards the end of the year, I received notice that we were moving. This was a purely politically motivated move, of course, a necessary preliminary to exile.

In fact we'd realised for some time that we wouldn't be able to stay in the pickling factory. I was only too happy to move, as soon as possible, to a place where I wouldn't have to face the disapproval of my fellow tenants. But at this point our pile of unburned Yangquan coal became a problem. Who would be willing, or even dare, to accept a present from a Rightist? As I worried about what to do with it, Jieruo told me that it was the only genuine privilege I'd ever got from being a creative writer, so we ought to take it with us as a souvenir.

Whereupon we moved our whole household, sacks of Yangquan coal included, out of our home of four years to a lonely lane in the northeastern part of the city.

Before I moved, two officials from the special group in charge of my case came privately and told me: 'It's been decided that you won't be sent off to hard labour. Instead you can return to your translating work at home. You needn't go to the office.' When I heard this I was of course very grateful. And I was elated not to have to go out to work. That meant I wouldn't have to see anybody. Having passed through several struggle sessions – having seen right and wrong turned on their heads, truth refuted, smiles suddenly becoming scowls – I felt that the further away from people I could get the better.

This was at the end of 1957. The Anti-Rightist movement was in full swing and organisations were sending their disgraced staff members away to work in the countryside en masse. Jieruo said that since I was the one in trouble, she should appear to be an even keener activist than the others and strive to be sent away to the country in the first batch her unit despatched. After thinking about it, I agreed. I could easily do my translations as a househusband, while I looked after the three children. Washing nappies and milk bottles ought to be just the thing to take my cares away.

When Jieruo went to take a look at our new home, in the city south of Jiaodaokou, she came back very pleased. She told me she hadn't imagined such places still existed. Then I went for my first look. It had a spacious courtyard. The five principal rooms, which faced south, were already half occupied by a man from my old unit. My family took the two rooms on the east end; we partitioned the central room between us half-and-half, using wooden boards.

The day we moved, I felt like a prisoner who was just coming out of his cell after a long time. I was unshaven and my hair stood out like a hedgehog. Since childhood, I had always been reluctant to leave any place I was used to, I'd look back over my shoulder as I walked away. But I didn't look back when I left the pickling factory. I seemed to be leaving a place I ought never to have entered.

The family with whom we shared our new home had recently been transferred there, too. Originally the husband had been extremely warm and friendly towards me. But as the Anti-Rightist temperature rose in May, he had joined in the criticisms. Now he felt awkward and when we chanced to brush past each other, he would turn his head so as not to meet my gaze. His two teenage daughters, though traditional oval-faced beauties, would yell through the windows at me: 'Some people get called writers just because they sit at home all the time.' I couldn't see how that applied. Since 1949 I'd been a writer for just a few months and I hadn't sat at home then.

Another man in our courtyard had studied at the same college as I. But he'd read the criticisms of me in the newspapers, so he didn't greet me when we met, but quickly turned away. Being a leper, of course, I had to make allowances. I knew how to behave and had no intention of involving others. So I always kept my head down when I went in or out.

Luckily the sun kept shining on me, just as on other people! The sun is very cheering at the start of winter; it offers encouragement as well as heat. In the months past, the ground beneath my feet had shaken but now it was solid again and I could walk on it firmly. When I went to market to buy vegetables, I straightened my back, happy to discover that I hadn't become a permanent dwarf.

Jiaodaokou was a corner of Peking that I was very familiar with. My mother's only blood sister had lived in an alley across the way. Big Third Lane, the site of my old Truth Hall, ran from Jiaodaokou to Northern New Bridge. When I was on work-study I'd driven a flock of Swiss mountain goats along the Jiaodaokou thoroughfare and through the Anding Gate, to put them out to pasture.

I felt as if I were back in my childhood. Since leaving this place in 1928 I'd been blown to and fro across the globe for many years, but now I'd returned to my old haunts. Even though I'd lost all my professional standing, I still felt consoled, as if I'd returned to the loving embrace of my mother.

We made new household arrangements before Jieruo went away

to work in the country. Our older boy would continue to live at school, our daughter would be sent to a nursery, and the younger boy, though still only a baby, would stay by my side. The day Jieruo set out, I accompanied her on my bicycle, with her luggage strapped to my back, to pick up the truck that would drive her to the train station. I took refuge in a shady spot and sadly watched the truck bear her off far into the distance. But on Saturday afternoon things livened up. Our school boarder and our daughter at nursery school were both at home. Our house was a home again, except that it lacked its mother, its heart.

In the days when I was happy and successful, I was busy running around all day long and had little time for my children. Now that I was down on my luck, I had plenty of chance to get close to them. They became my spiritual sustenance. Even changing nappies and emptying chamber pots brought me happiness. As I held the bottle and watched the milk being gulped down the tiny throat, I forgot all my misfortunes. Often I'd bury my face in a pile of children's clothes.

I was happiest when the four of us squeezed together on a bench, with Number Three on my knee, burrowing into my chest, and Numbers One and Two leaning against me on either side. I talked and sang to them, sharing with them all the nursery rhymes that an older cousin had taught me when I was little:

> Grandpa Moon has shoes with clamps,
> you be Grammy and I'll be Gramps.
> She sings till daybreak comes o'er the shed;
> but where goes baby once he's been fed?
> Gulp, gulp, gulp, going down the hatch,
> when this gruel's gone there's another batch.

Then there was:

> He ran up the lamp stand, little mousy brown;
> ate his fill of oil, but now he can't get down.

So the Party had struggled against me – over, under, around and through – but it had not wrested my memory from me.

I could sing 'In January we enter the lantern feast of winter', all the way through to the verse for December. When I was tired of that, I told stories. I told them about the foolish son-in-law, about the comic Ming dynasty painter Xu Wenchang and the fairy tales of Hans Christian Andersen and the brothers Grimm. I played stone, cloth and scissors with my eldest, a game I'd learned in the Baofang Lane lock-up at the age of sixteen. For the younger ones, I tied hankies into rabbits, and used my hands to make shadow figures of cows and horses on the wall. I thought to myself that if I couldn't do anything else, perhaps I could at least serve as an 'auntie' at nursery school.

Little brother and his sister were happy as could be. It was the eldest whose spirits I couldn't lift. He had a worried frown on his face most of that year. Even the most exciting story didn't interest him. One day, just as I was getting going, he suddenly interrupted. (For some time he'd stopped calling me 'Daddy' unless he absolutely had to.) Eyes glaring, he asked me fiercely, 'Why in the world do you have to be anti-Party and anti-socialist?'

These words struck me harder, coming from his lips, than those from the people who'd raged at me in meetings. I'd always hoped that he didn't know about all the bad things that had happened to me. How naive I was; he was already in the third form, away at boarding school. His eyes brimming with tears, he told me: 'They chase me at school, and call me "Rightist Junior".'

What could I tell him? If I told him the truth and he repeated it to someone else, then that could be taken as a 'counter-offensive' on my part, and would bring still greater misfortune down on him. All I could say was, 'You'll know what kind of person Papa is once you've grown up.'

'Yes, but it's right now that matters,' he said, 'and I can't stand it.'

I mentioned this in my letters to Jieruo, away in her farm production team, telling her that the wounds suffered by our children were like a knife through my heart. She answered: 'When the children grow up, you'll be a papa they can be proud of.' She told me I must grit my teeth and get to work. I had books to translate, books that I dearly loved, by authors such as E M Forster and Virginia Woolf.

Just then the streets of Peking were full of activity in connection with a general election. I wasn't clear what positions were being filled, and in truth I didn't care. I felt as if I'd already been expelled from the People's Republic.

Just as if I'd anticipated that I would come to such straits as these, I'd bought a lot of useful translator's reference books in the early fifties: dictionaries on the natural sciences, law, economics, finance, even the military. I always thought of technical dictionaries like these as fire engines – ordinarily they stood idle, but every now and then you needed them. Now with the books arranged in a row on my writing desk as my shield, I began to think seriously about translating again. I was glad that I still had my English. A creative writer could sell what he wrote only while his name was in good repute. What usually decided his success was not the quality of his work, but the soundness of his political standing. Once that went bad, everything he wrote would be worthless. But translation was different. Even if you were poorly regarded, so long as there were no problems with the original author, you could still translate for your bread and butter.

Little did I know what else was in store for me.

One evening a Party member from my unit, the *Literature and Art Gazette*, brought over a revised formal political verdict on me. Hadn't we been through all that in 1956? I asked him. He assumed a serious look. This time it was different; I'd understand when I read it. He pressed me to admit its truth and sign it on the spot. As I read it, I nearly fainted. I begged him to let me think about it. He gave me twenty-four hours.

The official verdict on me a year or so earlier, during the investigation of my background, had been based on my 50,000-word autobiography and its many appendices, all verified through repeated investigations over the course of six months. But now everything had been reversed. What had previously been confirmed was now denied; what had once been refuted was now fact. As I've already written in connection with my work on the magazine *New Road*, the original verdict had said that the journal 'was a periodical established in 1948 by high-level Democratic Personages in Peking and closed down by the Kuomintang'. Now this journal was said to be 'a mouthpiece for the Four Great Families', the Kuomintang ruling elite. The original said 'Hsiao Ch'ien ceased participating in its editorial work on the advice of underground Communist Party members'. Now I had become one of its 'mainstays'.

Never in my life had I been so distressed. I could bear all the false words at the criticism meetings, even if they did appear the next day in the papers. But this was a serious document, a 'political verdict' on a man's whole life, handed down by an imposing Party committee, and they wanted me to admit its truth and sign my name to it immediately.

Years later a woman comrade told me that on one occasion she'd been taken to a newly-dug grave and actually told she had to sign or be buried alive. She decided she'd rather die than put her seal of approval on a lie. And she survived. I, however, was a coward. I tossed and turned all night, thinking that since Jieruo had been sent away, if I sacrificed myself for the truth, how would the three children manage?

Although I despised myself for my cowardice, I still think that in a replay of history, under the same conditions, I'd have to grit my teeth and sign. Because of me, Jieruo and I had already lost one unborn child. I couldn't stand another sacrifice. I signed.

One day in April, I was ordered to attend a meeting at Zhang Guangnian's house in the big pickling factory. I arrived punctually. Three steely faces greeted my entry. I found a corner and sat down, head bowed. It turned out to be a select meeting to pronounce judgement, and it was to be conducted by Yan Wenjing, the one person in the pickling factory who'd maintained friendly relations with me. He read out my sentence in a voice that betrayed no hint of warmth: I was to be sent away to a farm to do penal labour under surveillance. And it was to be carried out immediately, within the week. I knew that he was undergoing difficulties of his own and had to do this to me.

Quietly I asked one of them: For how long? Now that I think back on it, I must have been confused at the time, for only an idiot would have asked such a question. I immediately felt ashamed for having spoken. Still, I was thinking about my three children.

How could they answer me? The one I'd addressed coughed discreetly and said, 'With good conduct, you *might* be able to return in eight or ten years.'

Once again I nearly fainted.

Except for the time back in 1926 when I'd been seized by Zhang Zuolin's police, I'd never had any brush with the law, never even entered a police station. A lot of things about the terror of the Russian Gulags that I'd read in British anti-Soviet propaganda during the forties kept coming to mind. Though I was worried about what fate awaited me, I was even more anxious for my family, for Jieruo and the children.

When I got home, I looked at my children as they lay in bed asleep. 'Poor things,' said my heart.

I must get in touch with Jieruo right away! I had this irrational faith in telegrams. I sent her a telegram asking her to come at once, with the thought that she might be able to hurry back before I had to leave. Only later did I learn that she'd been sent away to such an isolated little village that all communications, letters and telegrams alike, went first to the county town and then took at least a week to be passed on.

My beautiful dream of translating in between washing nappies and bottles lay in ruins. Once I was separated from my children, there was no telling when I'd see them again – perhaps never.

According to the railway timetable, there was only one incoming local train a day that stopped at Jieruo's little county town It arrived in Peking at 5 pm. For four days towards evening, I'd go to the eastern end of our alley and wait expectantly, leading child Number Two and carrying Number Three. In my mind nearly all the short-haired women wearing spectacles seemed to look like Jieruo. When it got dark, we'd go back home, crest-fallen.

At daybreak on the fifth day, I heard a sudden miraculous tapping at the window. It so happened that Jieruo had gone to the county town the previous afternoon to attend a meeting and so got the telegram quite by accident. As luck would have it, her train was delayed and arrived at the Eastern Station in the small hours, at about 2 am. So she'd just walked home, passing through the great plaza in front of the Gate of Heavenly Peace.

She'd thought one of the children must be ill. She instantly felt their foreheads. They were sound asleep. Only then did she turn to me: 'Why did you call me back?'

She took the news that they were going to send me away very calmly. I even repeated the 'eight or ten years' of the sentence and without the least hesitation she said, 'If they send you then you go. Eight years, ten years – I'll wait forever'.

Luckily Chinese society sets great store by the extended family. And luckily Jieruo still had her mother, Wan Peilan, her Older Sister Number Three Changwei, and her younger brother Xuepu. At this critical moment, my in-laws became my salvation. Jieruo told me not to think about my own future, only about how to avoid creating hardship for the children.

It seemed that the more mentally paralysed I became, the more resourceful Jieruo was. She was as resolute as a captain standing on the bridge after his steamer has struck a reef. We would shut up our home in this little lane and entrust our two littlest ones to Grandma and Third Aunt. The oldest lived at school most of the time anyway; during vacations he could live with her brother, or at a cousin's home.

Jieruo returned on a Friday. Our family spent one weekend together, most of the time disposing of our possessions. My reference books were tied up into a bundle, Jieruo collected the children's and my clothing, putting them into separate piles, and the family was ready to go. But we still had to prepare our children psychologically, particularly the younger ones.

Jieruo said: 'Papa's been called away on business, and this time it will be for a very long time. Grandma, Third Aunt, and Uncle will take care of you. You must be good. Mama will come home sooner than Papa, and after she does, she won't go away again. On Sunday she'll take you to the zoo, and you'll see the monkeys and pandas and elephants . . .'

She hoped the promise of the zoo would distract them, but our eldest saw straight through her. He asked, 'Will papa come back?'

'Of course he will.'

'When will he come back?'

As I heard this I almost wept, but somehow I managed a forced smile: 'Of course I'll be back. And I'll bring you some nice things to play with. Tell me, what would you like?'

The three-year-old fell for it. She said 'I want a doll, and a . . .' But the ten-year-old turned his back and said nothing.

Time never passed as quickly for me as it did during that period. All the arrangements were made and I saw Jieruo off at the station. She leaned out the window and said, making an effort to smile, 'Even the worst crises don't go on for ever.' As the train started up, gathered speed, then disappeared into the distance, she kept on waving. I gazed after her, tears running down my cheeks.

Now it was my turn.

I moved Number Two from her day nursery to a live-in one. That left only the one-and-a-half-year-old at my side. I ought to have let my mother-in-law take him away earlier, but I couldn't give him up, so I kept him with me to the very end. My old mother-in-law shared a simple supper with me in our little lane the evening before I set out. I hugged the child; he leaned against me as I ate. After the meal, I covered my writing desk with newspapers, as Jieruo had directed. One couldn't tell how many months and years of dust might collect on top of it now. Afterwards, I locked the door, kissed my child and went away.

That was in April of 1958; maybe the 17th or 18th. I just remember that the entire city went into action against the sparrows that evening, in obedience to an instruction from Chairman Mao. The idea was to whack at the sparrows with bamboo poles and sticks so that they couldn't alight – so that there would be no place left for them to land. It was said that a sparrow hadn't very much stamina. If you didn't let it rest on the ground, it would ultimately drop from the sky stone dead. So, as I crossed the streets and alleyways that night, every family was out chasing sparrows. I felt like one of them.

I arrived at my unit on time, at eight o'clock. There, a middle-level official from my unit was to hand me over to someone from the Party committee in charge of all departments under the central government (as opposed to the municipal government). The latter would take me under escort to the penal farm settlement.

The man in charge of turning me over to the custody of the other had been in the same department with Jieruo at college and so, like her, was a student of foreign literature. While waiting to make the hand-over, he was kind to me. Lightly flicking ash from his cigarette, he offered me his literary appreciation of Keats's 'Ode to a Nightingale'.

The train left at eleven o'clock. Meanwhile, laden with anxieties I listened attentively as this lover of English romantic poetry made conversation. I thought of something I had seen in the street when I was little: a funeral procession had passed on one side and a bridal troupe on the other, signifying two different lots in life, two different human dispositions and two different frames of mind.

Eventually I was at the Eastern Station again, this time as a criminal under escort. My new travelling companion carried only a document portfolio under his arm, but I shouldered a heavy bed roll, a travel bag full of clothes for all seasons and the few books I loved most. I had to shift the load to the other shoulder every few steps. With much effort we squeezed on to the train and found window seats opposite each other. Because of the difference in our status, we hardly spoke. He knew my name. Probably everything there was to know about me was in that portfolio. I knew my place, so of course I didn't bother him with small talk, least of all a discussion on the 'Ode to a Nightingale'.

The man had probably been on trips of this sort many times before. Although we were only travelling in hard-seat class, he was well-prepared. Around midnight he pulled out a bottle of wine and a couple of pickled eggs. After skilfully removing the shells, he smelled them and was satisfied. Then he began to drink from the bottle, smacking his lips after every mouthful. The wine and eggs smelled good enough to make my mouth water.

I pressed my face against the window. The glass was cool. Watching the landscape speed past in the moonlight, I thought back on the good old days when I'd held a chicken leg in one hand and a flagon of wine in the other. I also thought of my little ones, who were now dispersed here, there and everywhere. Just now, with any luck, they would all be sound asleep.

When we got to our station next morning, we had a bite to eat at a little restaurant in the town, then mounted a truck with a batch of other prisoners who were also going to the farm. I even saw a distant relative of mine on the truck. Each of us realised that the other must be in trouble. We didn't even exchange a nod.

Before the truck set off, a group of young people who were on a spring outing sang 'Hail Socialism' at us, as they shook their fists in condemnation. The song had been composed for the Anti-Rightist campaign. At least in those days they still assailed us politically unreliable ones with words instead of blows.

It was the Baigezhuang Farm on the Gulf of Bohai, a huge state farm set up by the Soviet Union in the fifties. High-grade rice was the main crop. The land had originally been saline, so in addition to farming, we had the task of improving the soil. The leaders of the farm at all levels were decorated veterans wounded in the War Against America on Behalf of Korea, while the backbone farm workers were young agricultural labourers recruited from eastern Hebei. Besides the headquarters farm, there were branch farms.

After we'd got off the truck at the gateway to the main farm, my escort, the Party man from the capital, immediately led me to an office. This wasn't the personnel office but the farm's police station. Clearly I was to be treated as a criminal – even though my offence was in fact a 'contradiction among the people', not a 'contradiction between the people and the enemy'. But I thought better of complaining. Why haggle over it? There wasn't all that much difference between the two.

The man from the capital opened up his portfolio and took out a stack of documents, probably to do with my case. He made his report, chatted to the people in the room, and then swaggered off.

The farm's Public Security Office appeared to have everything arranged in advance. The man on duty took one look at my documents and gave me a slip of paper. 'Report to Branch Farm Number Three,' he said.

This time I went off on my own. Presumably I couldn't run away, now that I was on the farm premises. Me, I was happy to be free.

Branch Farm Number Three was three or four miles east of the main farm. I walked there by way of dykes, my luggage on my back. The further I went, the harder the going. Though April wasn't very hot yet, I was drenched in sweat. I'd walk a while and rest a while, urging myself on by telling myself that my labours from now on would be much tougher, so I'd best start getting used to them.

In the morning sun I cast a long shadow. As I looked out from the top of the dykes I saw rice fields all around me. Light green seedlings swayed in the breeze. It was a pleasing sight. Having grown up in the city, I'd never come into contact with the countryside. So I consoled myself thus: In life you ought to experience everything. But then I remembered the 'eight or ten years'. Would my children recognise me when the years were over?

Number Three Farm was divided into several work brigades. I entered a team under the Second Brigade. It was accommodated in one of a row of brick houses. Farm tools occupied the corners of its single room, and beneath the window was a big *kang* for sleeping. The other team members and the leader were young agricultural workers recruited from along the banks of the Luan River. They welcomed me into their room, calling me 'good ol' Hsiao'. We hit it off at this first meeting, feeling as if we'd all known each other for years. They cleared a space for me on the very best spot on the *kang*, against the wall, and even spread out my bedding there.

This was another home. I had expected it to be gloomy and horrible but this warmth was the first I'd felt from people outside my own family in ten months.

How kindhearted and honest is the Chinese peasant. I told Jieruo in a letter. 'Don't worry, I'm living among the very best people in the world. There's no cheating or cleverness here, no double-dealing, still less any taking pleasure in other people's bad luck, or hitting them when they're down. These people who earn their keep from their labour aren't interested in advancement at the expense of others. The one thing they really care about is how the crops are growing – whether it's going to rain or shine. They're happy and they want other people to be happy too.'

In the middle of the branch farm was a big mess hall. There was a boiler dispensing hot water at its north end, and in the west wall an opening to the kitchen. When the time came, the farm workers would pick up their bowls and stand in line to ladle out their rice. The first day I didn't understand the system and hadn't brought any utensil to scoop up my rice. No matter, several young men competed to lend me theirs. One even wanted to do the ladling for me.

As I stood in line for rice, I saw some familiar acquaintances from my old unit, as well as some I knew by sight but not by name. We all shook hands and grinned at each other knowingly, as if to say, so we're all in the same boat. . . .

Indeed, though it had been less than a year since the Anti-Rightist movement, this was a separate world. Only later did I learn that some of them hadn't written a single improper line or spoken a single improper word. It was just that in discussions about other people they'd expressed an opinion that 'perhaps we needn't draw the line too rigidly between them and us', with the result that they, too, ended up at the Baigezhuang Farm. Others might have expressed their feelings about some minor political question in a short article which, even if unpublished, was still used as evidence against them. I also discovered that people like me who retained the love of their wives despite separation were a lucky minority. The marriages of some were hanging on; but there were many pathetic cases in which people had lost all hope for the future and had filed for divorce, abandoning even their babies.

An Indian proverb came to mind: 'I complained day in and day out that I had no shoes, until I saw a man who had no feet.' It wasn't hard for me to find people who were worse off than I. But what made me feel really guilty was the case of a lad not yet twenty years old.

His only crime was to have expressed sympathy with an article of mine that had appeared in the *People's Daily*. He was an amiable young man, the nephew of a composer from an old Communist base area. He didn't show resentment towards me, but I felt very distressed. His life had hardly started, yet it was already in trouble.

Me, I was used to sleeping on a *kang*. I'd grown up sleeping on one, and when I went to report to Darien (Dalian) as a newspaper correspondent in 1956, I'd slept on a big *kang* in a collective farm again. Those who shared my berth then had included a chemical fertiliser salesman and someone from an insurance company. We talked a little after lights-out, but we had no particular interest in each other and went our separate ways during the day. This time, tucked up together with the young men of my team, it was very different. The team leader who slept at my side asked me everything about my life: how many children I had at home, what my wife did, and so forth. My team-mates likewise questioned me. They weren't just curious, they were genuinely interested. Sleeping on the *kang* did give me one difficulty however. Because I suffered from weak kidneys I drank a lot of water, under doctor's orders, and had to get up to relieve myself several times a night; that meant rousing the young man who lay next to me. There were no torches and often I stepped in the wrong place. A solution finally occurred to me: I would drink no liquids after noon. It worked, but it also gave me kidney stones. Later in my life I lost a kidney.

On my first night at the farm by way of briefing us all about our tasks, the team leader said: 'Tomorrow we dig ditches and build dykes in that piece of heavy land to the east, so what work d'you think we should allot to good ol' Hsiao?'

One who was leaning up on the *kang* on his elbows said, 'He's just put down his pen, let's have him just look on for a while, and then decide.'

At that I had to interrupt. I said to the team leader, 'You mustn't feel sorry for me. I worked with my hands when I was young. And I'm still strong, so I'll just follow along and do what you do.'

The team leader was surprised to hear that I had done manual

labour before. 'OK' he said, 'We'll let you do as much as you can –
just don't frazzle yourself.'

His dialect was very like that of Peking, except for some
differences in tone, but the last sentence left me bewildered. I asked
him what 'shagged out' meant. A young lad bedded down in the
midst of the group stuck his head up and tactfully explained that
they were afraid I'd exhaust myself.

'All right, everybody catch some sleep now.' The team leader
cut short our conversation – we had to get up at dawn and it was a
long day.

As I lay there, looking in the moonlight at the pretty coloured
prints of traditional children's dolls on the walls and listening to the
snoring of my companions, I was overwhelmed with the real-
isation that this home was much better, and much warmer, than I'd
ever expected. I must write a letter to Jieruo the next day, to tell her
how friendly and helpful the young men were among whom I was
living.

With this thought in my mind I drifted off to sleep. Having
carried my baggage such a long way, I really was tired, so I slept
soundly.

Breakfast on the farm had to be got through quickly and took a
lot of skill. You had to hold your two steamed buns in your fingers
while balancing an enamel pot of rice porridge accompanied by
half a pickled turnip. I couldn't begin to keep up with the others.

'Don't rush,' the team leader told me when he saw me frantically
stuffing my face. He suggested that I hide a bun in my clothes to eat
at my leisure on the way to work.

Next he led me to the tool shed.

Along the way he told the rest of our team, 'We'll have to find a
good shovel for this ol' Hsiao of ours.' There were several dozen of
them and they all looked the same to me. He picked one out, hefted
it to judge its weight, then shook his head and put it back. He tried
out seven or eight before he came to one that he pronounced 'OK'
and he handed it over to me.

'This one is light and strong. The handle's smooth and the blade
is sharp. Take it and try it out.' He told me to make a mark on the
handle to identify it as mine. I felt very touched by his thought-
fulness.

That day the team's job was to dig ditches and build dykes
between the fields. The leader assigned me only a small section and

said that even if I couldn't finish, it didn't matter – before the day was over everybody would give me a hand and get it done. The lads worked stripped to the waist. I took off my shirt too. It was roasting in the midday sun. Larks circled overhead, their soft chirping like a benediction. During the last few months in the city I had hardly dared to breathe; now I felt like a new man.

I loved this vast plain and these simple straightforward young men who worked by my side.

Still, I worried that when they discovered I was a Rightist their attitude towards me would change. I weighed the matter and decided it would be best to let them know the truth immediately. So, during the midday break, I asked the team leader, 'Friend Chen, you're all so good to me, but do you know what I am?'

'You?' He grinned at me. 'You're ol' Hsiao.'

I bowed my head and said, quietly, 'I am a Rightist element. Did you know that?'

I watched him and the young men by his side to see their reaction.

'Of course we did,' he said casually, 'but Rightists are Chinese too, aren't they?'

A lad nearby chipped in: 'If you weren't a Rightist, we'd never have met, would we?'

Another gestured grandly. 'This is a fated encounter from halfway across the realm,' he said with mock pomposity.

This exchange not only freed me of my anxiety, it increased my respect for my young companions. They'd left school early, they weren't highly educated and certainly couldn't quote the classics, but their hearts were in the right place and they went in for none of the backbiting so common among intellectuals. In agricultural work, the more hands the better; how much more so in revolution – they understood that truth very well from their common sense alone.

Jieruo, working in her agricultural production brigade, sent me a letter every other day. In some ways her situation was very similar to mine. The official policy had been explained to her group before they left: the country folk were not to be told the crimes of the various spouses, the purpose being to keep them from being implicated in his or her offence.

But, no sooner had she arrived than somebody from Jieruo's outfit spread every detail of my situation. Throughout the village the news went around, 'She's the wife of a Rightist element!' What amazed Jieruo was that not only did she not suffer because of this, but in fact the country folk actually showed her special kindness.

'With both of you sent down,' they said, 'how hard it must be on your three little ones!'

Jieruo was able to reassure them, saying there was still a grandmother in the family, and an aunt, so they needn't worry.

Among the people who were sent down together with her, no one else was the spouse of a designated Rightist. She was required to describe my crimes in team meetings, and her leader did ideological work on her. He told her about the case of a female of high political consciousness in a certain unit who had been particularly thorough in exposing her husband's iniquities. Afterwards she was even admitted into the Party. He insisted that Jieruo think back – had she left out anything at the criticism meetings? The result of her being 'mobilised' like this was that Jieruo simply made a self-criticism instead. She said that some of the bad things appearing in the poisonous articles I had written were opinions that had originated with her in our home: if she had exercised more wisdom and had not spoken then, perhaps my problems now would not be so grave. The team leader got so furious at this that he accused her of falsely trying to take the blame for another's crime.

So it was that although Jieruo's attendance rate at meetings was the highest in her team, and although she used her midday rest period to combat illiteracy in the village, her official valuation at the end of her period of rustication dropped her down to a 'lagging behind in political thought' classification.

Things in this world are hard to predict. I'd thought that after being sent down for 'penal labour under the surveillance of the masses', my life would inevitably be that of a miserable convict. But I ended up happy and my cross was borne instead by Jieruo.

Some people will stop at nothing to show their colleagues how revolutionary they are. Now I have no quarrel with those who are proud of their commitment to revolution. The crux of the matter lies in the motivation behind the show, and in that were the seeds of tragedy to be found for many people after 1966.

I'd eaten rice all my life without ever witnessing the complete process of rice cultivation. After laboriously dredging out the fields and piling up the embankments, one had to transplant out each individual seedling. Field management was much lighter work.

While flooding the fields, we'd often catch fish in the ditches. Then we'd wrap them in a thick layer of mud, find a few twigs for fire, and bake the fish at the edge of the field. Soon the mud burnt back into a black lump. When we peeled it off, the fish inside was white and tender and the skin had come away with the mud.

In the course of our shared labour, I became close friends with the young men in my team. On rainy days, when we didn't go into the fields, we chatted together in our hut. It was in their district that Pingju (a lowbrow form of Peking opera) had originated. They'd sing in the Luozi tone scale, and sometimes I'd try to add the harmonies. I felt the wounds in my soul begin to heal. When I'd first arrived and seen the farm wall poster that read 'Take the Farm To Be Your Home!' I had thought it a cruel joke. Now, as I wrote to Jieruo in a letter, 'If it wasn't for missing you and the children, I'd willingly live out my life here.'

But, around harvest time, the situation began to change.

As I was getting my breakfast rice one morning, I heard from the canteen loudspeaker about the success of the Great Leap Forward. The head of the branch farm and its brigades were disabled veterans, but each brigade also had an agricultural expert, a technician who'd graduated from an agricultural college and, for the last few days, our technician had been strangely silent. Later that morning, he told us he'd been judged to have Rightist tendencies and, should anyone ask us about the average yield- per-acre of our farm, we must please remember to say that it was fifteen hundred kilograms. In fact we never had any call to report our yield to anyone; we were busy enough with our own affairs, so it made no difference to us whether we raised or lowered it. But we did notice that all the villages along our route to and from work started putting up from out of the blue wooden placards reading 'Youth Cultural Village', 'Advanced Scientific Village' and the like. And although the primitive conditions within the villages remained unchanged, the farm itself hastily posted up a 'five-year plan construction map' which included sites for a new airfield, museum, theatre, concert hall and meteorological station. Within five years, clearly, our district, like the rest of the country, would surpass England and almost catch up with America!

Five years were a long time; more relevant were certain immediate changes in the work teams. In accordance with instructions from above, a separate team made up only of Rightists was established, in order to focus the class struggle. The farm headquarters named one of us to be the team leader. The brigade leader, who concerned himself only with appearing to meet production quotas, sent another disabled veteran to superintend our moral regeneration.

That move terminated my days of contented labour and the gentle breezes that had been healing my wounds. Our moral regeneration quickly became a crude competition to see who was the most revolutionary and who could get the upper hand in class struggle.

Our work load too, increased to the point where I could no longer keep up. After the autumn harvest we had to carry the new season's rice plants in enormous bundles on our backs; if we lightened our loads by even a single plant we got into serious trouble. If anyone spoke a single indiscreet word out in the fields, it was immediately reported and a full-scale meeting was held, raising the matter to one of important political principle.

Not only I, who was of course not a Party member, but even a nice old fellow from Yan'an who'd entered the Party back in the thirties was a frequent target for struggle and criticism. Posters went up on the farm and my fellow-Rightists miraculously changed into Leftists one after another.

At the end of 1958, one woman ex-Rightist was ordered by the authorities to write up political appraisals of us all. There she was, working by lamplight, a green padded jacket thrown over her shoulders, inventing character references that would stay with us for the rest of our lives. When she got to me, she must have curled her lip in contempt, for she used every venomous word she could think of. She even referred to the one time when I had worn leggings over my trousers while weeding rice seedlings as 'a deliberate smear against socialism'.

These appraisals were by no means unimportant. Very significant rewards and punishments resulted from them. The minority who had behaved well, headed by the woman in her green padded jacket, were allowed to visit their families for the New Year celebration, while the rest of us had to stay at the farm and continue with our moral regeneration.

During class struggle, showing a chivalric interest in justice for the weak was virtually out of the question. Certainly I myself never expected anyone to come forward and speak on my behalf. But at least there were people in a position to damage me who refused to do so, and for them I am still filled with gratitude.

In the northeast corner of the farm was a tall building which housed a fine Yili breeding horse from Sinkiang. He was said to be worth several tens of thousands of yuan. Two agricultural workers who knew about horses waited on him day and night, in shifts. Besides feeding and watering him, they exercised him every day.

This thoroughbred was enormous. He trotted with his head held high, in a most imposing manner. And during the breeding season he was attended to with particular care: the brigade head, even the farm head himself often came by to pay their respects.

Every time I passed that Yili horse, I asked myself how much less a Rightist element like me was worth than he was. I had my reservations about the popular Russian phrase, 'Of all things in the world, people are the most precious'. It depended on whom you were talking about, and their class status. That horse gave me a salutary sense of my own insignificance.

My low morale was most obvious in the manner of my eating. It was in that that you could see best who was succeeding in his reformation and who was failing. We passed through villages on the way to fields and sometimes I'd creep away to a shop and buy a pickled egg and sometimes even a little cup of white spirits. I'd gulp them down in a great fluster as I leaned on my shovel and several times I choked on them in my anti-socialist greed.

On the way to the fields, too, I often caught a glimpse of big, white, red-headed birds on the embankments between the rice paddies, crooking their necks at us. At first I thought they were cranes, but then I learned that they were storks. One day a local peasant shot one with a homemade gun. He secretly brought the succulent bird over to our hut to sell it to us. Those who were striving to regenerate themselves resolutely turned away, saying that if headquarters found out, they'd be bound to disapprove. Others of us said, 'Let's go ahead and eat it – it'll be worth a few harsh words during criticism.' Naturally I joined in. It was a big bird, enough for several meals for the three of us who finally bought it. We got a bottle of stork oil out of it, too.

The subsequent criticism meeting was inevitable. When you've been criticised so many times, you grow calloused and cease to care. First, they may criticise you for various things, but it all boils down to the same stock words. Second, when you've been brought so low, if you fall again, where is there to fall to?

When Jieruo came to see me in 1959, during the October First national holiday, she said that food shortages in the cities were much worse than on the state farm. But she still brought me festival moon cakes and sausages, procured only after waiting in interminable queues and spending a great deal of money. I took my little enamel basin to the canteen for our rice. Even though I heaped it way above the brim, we gobbled it down and still felt hungry.

I was doing heavy labouring jobs in those days which consumed a lot of energy. Our rations were so small that I sometimes grew lightheaded. Once when I was carrying boiled water on my shoulder pole to the fields for everyone to drink and had managed to make it there with great difficulty, I felt dizzy just as I was setting the buckets down. They overturned and I spilled everything.

There was a rice mill on the farm, operated by a reasonably kindhearted young fellow. Sometimes I'd run in, grab a fistful of rice bran from under the machinery and stuff it into my mouth. I think it amused him to see me brought to this sorry state, but he never stopped me. With white rice bran sticking to my face, I must have looked just like a circus clown.

Of course I was criticised for being greedy even when I wasn't. For instance, one day I'd been assigned to help out a master woodsman whose name was Lin. I had a crick in my back that hurt when I squatted and after a while I began to make little moaning and groaning sounds. Master Lin and I worked the whole morning; after that he contacted the brigade office to send someone to replace me. This turned out to be a disaster, of course, for they said I was refusing to work. That evening, Master Lin quietly called me out from the hut and invited me to his house. As we entered, I saw he'd already set out a pot of wine and a dish of peanuts on the warming ledge of his *kang*. He offered me a seat, sighed, and said 'Brother mine, I'm so sorry – I had no idea I would get you into such a mess.' I didn't eat a thing, nor did I drink his wine, but I was cheered by this proof of ordinary people's inner goodness. When I got back to the Party officials, though, they insisted that I'd taken greedy advantage of Master Lin's hospitality. The criticisms were much worse than usual.

In 1960, when Jieruo heard that I often ate raw food, she enclosed in her letter a little packet of potassium permanganate so that I could dose myself against hookworm. It couldn't have cost her more than five cents. Nevertheless, a fellow Rightist immediately reported it to our rough and uneducated brigade leader who then accused me of receiving high-grade medicine from the capital. That, needless to say, showed that I was obstinately clinging to my reactionary attitudes and resisting reformation.

It was on another occasion that I really hit bottom. Every time I think about it even now, I'm still embarrassed. It was in the spring of 1960; our work had been moved from the fields indoors, to the production of bacterial manure. It was light work, but sometimes you had to stay up all night, periodically measuring the temperature of the compost.

First, I must describe a big event that took place in 1959; the farm 'uncapped' some people [removed the symbolic high hat of political shame: ie declared them rehabilitated]. Naturally I wasn't one of the lucky ones, but the event did send a ray of hope into my heart. I might not have to be there for eight to ten years after all. Several were uncapped in my own brigade, including one man who had put up an outstanding performance by being the first to copy out the necessary manure manufacturing instructions from the appropriate manual.

One evening I was on night duty, watching the fertiliser. A stove had been lit in the corner of the room to maintain the temperature. Stewing on top of it was a fat hen that had been raised and killed by one of the uncapped fellows. He added some spice or other and asked me to keep an eye on it during my shift, while he slept. So I put a cover on the burner, which reduced the heat. The stewing went on till midnight and the smell of it was enough to send you crazy. I'd gone on duty right after dinner and happened to have my bowl and chopsticks; telling myself that I was just testing to see if it was done, I took a little taste. Unfortunately, by the time the uncapped fellow woke up and wanted to eat his stewed chicken not much was left sticking out of the broth but a bare skeleton.

It was serious enough to steal food, but I'd actually eaten the chicken of someone who was now uncapped. I knew I had to confess to something more political than mere gluttony. I said I wasn't reconciled to the fact that uncapped people could raise their own chickens while I could not. But that only made the thing worse. It elevated my crime into a matter of dissatisfaction with the farm and with the reform process: eating chicken on the sly became an act of class retaliation.

We who were seen as stubbornly resisting reformation were not permitted to return to our families for the New Year celebrations in 1959. Some ordinary agricultural workers whose homes were far away stayed at the farm, too. Dance parties were popular in those days, so the brigade leader superintending our reformation announced that a Spring Festival ball would be held in the mess hall. He wanted any Rightists who could play musical instruments to organise a band. He found only one, a man who could play the fiddle. I don't know who let it out, but someone had heard me playing a harmonica behind the ricestraw stacks after the autumn harvest, so they wanted me to join the group too. In order to show my positive spirit for once, and also to cheer myself up, I agreed.

The two of us playing on fiddle and harmonica were the most pathetic band you could imagine. Fortunately those who came to dance were hardly the top-hat elite. The only female guest was the wife of the brigade leader. All the rest were male farm labourers. We had no sheet music – we played only what we could remember, that is to say, what we could both remember. The tune the two of us knew best was The Merry Widow Waltz, so we filled in with that whenever we could think of nothing else. And when we needed a breather, the brigade leader sang some Hebei opera at the top of his voice. He sang 'Chen Shimei Forsakes His Wife.'

Anyway, most of the people at the dance were just there for some fun. They just hopped round and round, not caring what tunes we played.

As the New Year began, wheat flour and meat were distributed, so even people who were labelled 'stubborn elements' actually got to eat a meal of *jiaozi* (meat dumplings).

In my three years on the farm, I returned to Peking only once, in 1960. Even then it certainly wasn't because I'd been reforming myself well, but just because those above had decided that for once all of us could go home for the New Year. Before we left the farm, each of us was given a slip of paper: it stated the date we were to be back at the farm and stipulated that the moment we arrived in Peking we were to report to our local police station. Before returning to the farm, we were to go there again, so that the police could sign and stamp our form. Though the farm wasn't officially a prison, these procedures made us feel as if we were being released on parole.

I hurriedly got on the train; there wasn't time to write to Jieruo beforehand. My heart had already flown all the way to Peking, but I didn't know where I ought to go once I got off the train.

For I was already homeless again. Lots of factories had been set up in residential areas in the summer of 1958 and the courtyard we moved into had been requisitioned. My old unit had found us a place just large enough to store our furniture. After Jieruo's period of rehabilitation was over down in the country she squeezed in at her mother's place with her older sister. Our children were boarding elsewhere now and came home only at weekends.

I didn't want to look for Jieruo at the publishing house where she worked for fear of causing her to lose face, so I ran from the station directly to my mother-in-law's house. Unfortunately my mother-in-law was out and her rooms were locked. I inquired with the family across the courtyard. An old granny came out to meet me. In the past she'd been extremely polite to her honourable neighbour, but today she acted as if I was a convict just out of jail. She looked me up and down, said 'I don't know anything', and slammed the door in my face.

I had a sudden inspiration. I'd find a public phone in an alleyway, make a call and have Jieruo summoned to the telephone. Fortunately she took the call herself. She had a study class that night and simply couldn't get off, but she said she'd call her younger brother right away and ask him to help get me settled.

After hanging up, I walked impatiently through the streets. By the time I returned, Jieruo's mother and sister had already come back. After dinner, my brother-in-law Xuepu arrived. He had a key to where my furniture was piled and sometimes he helped Jieruo clean it up.

The place was in a little alley east of the Drum Tower. When I was little, the grandmother of a classmate had lived behind magnificent red doors east of the opening to the alley. I often went there with my friend to play; the old woman worshipped Buddha and was a vegetarian. Every time I went, I saw her kneeling on a rush mat in the family's devotional hall. How I'd loved the wafting incense and the sound of the hollow wooden fish block as it was struck. Now the place had been turned into a neighbourhood factory.

Groping in the dark, Xuepu found the door and opened it. The room inside was as cold as an icehouse. Fortunately it faced south and also had a skylight. Every month, when Jieruo and Xuepu came to pay the rent, they took the opportunity to air the place, so it wasn't as dirty or dank as I'd imagined it might be. Although our chairs, tables and stools were stacked in piles on top of one another, the bed and stove were in place so that they could be used. Even the stovepipe was installed. Xuepu immediately built a fire with our precious Yangquan coal. We'd already had a cup of tea by the time Jieruo hurried in.

The next day was Lunar New Year's Eve. Jieruo had arranged for me to visit my elderly cousin, Venerable Elder Sister, and my older son, Tiezhu.

That cousin, now old and deaf, had been half a mother to me. She hadn't seen me these past several years, but she patted me and stroked my head just as she had when I was little. Not long after I was back on the farm, I learned that she had died. The upset of my visit had been too much for her. Jieruo's letter described how she and the other cousins had gone together to buy a coffin and erect a tombstone for her. I threw myself down on the haystack and wept, grieving that I'd never been able to return to her a single day of happiness.

I hadn't seen Tiezhu in nearly two years and he'd grown half-a-head taller. At Jieruo's urging he'd written often to me. In the main he described his weekend outings with his little brother and sister. But he was the only one in his class who didn't wear the coveted red bandanna of a Young Pioneer. That of course was the result of my political circumstances.

Jieruo now said that she'd already arranged to complete her labour service in the first part of the year (at the time, all in her group had to work in the country for at least one month out of the year). During the summer vacation she'd have him live with her in the storeroom. Perhaps that would cheer him up.

When we returned from Venerable Elder Sister to the storeroom, Jieruo went and collected our daughter Lizi. She had grown from a baby into a young lady, with a little round face and her hair tied up in a knot with a red satin ribbon on top of her head. Jieruo asked her to call me Papa. She stared at me for a good long while before finally saying it. Jieruo told me that once when she took Lizi to the main shopping district in Wangfujing and stopped to talk with a male acquaintance, Lizi suddenly clasped his leg. Afterwards Jieruo asked her 'What did you think you were doing there?' She said, 'I thought he was my daddy.' In fact my sudden disappearance at that crucial stage in her development had left a deep emotional scar on her. Jieruo remembers Lizi's natural cheerfulness as having changed from that time forward. Even at that early age she began to look anxious and depressed.

The saddest thing was that I didn't get to see Tong, my youngest. Before his second birthday he'd entered a privately-run nursery and nothing I could do was enough to persuade it to let him out or me in. Having won the honour of being judged the Red Flag Unit of its Eastern District, the nursery had instituted a policy of not letting any of its children go home – not for the whole winter – in case one of them came down with a cold!

Jieruo pressed me to go to the pickling factory to see my old boss Zhang Guangnian. At first I couldn't pluck up the courage, but she seemed to think my fate was still in his hands, so I decided I'd better go to see him.

How naive we were, how unaware of our new standing! It was New Year, so all were enjoying family parties behind their closed doors. As I knocked on the leader's door, I heard songs on the radio inside and peals of happy laughter. But when they opened the door and saw me, a shabby and sorry sight, everything suddenly became quiet. Grudgingly they let me in. Then they turned off the radio and the whole family hid in another room, leaving only my old boss. Sitting very righteously in his hardwood Imperial Tutor's Chair, absolutely still, he asked me how my rehabilitation was going. I spoke the words I'd rehearsed to myself on the way over, saying that even though I hadn't reformed myself very well, I remained optimistic. The Central Committee of the Communist Party had now released even Kuomintang war criminals like Wang Yaowu, so I felt that surely when it came to me they'd. . . .

Ashen-faced he stopped me in mid-stream. 'You are worse than a Wang Yaowu in the literary world!'

I said no more, but quickly withdrew, blaming myself for being spineless as I went out, and also blaming Jieruo for having suggested this visit in the first place.

My one week of leave quickly expired. No matter how far I'd come down in the world, so long as I had Jieruo, the children and a storeroom, I could say I had a home. I set out at 9.30 pm to catch the 11.30 night train. Jieruo braved the piercingly cold north-west wind, insisting on seeing me off at my trolley stop. Knowing the front gate and door to the house were left unlocked and our Number Two might be frightened to wake up and find herself all alone, I urged her to go home. We parted.

Jieruo came to the farm to see me again on New Year's Day, 1961. By then, in the wake of the backyard steel furnaces and communal mess halls, even in Peking only a small elite could eat their fill. Instead of asking us to eat cake in place of bread, Chairman Mao had called on us to eat 'melons and vegetables in place of grain'. So although Jieruo went all over the city to find some extra nourishment for me, this time she was only able to buy medicinal wine and a carton of fruit juice. She told me that someone had disclosed to her that the publishing house was trying to get me back to the city to translate an English novel for them: *Tom Jones*. She hoped to be able to rent us decent accommodation convenient for work before I returned. I was very sceptical about all this. By that time I'd learned to keep my feelings bottled up and never to trust anyone.

In the early summer I was transferred to a community vegetable patch which I tended with a local peasant. During the day we put irrigation water into the ditches bordering the fields and spread pesticides. Night duty rotated between us. I was only with my team of Rightists during meetings and study classes, so I was much easier at heart.

One day, as I was picking aubergines, a basket on my arm, the brigade leader himself suddenly appeared in the field. He said Peking was planning to recall me and that I must return to my team immediately to undergo reappraisal.

In fact, although we couldn't have known this at the time, it wasn't long before large numbers of Rightists were returned home nationwide; none of my group had to stay on. But at the appraisal meeting, the entire record of my past misdeeds was gone over once again – my eating on the sly, my shirking while carrying rice plants, my cynical comments, even my wearing of leggings in order to smear the good name of socialism. I tacitly acquiesced in the accusations. Only one person, a disgraced Party film expert (Zhong Dianfei) attacked my future rather than my past. He asserted categorically that sooner or later I'd defect to England or America. Of course there were people who said good things about me too – that I had suffered much and worked to the best of my abilities even though I was the oldest one in the whole group and suffered from kidney disease. And they hoped that after I left, I would be careful not to let myself go again. Naturally I was extremely grateful and promised to do my best. But frankly I was puzzled. Most of the people in my team were backbone ex-Party members, men who'd entered the Party in the fifties, or even earlier. They were all clearly judged to be more rehabilitated than I, so why was I going back to the city before them? Indeed, several of them couldn't see the reasoning behind it. They refused to accept the idea and I sympathised with them.

Afterwards, I packed my bags and went to the assembly point at the main farm. Other people from neighbouring branch farms were returning to the city with me. This time we weren't travelling under escort. We received our living expenses for the month, rode the farm's truck to the train station and then went our separate ways.

After getting off the train, I found my way to the address that Jieruo had enclosed in her most recent letter: she'd actually been successful at getting the housing bureau to exchange our storeroom for something better. It was in a dead-end lane off a small northern street. Following the house number plates, I entered a big courtyard occupied by several different households. I found the three-room unit her letter had described. No one was at home, but peeking through the crack between the door and its frame, I saw familiar pieces of furniture. I set my luggage down outside the entrance, said hello to the old lady across the way, and walked round to my mother-in-law's. She and Elder Sister Number Three had been expecting me and were overjoyed. After having a meal with them, I went back home, by which time Jieruo had arrived and had already carried in water for my bath. She'd missed me at the railway station and had waited by the ticket inspection gate in case I'd had to catch a later train. Now there in the courtyard, using a big basin, she helped me wash off the accumulated dirt of three years and two months on the farm.

The good things about our new lodging were that it was bigger and had more rooms than the storeroom, and was conveniently halfway between my mother-in-law's and my work unit. The disadvantages were that it was cold in winter and hot in summer, lacked a finished floor and ceiling and running water. So I'd still be carrying water, even now that I was back in the city.

But, so long as we and the children could sleep together under the same roof, we could say we had a home again. In fact we were very lucky. After all, there were plenty of people much worse off than we. There were men who returned from their penal servitude to broken marriages and loneliness. There were others, long-time Peking residents like myself, who were now sent to work in far-off districts. Every day I reminded myself how lucky I was: not only was I allowed to remain in Peking, my birthplace, I could also resume my literary work. I didn't care that I'd been demoted several ranks and was permitted only to translate (so long as I did so anonymously) and not to write. However far I'd fallen, I was earning a great deal more than the living expenses I'd received on the farm, so the burden of raising the family would no longer be borne by Jieruo alone. Besides which, in this society writing appeared to be so much more hazardous than any other profession that I had resolved never to write again. I also prayed that my children would choose any line of work but writing.

My working conditions, now that I'd returned to the city, were just about perfect. My employer, a branch of the giant People's Literature Press, was situated in a fine tall new building and the majority of my colleagues, like me, had been targets of attack for one thing or another. Most of them did translation – of fiction, poetry and theory, from various foreign languages. We tended to be relatively old, and each of us concentrated on his own job, seldom concerning himself with the projects of others. Also, since we were not doing editorial work, we had few relationships with people outside the department. It was an ideal haven. The man in charge was an old author in the Party, Lou Shiyi. He was amiable, brimming over with energy for his work, and always approachable.

Except for the chief, who had a separate room, there were three or four people to an office. The big reception room had a ping-pong table. When the bell sounded for our work break, several old chaps who were ping-pong addicts took up their bats and descended on it. I wasn't good at ping-pong, but I became addicted too. That bouncy little ball somehow seemed to symbolise the combination of freedom and restraint that I now believed I needed.

There were still plenty of things to worry about. First was the problem of finding a larger place to live. Our daughter Lizi would soon be leaving her nursery school and our little rooms were already so crowded that no one else could get in. When Jieruo heard that Lizi's little playmate from the big pickling factory had been chosen to study foreign languages at the socially elite Coal Hill School, she decided that we would have our daughter learn to play the piano instead. Having just received payment for a manuscript, she went out and spent the whole lot on a piano. It created a lot of trouble for us – once the piano was squeezed into the house, there was no place for the young lady who was supposed to learn to play it.

Although two old friends were making enquiries about a new residence for us, they were busy enough with their own affairs, so I went to the chief of my new unit, the People's Literature Press, about it. He expressed sympathy and was willing to help, but had no means of doing so. I had been transferred from my old unit (the Chinese Writers' Association, publishers of the *Literature and Art Gazette*), but I was much too late to get in line at his.

Crowding was something I could endure. But I quickly discovered that my shameful Rightist status was common knowledge all around our shared courtyard. Nearby, across from the latrine, lived a family of five. The woman of the house had once been arrested by the Public Security Bureau for 'getting around too much', the quaint official phrase for prostitution, yet whenever I went to the toilet, she would stand outside and spank one of her children, yelling so loudly that even Jieruo could hear, 'You little rascal – when you grow up you can be anything you please, just don't be a Rightist!'

We had another reason for wanting to move. My elder son had already begun to attend secondary school. When Jieruo went to see his form teacher, she learned that Tiezhu was extremely happy because he mistakenly thought my return to Peking meant that all my problems had been solved. Also, since my two younger ones hadn't yet realised that we'd been in trouble, we made up our minds to find ourselves peaceful surroundings before they had to learn the truth from unfriendly neighbours.

In those days notices for buying and selling houses were posted on walls, electricity poles, even public toilets. Why not give it a try myself? I wrote out an ad that very night and stuck it on an electricity pole north of Dongsi.

Amazingly I had an answer within only a few days. As soon as Jieruo and I got off work, we went to see the place. The location was attractive: just one bus stop away from our work, less than ten minutes by bike. A five-room apartment at the south end of a courtyard, it had a porch as well as a little room on the west end that was about to collapse. There was a storeroom out by the latrine, and three little pieces of land you could plant something on. The owner lived in a row of rooms to the north end of the courtyard and the two families would be able to keep an eye on each other's houses.

The owner explained that during the Great Leap Forward, these six spare rooms had been requisitioned for a nursery. Now that the communising wind was in a lull the nursery had been closed and the rooms returned to their owner. But for all he knew the wind might blow again, so he thought it best to sell them off quickly for whatever he could get.

At last we had a proper home again. As soon as we'd bought it, Jieruo began to make plans. She suggested we fix up the western room for me, as a study. The row of five rooms were a bit like railway carriages, but the two rooms in the middle had no firm divider between them, so they'd make a good living room. It was a perfect place for the piano. Although our house had a northern exposure it had two rear windows that let in the sun. We constructed a long table along the window by putting a wooden plank across our two old-style trunks, just wide enough for two children to sit at one end, shoulder-to-shoulder. We saved up our money to replace the old-fashioned doors and windows with western-style ones, and to replace the paste and newspaper on the rafters with a proper plaster ceiling. We brought in pipes to supply running water to all three rooms and put a washbasin in one of them. All we lacked was a toilet.

How wonderful it was to have a house again. Jieruo's Elder Sister Number Three, Changwei, moved in to help us keep house.

After repairing the little room on the west side, I built a grape-trellis in front of the door. I thought that after it had served as my study for a while, we might use it to accommodate my mother-in-law in her declining years.

At that time you could occasionally buy your own building materials at construction goods stores. And a mill outside Anding Gate sold scrap lumber. In those days I still had lots of energy. Whenever I also had some money to spare I'd bike all over town, buying bricks, tiles and cement here, a full set of carpenters' and masons' tools there. And on Sundays I'd take up my tools and set about doing up the house.

The one bad thing about it was that there was a plastics factory just across the road, and when the wind blew from that direction the fumes were so noxious that we didn't dare open our windows. And a loudspeaker there played loud revolutionary songs all day long. But we didn't complain.

Jieruo took a lot of pains with our children's education. Our eldest child had always had more of a bent for the humanities than the sciences. He was no good at maths, so every weekend Jieruo had him do exercises and helped him with his mistakes. Ultimately he was able to pass the exams to enter an excellent middle school. When it came time for the two little ones to enter primary school, Jieruo managed to have her household registration moved to the house of a friend who lived near a key primary school, so that our children could attend there. She even took the children to live there for a time. I was fiercely against it, but I couldn't dissuade her, and when later I was held and struggled against during the Cultural Revolution, I realised what a good thing it was that our children hadn't attended school near home and seen the parents of their classmates ransack our belongings.

My work was to translate the eighteenth-century English writers. It was a world so far from my own reality.

I had returned to the city just at the tail end of 'the three years of bad harvests from natural disaster'. My ration of staple foods suddenly went down from the twenty-seven-and-a-half kilograms I'd been allotted on the farm, to fifteen. I was allotted no non-staples either. I was always hungry, but when I complained Jieruo told me to be satisfied with what I had, since she as a woman got only thirteen-and-a-half kilograms. Whenever there were Korean fish on the market, tough and unpalatable though they were, she'd buy big batches of them, just so long as they were edible. She took every precaution to see that we didn't come down with hepatitis.

The following year, things quickly improved. Not only were non-staples available, our cultural life was richer, too. At New Year there was a Lantern Festival once more, and the temple fair was revived at the Changdian marketplace. In the summer I took the children to hear a lakeside concert at Beihai Park. Peking had become a city of art and music again.

In the early 1950s I'd had private reservations about the Sino-

Soviet Treaty of Friendship and Alliance. In 1957, some people were capped for being 'anti-Soviet'. I congratulated myself for having kept quiet. After the split with the Soviet Union was made public, I kept my mouth shut as before, but inwardly I admired the Chinese Communist Party for putting principle before material interest. In spite of the atomic weapons brandished by Moscow the Party had maintained our national dignity and steadfastly opposed great-power chauvinism.

How the temperature warmed up in 1962! I was elated to hear that some were advocating that intellectuals should be rehabilitated as a group – even though I was myself only on the margins of the intelligentsia. There was one meeting after another, to consult with intellectuals, and for them to open their hearts to the Party. Even so, Jieruo and I reminded each other daily that we must watch our tongues. Secretly I hoped that in addition to opposing Soviet revisionism, the Party would criticise the Soviet Union's mass murder in the thirties of its own comrades, but fortunately I didn't breathe a word of this to anyone, for history was about to repeat itself: in China a similar tragedy was about to unfold.

Suddenly the assault on revisionism turned round and faced inward as the attackers turned to their fellow countrymen for new targets. Suddenly this, that, and every other thing was revisionist. Soon the flames were licking at our safe haven. Having been a victim of the Anti-Rightist movement, I was a natural for the Anti-Revisionist one. And this time a man wearing the Rightist cap had had the impudence to buy both a house and a piano. Not to mention having arrived with at least two bags of excellent Yangquan coal.

This time though, I'd already learnt some basic revolutionary skills. While at the farm I'd recognised that you couldn't hide from class struggle, you could only hope to hold your own in it. I'd seen how my own leader could secretly buy antiques and collect pornography and yet escape suspicion by making big revolution-ary noises and loudly criticising the revisionism of others. He might even go up in the world, very rapidly. The nub of it all was that in a struggle to the death, you didn't lie down and let yourself be bloodied. If you didn't want to be a mouse, you had to be a cat. And this time round, I was going to be a cat. Thinking back on it now, it seems both ludicrous and shameful. Among us old men, I – an old Rightist who should have known my place – rallied round the standard of anti-revisionism myself, and at a criticism meeting exaggerated the most trivial matters into questions of principle, just like the others. It was, of course, a pathetic defence, prompted by the fear that my having purchased a house and a piano might bring the scourge down on me.

But I had once been labelled a Rightist and, although by 1964 I was supposed to have been rehabilitated, I was still an ex-Rightist. So not everybody could become a cat simply by behaving like one. And in the summer of 1966, even before the real storm of anti-revisionism had broken, I was hauled off anyway, just in case.

In modern history there have been many movements with noble names, the true meanings of which were nonetheless vile and ugly. An example is Nazism. The 'na' refers to nationalism and the 'zi' to socialism, two of the most popular and best-loved words in twentieth-century political history. But what bloody import the word bears in reality.

Similarly the first time I saw the phrase 'cultural revolution' I immediately thought of the May Fourth movement in 1919, which supported democracy and science. Little did I know that it really meant a dual enslavement to feudalism and fascism. The revolutionisation of culture must signify a further step in the liberation of man, I thought.

But the movement that professed to enlarge people's souls actually killed them by the millions. At first, admittedly, verbal struggle was preferred to armed violence, but in the end the machine guns and heavy artillery were rolled out. If a sudden turn of events had not stopped the campaign, atomic bombs might well have been used. Driven by the lust for power, people became wholly indifferent to the suffering of their own kind, and cruelty ceased to have limits.

The upheavals of 1957 came suddenly, out of a clear sky; the great calamity of 1966 had been brewing for some time. At the start it did not go beyond the sphere of culture. It only found fault with certain films and plays; characters wearing ancient traditional costumes were driven from the stage and replaced by characters in revolutionary outfits carrying hoes. I didn't go to plays anyway, so I tried to believe that the Cultural Revolution had nothing to do with me.

I cultivated flowers and maize on the three little plots of land facing our rooms. I'd found several rare varieties of morning glory, including snowy white ones and striped purple ones. They clung to an entire wall of our home. A poet friend also gave me a load of tropical plants. My mother-in-law brought over the fish tank she'd had stored away for years. I put it in the centre of the courtyard and planted my favourite water lilies in it.

While our eldest child was learning about ancient mythology, our younger two told revolutionary tales at the municipal Children's Palace and won prizes for their outstanding performances. On Sundays I'd ride my bike to Santiao, taking my daughter on my back to her piano lessons. Meanwhile Jieruo took off the youngest so he could sketch flowers in the municipal gardens. His pencil drawings won a prize at the children's exhibition put on by the local television station.

One day a grand lady who'd seldom had much to say for herself before, took the political centre stage. In the privately circulated copies of Madam Mao's speeches she didn't seem particularly fierce, and she spoke of cultural matters, novels like *The Dream of the Red Chamber, Water Margin* and so forth – nothing seemed too highbrow for her. Her views indirectly represented instructions from Mao Zedong, too, so one could not but have the profoundest respect for them.

On public occasions I went all-out, adding my voice to the criticisms of revisionism, desperately trying to preserve my family and its relatively comfortable circumstances. Like me, Jieruo simply wanted to keep our little home together. To prevent the re-emergence of revisionism, we bought our children gramophone records of revolutionary songs. We taught them to remember the heroes who crossed the Dadu River during the Long March, and from the songs of *Third Sister Liu* and the figures of oppressed tenants in the 'Rent Collection Court' sculpture, they learned to love the peasants and hate the landlords. We skimped on food so that our children could grow up in a peaceful environment and fully enjoy the warmth of socialism. We only wanted to contribute to the new society a few of the things we'd learned under the old one – to rise and retire with the sun, living out our lives in peace.

Having suffered before, we'd learned not to look at non-revolutionary things and not to listen to non-revolutionary words. We had a big Czech-made short-wave radio in our home, but we listened only to Central Broadcasting. Once I accidentally tuned in short-wave to a Christmas carol. Jieruo immediately turned it off and demanded to know down what dangerous path I thought I was leading the children. We truly had no other desire than to do our duty and be law-abiding citizens in this Socialist paradise.

Jieruo was worried also by the prints of British graphic art I'd hung on our living room walls. She said I must never forget how in 1957 I'd been reviled as a slave of the foreigners. She went with the children to buy several posters of Mao Zedong, then put them in the frames in front of the art prints. One Mao portrait was fully two-and-a-half feet wide and four feet high. She hung it in the centre of the living room wall, so that the children could see it day and night and constantly be reminded of our leader, the Red Sun. Yet even these painstaking efforts of hers, come the storm, were to be turned into crimes.

One day in early June 1966, it was announced that a new high-level Party committee had sent a special team to assume control of our unit. That day we all went downstairs from our offices and lined both sides of the street to welcome them. The new leader was a middle-aged woman. She was short, plump and dark and she flashed a harsh, cold glare from behind her spectacles.

Our former unit leader invited her and her retinue onto the dais, after which she read out a list: the names of the first batch of class enemies, calling them cow demons and snake spirits (in a reference to Buddhist mythology). It came as no surprise that I was on the list, but the former leader was on it too. That was on a Saturday. We were notified to report early Monday morning with light baggage. Our leaders planned to make revolution by 'putting us back-to-back' – in other words, by getting us to criticise and so condemn each other.

I'd just set my home in order and now suddenly it seemed to be in imminent danger. Seeing me return home in a daze, my children anxiously asked me what was the matter. I hugged them tight, unable to answer. It was as if an invisible hand was breaking my family apart.

I thought we would be sent to some farm again. Instead we were billeted in a high-rise college building, now out of service, in the western suburbs. Here were assembled about seven hundred top men and women in literature and the arts – hence revisionists one and all. Some wrote novels. Some sang Peking opera or danced the ballet; some were archaeologists. Others painted or composed music. We settled in, two to a room. The sheets were white and the food was delicious. In the daytime we went to meetings to criticise our own revisionism and in the evenings we watched old films from the thirties. It was announced that we were not allowed to leave the premises, but at weekends limousines came to take us to the city and return us, so that we could be reunited with our families. The inscrutability of class struggle lies in its unpredictability. When I look back on that period it seems macabre.

In July, the term 'Black Gang' appeared. The Gang was supposedly headed by Zhou Yang, and had a whole network of followers. At first I thought it referred only to officials above a certain rank. I quickly discovered that the seven hundred here could not escape being implicated.

Luckily the Anti-Rightist movement had long since brought me down several ranks, making me a very minor figure. By the end of July, many of the seven hundred had been seized and struggled against. Some were already mortally wounded. I drew my neck in and took cover.

One day in August, a big truck arrived to take a group of us off. When we got on the truck we discovered that the people from our unit there to meet us had become fierce and truculent, not at all like their old selves. The difference between us and the more famous musicians and film-makers who suffered at the time was that we hadn't been attacked and beaten half senseless before we climbed aboard.

The truck entered the big courtyard of our office compound. Immediately we heard the shouting of slogans. When we got down, those among us who had been on the old Party committee were all made to wear dunce's hats. One of the younger Party members was made up as a clown and given a little gong to beat. He was to go ahead of the others and clear the way. I followed at the rear of this parade. It went round from one building in our compound to the next. Every floor of each building was crowded with revolutionary masses yelling themselves hoarse with slogans denouncing us as filthy revisionists.

After the parade, we were permitted to go home. If that was all there was to the Great Cultural Revolution, I thought, it wasn't too bad.

But a few days later, the Black Gang was summoned. That is to say, we brought our bed rolls and were locked up inside our unit's compound. Meanwhile our colleagues were mobilised to put up posters exposing our sins. When it was all over I learned that at this time, Jieruo and her elder sister had been pressured to expose me, too.

As even a man who'd filled a whole wall full of posters against me had to admit, I'd never dared do a thing wrong since returning to work from the farm. I hadn't put up the briefest of wall posters without first calling for joint deliberations on it and obtaining the consent of several people. And yet, in that same batch of posters the man described me as cheering and clapping in the office at the news that Soviets had beaten up some Chinese students in Moscow, or that American planes had bombed the town of Laojie in Yunnan province, near the Vietnam border.

The posters hadn't been up for more than two hours before this poor man was himself thrown into a cow shed (as any place where 'cow demons' were confined was named). He was accused of having been a professionally trained secret agent in Kunming before Liberation; they said his job had been to mix with leftist students so he could report on them.

I'd read about gun-toting workers and peasants tyrannising intellectuals in novels about the early years of the Soviet October Revolution. Now, in 1966, in our unit, the business of which was book publishing, drivers from the motor pool behaved as if they were in charge of the agency, and our kitchen staff acted as Party commissars. My batch of cow demons and snake spirits was put under the supervision of the lad who used to deliver our manuscripts to the printer. Early every morning he assigned one of us to clean the toilets, someone else to heat the boiler and so forth. He also functioned as jailer. When a unit wanted to struggle against someone, they came to him for their man. He handed the person over and, when it was all over, took custody of him again.

There were of course incessant criticism and struggle sessions in the cow sheds. The name of the target and the time of the meeting were all decided on by the chef from our mess hall. I had not been respectful enough in speaking to him. He got every cow demon and snake spirit in the cow shed (all sixty of them) to criticise me in succession during one three-day marathon session. Then he transferred me from ordinary heavy labour (such as moving the rolls of newsprint) to the heaviest and dirtiest work in the boiler room. Fortunately two of my fellow-workers, Wang Ziye and Fan Yong, looked after me. It was they who saved me from total collapse.

I had expected that I might eventually become one of the targets within my unit. What I could never have dreamed of was that my neighbourhood had a score to settle with me too. At noon on 23 August, as I was nibbling on my steamed bun, the jailer escorted me to his office – the very room that used to be the office of our leader. I was informed that at one o'clock, workers from the plastics factory opposite my house wanted to struggle against me, so I should prepare myself psychologically.

Several burly fellows with red armbands waited for me at the gate with angry scowls on their faces. They rode their bikes with me as I pedalled home.

I'd seen landlords struggled against during land reform. And during the suppression of counter-revolutionaries, I'd seen the boss of the Southern District attacked. Now it was my turn. But I'd lived opposite them for only four years: we'd always kept our door closed and never bothered anyone, so what were they going to complain about? I puzzled over this as I rode.

As I neared home, I saw that the walls on both sides of the lane were covered in posters calling for my humiliation, but they only called me a slave of the foreigners, a longtime Rightist and other such insults to which I'd become accustomed since way back in 1957.

After I was led in, though, I was appalled. Plastics workers whom I'd never met and who didn't know me filled the courtyard. They were shaking their fists and shouting slogans. I saw that the little flower garden I'd painstakingly cultivated was in ruins. The creeping vines were torn down and trampled on; the potted plants had been smashed to pieces. Not even my grape trellis, nor the little apple tree that had given us a few green apples for the first time this year had escaped. I peered inside the rooms and saw that the cabinets were overturned. Everything breakable had been smashed. Pieces of glass and manuscript pages littered the floor. Even the picture frames on the walls had been searched; the prints of British artists had been found and torn to pieces. At the criticism meeting I was accused of using the Chairman's portrait to cover up bourgeois rubbish. A high crime, for which I was obliged to wear a big wooden placard. It said 'active counter-revolutionary element'. Fortunately Jieruo was at work and my children away at school, but then their Third Aunt was compelled to kneel with me on a table in the middle of our courtyard.

Only after the event did I learn that this struggle meeting was just a token. Apart from the pictures there'd been no revelations about me, so of course there was nothing to criticise. But the real purpose of the meeting was clear from the speech of one of the women present. She said, 'Me and my seven kids, a household of nine, have to live in one little room. You have only two children. *And* they're away at school. How do you get away with living in such a big, tile-roofed house? There's revisionism for you!'

The struggle meeting was concluded when she was moved into our tile-roofed house and we were forced into a little eastern room with a newspaper ceiling in a multi-family residence courtyard nearby.

After the meeting, I got on my bike again and was escorted back to my unit. Afterwards I found out that my elder son, who was about to graduate from high school, had come home that day. He had brought along his bedroll, to be opened up and washed. When he entered the lane, the many posters and the denunciations he heard coming from our courtyard had scared him so that he turned round and fled. Peking still had its moat in those days. He wanted to end his life in the dark, still water, but he just sat by the bank until it got dark. He was a homeless child.

The ruffian with the armband insisted that I keep wearing my placard. Thus was I paraded by bicycle through the streets as an example to the public. As soon as I entered our work compound I saw Jieruo, wearing a dunce's cap and standing on the platform of a parked pedicab. She was being struggled against. The 'masses' were clustered around her, shaking their fists and shouting insults. Actually they were half a dozen or so workers from her department, some of them from her own office. Later that day the responsible person from the People's Liberation Army Mao Zedong Thought Propaganda Team called me aside and questioned me. 'Your woman confesses to being a spy. She has a radio transmitter and receiver. Will you divorce her?' I said, 'If she really were a spy, how could I not be one too, sleeping in the same bed with her?'

The revolution, which had been cruel enough during the Anti-Rightist campaign of 1957, was, in August 1966, about to become bloody.

A few weeks later six corpses turned up on the garbage pile in our alley. They were consigned to the flames of the nearest crematorium – while still breathing, according to some accounts. My older son told me the story of a dedicated teacher at his high school who was accused of class crimes and beaten to death. Afterwards the school principal was forced by the rebel faction to mount a balcony where he could be seen, put his arms around the corpse and dance with it. He jumped to his death. For many people in those days death was pleasanter than life. I came near to joining their number. Seeing my house smashed into smithereens, my pictures torn up, my precious gramophone records of European music, acquired with so much difficulty in London, New York and Paris, all shattered, and Jieruo in a dunce's cap, abused and humiliated, I lost all interest in living for a time.

What crime was my wife guilty of – a woman who'd gone straight from college into her unit, reading proofs on her own wedding night? What was she being struggled against for?

By the end of August, I was asking myself day and night why I stayed on this earth.

I was still in my cow shed; on every trip to the latrine I reconnoitred the possibilities – which pipe could I hang my belt from? If I was going to jump, where might I do it? One afternoon I tried to climb to the fifth storey and end it all: to make my bloodied corpse into an instrument of protest. But a sentry posted in the corridor prevented me from going.

Finished – it was all over for me – or so I felt at the time. I felt that death alone could release me from this humiliation and torture. I knew what it would be like for my three orphans if I took my own life. And what if I only crippled myself? Still, the thought of death would not let me go. Patiently and persistently it asked me: are you any good to your children as it is? Aren't you in fact making it harder for them? So, on the night of 3 September I swallowed a bottle of sleeping pills and half a bottle of distilled spirits. By noon of the following day, however, I had regained consciousness and was lying in a bed at the Longfu Hospital.

In those days hospitals were free to refuse cases like mine – a lot of people died because of this policy. But for some reason the Longfu Hospital saved me. Several years later I got a look at my medical record and saw the words 'Rightist element attempted suicide to escape punishment for his crime'. It had of course been necessary for the hospital to write that, simply to cover themselves. They had, after all, aided a member of the Black Gang.

Not only was my attempt at suicide unsuccessful, it drew more criticism and struggle down on me. Although in my last will and testament, composed in red ink and left behind for my persecutors to read, I had protested my loyalty and enjoined my family to obey Chairman Mao and become genuine members of the new society, my words were criticised as lacking sincerity. And indeed, they were not wholly genuine – probably no more genuine than the Soviets about to be executed as counter-revolutionaries in the thirties who had wished a long life to Stalin. Up to that September night I'd never been able to understand how they could wish him well when he was wrongfully putting them to death. Now I realised, from my own experience, that since I was destined to die in any case, I might as well do something for Jieruo and the children, thinking that they'd be treated better if I appeared repentant.

At my criticism and struggle meetings they wanted me to confess my black thoughts all over again and explain why I had tried to use suicide to resist the revolutionaries' rightful authority over me. This time I told them everything. Since they wanted me to confess my black thoughts, I told them it really wasn't easy for an intellectual in New China to die a natural death. I told them I was thankful that people like the author Zheng Zhenduo and the opera singer Mei Lanfang had died before the Cultural Revolution – if they'd lived longer, they'd have been executed. This then was the logic behind my suicide: under such a regime it was better to die sooner rather than later. Death was preferable to life, for death put an end to suffering.

When I finished there was of course a stern denunciation. But my words had come too close to the truth; I had simply spoken what many of those present must have felt but dared not say. To my surprise, Jieruo and I were released and allowed to return to our home (in so far as it was still a home) when the struggle session was over.

Following the raid on our house, the two of us had been separated from each other. When we finally met again, I learned the story behind the attack on Jieruo. She told me that because her elder sister had married an American professor and had taken out US citizenship, the people in the red armbands had insisted that she and her mother were spies. When they'd raided our home, they'd found a radio in her mother's room. Though it had been assembled quite openly by her younger son, a technician who worked in the city of Datong, they had kicked and beaten her, charging that it was a transmitter and ordering her to confess her crime. That night, being a dutiful daughter, Jieruo had taken chicken soup to her mother at the place where she was being kept, behind a door plastered with denunciatory posters. That brought further disaster down on Jieruo. Come midnight the interrogators arrived to tell her that her mother, Wan Peilan, had hanged herself in her room. What Jieruo found most painful was the gloating on the faces of those thugs. They made her stand before the corpse of her seventy-year-old mother, which was not yet cold, and yell out over and over again: 'The death of Wan Peilan has relieved the world of another stinking scourge.' Now that the old lady had been driven to her death, responsibility for the crimes of espionage and having a transmitter fell upon Jieruo. When the men in armbands got tired, they called in a gang of students so that they could go home and get some sleep. Jieruo estimated that they were fourteen or fifteen years old at the most. They whipped her with the brass end of a leather belt and tore out patches of her hair. They chanted at her: 'You're getting off lightly! Others have had their eyeballs dug out.' Afterwards we learned from Red Guard publications that the school which these students attended had set up a 'water dungeon'; prisoners were kept half-immersed in a basement. Many of them died.

Next morning, Jieruo was chased around the city barefoot with black ink smeared over her face as an example to others. Then she was led under guard back to her unit.

People's temperaments are not immutable. In the last thirty-odd years, I've seen a marked change in Jieruo's disposition. Before 1957 she was shy, even meek. Once she was declared the wife of a worthless Rightist, though, she became more assertive and combative by the day. That's how she endured for the whole ten years of the Great Calamity.

When I contrasted my mother-in-law's treatment with my own, my plans for killing myself faded. Her children had all grown up but I had one in secondary school and two still in primary school. I must not die: my sense of family responsibility grew strong again.

One technique in the Cultural Revolution, less spectacular than criticism and struggle but even crueller, was being subject to anonymous accusations from far away. The former involved a noisy cracking of the whip; the latter felt more like having little pieces of your flesh cut off with a knife. Many of my friends took their struggle sessions and criticism and then went on almost as if nothing had happened. But after the insidious torture of being accused from afar they committed suicide.

Most of the information used for struggle and criticism came from 'background investigations' within your unit. With information transferred to your unit from somewhere else, however, you had no idea where it had come from. And here was something sad about intellectuals: just like the tigers of the Three Antis campaign, intellectuals down on their luck were eager to drag down anyone they could. Therefore while someone out in Gansu was turning in documents saying you were a class traitor, someone else down in Hainan Island might be testifying that you'd gone over to the foreign enemy. All this information would be forwarded to the revolutionary committee of the unit that housed and fed you. Sometimes it was your own revolutionary committee that would order you to confess; sometimes the revolutionary committee of the unit that had obtained the incriminating evidence would send someone to interrogate you. The procedure was fairly uniform. They would never tell you who your accuser was, nor would they so much as hint at what you were accused of. They simply pounded the table and shouted 'Confess!' This happened to my old friend Fan Changjiang, founder of the *Liberation Daily*, after he'd already been cleared and sent back to work. He drowned himself in a well.

I was lucky in this regard. I avoided having to frame anybody and nobody framed me. My one encounter with 'accusations from afar' in fact ended comically, and not because I was a brilliant talker, but because the men sent to interrogate me were so stupid.

One day when I was in the boiler-room stoking coal, I was suddenly called out to meet them. The moment I walked into the room, two young fellows whose combined age must have been less than forty pounded on the table and ordered me to confess. What had I said to my ex-wife Wang Shucang in 1938, when I'd refused to throw in my lot with the Party at Yan'an? I kept trying to remember, but was unable to. I had no way of even guessing what I'd said to her.

Finally they showed their hand (most people in their situation did not; this was one indication of their inexperience). They said that I'd once told Wang Shucang, 'I'm unwilling to accept the leadership of Zhou Yang, so I'm not going to Yan'an.' At this I couldn't help smiling. I asked them if they had any idea just what kind of person Zhou Yang was. (That took them aback.) 'Someone must have forgotten to fill you in – he was uncovered as the ringleader of the Black Gang in literature and the arts at the very start of the Cultural Revolution. If I refused to accept his leadership even then, that not only proves I must be outside the ranks of the Black Gang today, it proves I must have foreseen the course of the whole revolution!'

When the lads heard this, they clearly realised that they'd blown it. They waved me off back to my boiler room.

I had of course been faced with relatively *benevolent* blockheads. If their shame had turned to rage, they might easily have beaten me to a pulp instead. Every time I think of it, I'm grateful that I was only faced with two such charmingly naive young people.

At the beginning, the Great Cultural Revolution seemed a little like the throw of the dice in China's favourite traditional gambling game. An invisible hand shook them up and cast them out on the table. Then an upside-down bowl came down with a thud and covered them.

From June to August, the dice were under cover. No one knew who was to be in trouble this time, so Red Guards seized on the already-designated Five Black Elements: the landlords, rich peasants, counter-revolutionaries, bad elements and Rightists. A lot of innocent citizens came to grief out on the streets. Fortunately we still had our work unit.

In October and November, the bowl was slowly lifted. Mao wanted to get rid of his grey eminence Liu Shaoqi, who was then president of the People's Republic. There was clearly a power struggle on the highest level. Rightists were out-of-date; having long been in disrepute, they held no power: they were the dregs, garbage – anything people wanted to call them – but they could no longer convincingly be the main targets for attack.

Our unit's original leading group were named key members of the Black Line. This kept them extremely busy, being hauled off at every other moment for attack sessions big and small. We of the five black elements on the other hand were left idle. We sat all day in our offices (which were now cow sheds) with the Little Red Book on each of our tables. We'd leaf through it occasionally, then stare at the ceiling. If a bee or a ladybird chanced to fly in, we were united. A dozen pairs of eyes would follow it as it walked about on the ceiling or crashed against the windowpanes. Otherwise, we just sat there.

The important thing was that we could go home at night. Even if there was little left of home but the people in it, it was still a warm haven. Outside, human relationships had become so unreliable that those in the family were all the closer.

Our home at that time was a two-room shack hardly two metres deep, sharing a gable with another unit – a structure of the kind put up under the old society as the rent collector's shed. The eaves were so shallow that water came through our paper windows when it rained, soaking the whole floor. Cold winds blew in during winter and the sun turned the place into a furnace in summer. The original owner, who'd been driven off to the countryside, had left half a curtain over the window. Jieruo said, 'Heaven knows how long we'll have to put up with this, but it's not worth buying a reed awning. I can sew one myself.' Being used to working, she had to find things to keep her busy. Stitching together rags and old clothes salvaged from the looting of our old place, she hung the result under the eaves, like a tent in the desert. And I, using boards and asphalt roofing, built a lean-to kitchen outside our window. I'd never considered housework to be the special duty of women. After 1957 I'd told Jieruo on several occasions that I was willing to become a househusband. From 1966 to 1969, I kept my promise. The neighbourhood leaders had separated us from Third Elder Sister, so I made three years of family dinners in that kitchen myself. In those days we still had three thermos bottles. I hung signs on them: 'unboiled', 'boiled and cooled off' and 'still hot'. We used the boiled water for drinking, never to wash our feet. I felt very proud that I could perform these simple tasks so competently.

There were no books around to translate, but being accustomed to literary work, I was longing to get back to it. At the time all sorts of annotated editions of *The Poems of Mao Zedong* were in circulation. After making reference to all the earlier versions, I prepared a new definitive edition. Jieruo pressed into service a talent she'd had since childhood, of writing very tiny characters, to transcribe one copy after another. Our daughter, Lizi, copied out an edition herself, while the youngest, Tong, was our bookbinder. It was as if we'd opened a family publishing house.

Since August 1966, Jieruo had entered a cow shed too. Unlike me, she couldn't resign herself to staring blankly up at the ceiling. When she'd finished the awning she took the annotated Mao poems into the cow shed with her, to copy. And that was not all. One day, seized by a sudden urge, she took in my four-volume paperpack edition of *Selected Works of Mao Zedong*. With an eraser she rubbed out the notes I'd made in the margins in 1956, when I was temporarily released from work to attend an ideological study group. She wanted to make it like new for the use of Lizi, so she wouldn't need to buy a set. I'd written a lot in those margins, in closely-set characters, so by afternoon she'd only tidied up the first volume. But she'd already come to the attention of one of her companions in the cow shed and they turned in a report on her. The Revolutionary Committee then ordered Jieruo to turn in all the four volumes of Chairman Mao's works, with her hand-copied version of the poems. She was given until morning of the next day to hand over all the hand-copied books she and the family had ever made.

Lizi, who with her little brother Tong had been a 'Five-Good' student and a Young Pioneer troop leader, had already given away the book she'd copied out to her form teacher. Jieruo went with her to school that very night, to ask the teacher for its return. Despite her ten years of service, the teacher herself had been falsely accused as a 'rich peasant who managed to slip through the net'. Just then she was being held incommunicado for investigation.

At that time however, the revolutionary committee in command still occasionally listened to reason. Despite repeated investigations by a special small group, no problems were found with the hand-copied book of annotated Mao poems and the volumes of Mao's selected works; everything was finally returned to us.

In spite of this alarm, our family still refused to remain idle. Lizi and little Tong made a lantern slide show and projected it in the courtyard after dark. Naturally all the slides presented revolutionary propaganda, such as the exploits of the hero Lei Feng. I taught them to draw maps of the world and a time-chart showing events from both Chinese and Western history. I wanted them to know that China was part of a wider world, and that the Cultural Revolution was only a moment in history. It was also a means of comforting myself.

Besides intellectual encouragement, the children needed physical exercise. It seemed wrong to shut them up in our little apartment all Sunday long. We didn't dare to enter the parks in those days, so I took little Tong on my bike to a flooded quarry out behind the Agricultural Exhibition Hall to swim. We would take along food and stay all day.

One Sunday we were observed returning home by a member of my unit's revolutionary committee who used to belong to the kitchen staff. The next day I was called into the committee's office. The revolutionary committee had a very civilised way of punishing Black Gang elements in those days. In an early-morning ritual, offenders stood in ranks and pleaded for forgiveness. Then they were slapped twice in the face, loud enough for everyone to hear, but there was no beating or kicking. Also just a few were punished to warn everybody. Two in my group had already received this punishment and I guessed it was now my turn. But the comrade in charge of the cow shed (who had been an art publications editor) was surprisingly reasonable. I explained that I had gone to the pool not out of bourgeois self-indulgence, but for the sake of my child, and that he was innocent. After hearing this, the comrade nodded and let me go.

One day I went across the street from the publishing house to have my shoes repaired. Three cobblers sat there in a row, each with a big Mao badge pinned on his breast. One of the men stared at me. Suddenly he said 'Aren't you Lezi (Happy Boy)?' I was struck dumb. How could he know my childhood nickname? Warily I pretended not to have heard. But he continued to stare at me, 'Don't you recognise me? I'm Er Tuzi (Second Baldy)!'

Only then did I look at him properly. He was very familiar after all. His name was An – he was the son of one of my aunts. Wondering how he could still recognise me after fifty years, I tried to recall some events from our past. Once I'd gone with him to steal some fruit from a neighbour's tree and the dog that was set on us took a bite out of his pants. Another time, our house 'couldn't lift the cover of its wok' (had no food in the larder), so his mother, my aunt, had come over with her little son to bring us a bowl of cornmeal.

My cousin arranged to meet me at six o'clock that evening in front of a little restaurant on a street west of the Dongzhi Gate. I arrived right on time.

While stitching his shoes he wore very old clothing, but now he'd put on a smart new uniform in dark blue. Since at the time I was often under surveillance and feared getting into trouble with the revolutionary masses from the publishing house, I'd got into the habit of slinking around. He on the other hand thrust out his chest and boldly led me upstairs, where he selected a secluded corner table.

He asked me what I wanted to eat. I said I'd come mainly just to talk about old times. With a flourish he ordered us several dishes and a pot of wine. He told me that because many years ago he'd mended shoes gratis for the dependants of army martyrs, he'd recently been chosen as a living example of Chairman Mao's works in action for the Eastern District. He was often asked to lecture.

When he asked about me, I gave a big sigh and told him, 'If I'd kept on weaving rugs as I did in the beginning, instead of becoming a Stinking Ninth Type (an intellectual), maybe I wouldn't have fallen so low.' He shook his head and said earnestly, 'Brother, the book learning you've stored up in your head will have its use again.'

I thanked him for his encouraging words, but at the time I really didn't believe him.

As the Cultural Revolution wore on, the supreme leader, Mao Zedong, realised that it was a mistake to designate the entire Black Gang, together with all their children, as enemies. Thereupon the sons and daughters of the Black Gang acquired a new classification, 'the educatables'. Although they were junior, they were treated better than their Black Gang parents.

In the autumn of 1967 then, a Red Guard suddenly appeared at our house. We were scared half to death, but it turned out to be Tianji, the nephew of one of Jieruo's old schoolmates.

Ever since our eldest had been sent to the Great South West to 'exchange revolutionary experiences' and had written back that he wanted to make revolution among the Tibetan people, our two littles ones often made a fuss about wanting to go too. They'd suffered a lot emotionally after we were driven out of our house. There were still people who reviled them and kept threatening them with more raids on their new home. So when Tianji arrived the two children thought they saw a chance of escaping their cage. Little Lizi kept yelling about how she wanted to join a military unit on the frontier and little Tong went on about becoming a hunter in the Changbaishan, the Long White Mountains near the Korean frontier. To distract them, Jieruo asked Tianji if he could take them to Qingpu for a bit of fun. She never dreamed he would agree. Next day, off went our two children, in a great state of excitement. There was nothing I could do to stop them.

They had no idea how dangerous the trip would be. Afterwards I learned that they got off the bus in Qingpu, near Shanghai, just in time to witness an armed clash between two revolutionary factions. Five people were killed before their eyes. It was the children's first brush with live firearms, and the first time they saw dead bodies. On the way back they encountered a similar battle in Xuzhou, on the border between Jiangsu and Shandong. All this must have left a deep imprint on their minds.

When the papers began to write enthusiastically about the Liu He (Willow River, a village in Heilongjiang) May Seventh Cadre School (where cadres were sent to study Mao's thought and do manual labour) I had a premonition that things were on the move again: that we weren't even going to be able to keep our home with the ragged curtains.

Sure enough, we had to be sent away again. The list of names announced now included all intellectuals, not just the Five Black Elements, so this time, Jieruo and I wouldn't be separated. That was cause for rejoicing. But we'd have to leave our children again. This time there was no grandma, so we would have to leave them with their Third Aunt, Changwei.

Before I left, I took little Tong on a bicycle trip to Xiangshan, the Fragrant Hills Park. Along the way, we recited the Three Venerable Articles, the most heavily publicised of Mao Zedong's writings. We stopped halfway up the hill. I embraced the child I was so reluctant to part with and silently looked off into the distant smog. Beneath it lay the city of Peking.

'Papa, will we have a home again sometime?' he suddenly asked me.

'We will,' I said, hugging him tight, 'and it will be a good one, one we won't have to move out of ever again.'

But I didn't believe in the optimism I was offering my child, and he didn't ask me again. Perhaps he knew that what I'd said was just wishful thinking.

In principle it's a good thing for intellectuals to experience productive manual labour and share living conditions with the broad masses of workers and peasants. Everybody can support that. Unfortunately in those days it was regarded as punishment.

The sending down of the Rightists in 1958 was bad enough, but it was followed by the May Seventh cadre schools of September 1969, when the scope of the coercion was broadened with the intention of driving virtually every single intellectual out of the superstructure, thus preserving in perpetuity the power of the ruling gang. Only after the scandal about Mao's successor Lin Biao and his death in a 1971 plane crash as he fled the country did we learn that the fate of intellectuals had been sealed in 1969 with a General Order No. 1 aimed at rusticating them all forever.

When I got on the train in Peking, I wasn't looking that far ahead. I simply had misgivings about our being turned over by the Workers' Mao Zedong Thought Propaganda Teams to the custody of the People's Liberation Army Mao Zedong Thought Propaganda Teams. And rightly so: not long after I arrived at our 'school' in Xianning, Hubei, the PLA team worked on all of us 'May Seventh Warriors' one at a time, trying to persuade us to move down all our family members to live with us. It was a bad sign. Jieruo naturally consented. She returned to Peking to retrieve our two children.

Still, after being shut up in Peking for eight years and surviving so many hardships, it was emotionally liberating to look out upon the rich red soil of south-eastern Hubei – upon its gracefully undulating hills, the distant mountains and rivers, the villages that seemed straight out of landscape paintings.

We were billeted in a village situated on the road from the county town of Xianning: because all the villagers were named Hu, the village was called Guoluhu, or Hu's-By-the-Highway. All of us were quartered in peasant homes. Fierce slogans were plastered on the village walls, but the village itself was peaceful enough save for the clucking of chickens and barking of dogs.

Since the cadre schools were run by the army, everything was arranged according to military principles. Our unit was a company of a brigade; it was divided into platoons and squads. The roster of unit leaders at each level had long before been drawn up by the Workers' Mao Thought Propaganda Team, to be activated once we arrived. Jieruo and I were in the same company and platoon but not the same squad. During the first year and a half, males and females lived apart.

I shared a room with two other men. One had a fairly spotless record. He'd contrived to dodge trouble so well that he'd been recognised as a 'veteran revolutionary pace-setter'. The other, less nimble, had ended up accused of joining a spy network. From the start I found the pace-setter to be very arrogant. Later I realised that he was furious about his rooming arrangements. After all, our present statuses were miles apart. No wonder he was outraged at having to live with us.

In the evening, the head of the house asked his daughters to bring in steaming hot water so we could all wash our feet. Because of the differences in dialect, we couldn't always understand what the other was saying, but the honest warmth behind it was very similar to that in eastern Hebei. Living with country folk again made me very happy.

Soon I discovered that this village really was 'poor and blank' [a quote from Mao: China's people were poor and therefore ready for revolution, and blank, like a white sheet of paper on which any beautiful character could be written]. The villagers worked hard at their farming all the year round, but when workpoints were assigned to them after the autumn harvest, each household got hardly any spending money at all, just its grain ration. There was no electricity. The youngest children tended water buffaloes, leading them with a hemp rope. I don't remember seeing any of them carry the bookbag of a student but they were intensely interested in everything I'd brought from Peking. The whole family, young and old, gathered round for a look at my transistor radio. They were curious – and envious.

It was the custom in the village not to bury a person immediately after death. The villagers kept watch over the body in an open coffin all night long. The night of the third day after our arrival, the head of the house said that his grandfather's brother had died; he asked if he could take along my radio as a diversion for the relatives keeping vigil beside the coffin. Naturally I said yes. People were crowded into a dark room as big as an ancestral hall. I turned on the radio and placed it next to the open coffin. The country folk keeping vigil smoked as they listened to it, very happy, as if it was a consolation to the spirit of the deceased as well as to them.

At first I thought that living with peasants like this was part of an official plan, but soon I learned that the arrangement was only temporary. Yet the first order that came down to us was to engage in 'basic construction' – that is, build your own housing. We were preparing for a long stay.

Our worksite was about two miles from Hu's-By-the-Highway, on a hill that bordered a lake. After we had finished building the houses, we were to build dykes and reclaim lake bottom land for agriculture.

Bricks and tiles were our stock in trade. We marched out to the worksite first thing after breakfast. Dykes did not yet surround the lake, so the bricks could be transported to the lake down a waterway. There they were transferred to a big cart and hauled off to the worksite where they were unloaded with tongs, four bricks at a time. We then formed a chain and passed them from one person to the next. Those who were young and strong kept up easily, but we older workers were often left panting and gasping. Work tasks were usually assigned according to political criteria: uncapped Rightists like me naturally had to work harder than the revolutionary masses. When the boat bringing in bricks, tiles and lumber didn't turn up until midnight, the company captain would arrive outside our door and call off names for a second workshift. Those he summoned had to crawl out of bed and go to work even if they were sick or already asleep. To have to do a second shift after a full day of labour was very hard. Once the squad leader assigned me to dredge up mud from the river, work that only the strongest were up to. Jieruo got me out of it on the grounds that I hadn't brought my paddy field boots, but afterwards she was criticised for it.

One day I was sent to the warehouse at brigade headquarters to get asphalt roofing. I saw at a glance that the person in charge of the warehouse was the editor of a major foreign-language dictionary. He had cancer and his right leg had been amputated, but he had to carry on, limping along with his keys. I was stunned to see him. Whenever I felt that my burden was too heavy I thought about him.

In building the houses we started at the north and worked southwards. Economies were called for and building costs per square metre dropped lower and lower as we went. At first we built entirely of brick. Then we changed to half brick and half adobe. In the end our houses were made entirely of adobe. People moved into the houses as we built them. Jieruo and I were given a room in the southernmost row of adobe houses only after the old, the weak, the sick and the crippled – some of whom were dying – had been moved out of them and relocated in another area. Tong moved in with us at this time. The three of us were reunited, so we had something of a home once more.

People's feelings about the sun change with the season. They like it in the cold of winter and fear it during the heat of summer. I've never heard of anyone fearing the moon, though. That the full moon symbolises family unity indicates humankind's deep love of the moon. But while I was at Xianning, I feared the moon above all, particularly the full moon. It was then that the Army Propaganda Team might suddenly blow a whistle in the middle of the night, signalling 'marching and endurance training', a special military drill used in the ranks to promote combat readiness. When we warriors lying abed in our sleeping bags heard this whistle, we had to be out on the parade ground in full battle equipment within minutes. Frequently I was the last one to get there. I tried to tie my shoelaces as we were drilled. As a result, we who were taking the May Seventh Road hoped it would always be dark at night. When the moon was full, we got nervous – we would sleep with our clothes on and prick up our ears in our dreams, listening for the whistle.

The development of our two children began to diverge after we were sent away. Our son, being still in primary school, boarded in the Xianning county town, where he continued his schooling and caught a truck ride back to the village to spend the weekend with us. But his sister, because she was nine months older and had already enrolled in a secondary school in Peking, was enlisted in the great army of labour the very day after she got off the train.

Lizi was intellectually naive, and stubborn in her disposition. After seeing her house raided and her father attacked, she promised herself that she would 'resolutely grasp politics'. She tried to emulate Lei Feng and Wang Jie, heroes who had ignored all dangers on behalf of the revolution. She competed to be assigned the hardest work in the company. When it was time for the company to lay cement power poles in the middle of the lake, this fourteen-year-old girl was to be found alongside us May Seventh Warriors, working in the freezing water. After work, while her companions went home to bathe and rest, she would help out in the household of a man whose nickname was the 'Saint'. Finding such a dedicated maidservant must have been difficult, even for a saint. He put up a poster lauding her as a 'living Lei Feng'.

The Saint was well versed in our National Learning, having read some prose and poetry in his younger days. His favourites were a few stanzas of doggerel eulogising the backyard steel furnaces and communal messhalls of the Great Leap Forward. He was also famous throughout our company for his recitations from memory of the Three Venerable Articles. He was tall, and his voice was strong and clear as he recited Mao's works melodiously and expressively, in a manner full of proletarian sincerity. The Saint was not only good with words, he was clever with his hands and particularly skilled at repairing things. He'd provided himself with a tool kit well before he was sent away. Just after his arrival in Xianning, he heard that the head of the Army Propaganda Team had a broken watch and immediately took charge of the situation. He fixed the watch by lamplight that very night and took it over to company headquarters in person. Thereafter, while the rest of us waded barefoot through the marshes in wind and rain, head-quarters assigned him a little thatched shack next to the dormitories so that he could devote himself full-time to repairs. If something belonging to the honoured personages of the company broke, he mended it on the spot. But how quickly he managed with things sent over by the regular May Seventh Warriors depended on his mood.

The moment she heard the Saint intoning the Three Venerable Articles, our little Lizi was ready to throw herself down at his feet in adoration. She volunteered to move in with the Saint's daughters and do their washing and scrubbing for them. Several women felt aggrieved and one woman Party member from the old leading group sought out Jieruo and said: 'Those girls are really the limit. I just saw your daughter come back from washing their clothes at the pond and immediately start polishing their shoes. After they finished supper they didn't go to help her, or even invite her to the table. They just sent her back to eat at home and had a good laugh about it when she was gone.'

But the Saint told Lizi that Lei Feng was to be emulated for his endurance and thoroughness and she ought not to let spiteful rumours be an excuse for slacking off. When our little nun of a daughter heard this, her services became even more compre-hensive.

Our son, Tong, on the other hand, didn't think he had anything much to atone for, just because his parents had been struggled against in the Cultural Revolution. A long essay he wrote about Chinese folk songs was praised by the teacher in his Chinese class, and he began to study English with me. He never did become a hunter in the Long White Mountains, but he did become a local expert at catching snakes. In his three years with us he caught more than two hundred of them. Once his finger was bitten by a cobra and he had to go off to the clinic for medical treatment. Some nights he brought home bullfrogs. That gave the three of us a special treat for dinner.

Our houses, as I've noted, were on top of a hill, so getting drinking water was a problem. The lake was right at the foot of the hill, so we pumped up our drinking water from there. We needed a diesel engine operator for the pump, and when we got one he needed an assistant. He tried out several but was dissatisfied with them all, and, in spite of my clumsiness, picked me. So I was lifted out of the squad and given probably the cushiest job on the farm.

Before, when the company captain blew his whistle after breakfast, I'd had to shoulder my farm implements and be marched out to the fields, all the while singing choruses of Mao slogans like 'Fear neither hardship nor death'. Now I just stood outside the shed where the diesel engine was housed and watched the brigade go by. There was nothing I could do to improve the quality of the water, though. At any given time several dozen people might be bathing in the lake and still more head of water buffalo. But when you found a piece of cow dung in your glass of water, it was taken not so much as a sign that better purification was needed, as an opportunity to square your shoulders and shout revolutionary slogans.

Soon after the brigade passed by, the captain would sometimes take his net down to the lake and go fishing. This fellow, who'd been promoted on the basis of his class background and his skill at roughing people up (he'd been our porter in the old days), loved to fish more than anything – though he also took a woman helper with him, for good measure. The company treasurer had put out a good bit of money to buy his net. When the fish were biting, that improved his diet. Even when they weren't, he didn't return entirely unfulfilled.

One day, just as he was spreading out his net, a hundred or more angry peasants appeared round the side of the hill. Rights to fish in the lake had been newly assigned to our commune, but neighbouring villagers refused to accept that. With the head of their fishermen in the lead and ancient custom on their side, they had come over to seize some fish. When our company captain saw them he decided for once not to interfere with their historic rights: he pulled up his net and returned to camp.

As the reclamation of fields went ahead, conflicts between us and the local peasants grew sharper daily. Apart from their grain, the peasants' only income came from the lake, which yielded fish and shellfish, lotus seeds and roots. The cadres were draining the lake, planting sorghum in the high spots and creating wet fields in the low places. In retaliation our corn would sometimes be stolen by the cartload late at night, or we might wake to find a pig missing from the sties.

At this time the cadre school of the Party Central Committee General Office, then in Jiangxi, raised the banner of the Four Self-Sufficiencies (in grain, oils, meat and vegetables). It also called for cadre schools to earn back what had been spent on them in that year and become completely self-sufficient in operating expenses and wages the next year. Originally the theory had been that we were sent to the country so that we could be tempered through labour. Now they were forcing us to earn our living from the soil. Naturally our company was not about to lag behind the others, but in answering the challenge it increased our work-load until life became unbearable.

I was almost sixty when I was sent down, and yet until the pumping-engine job I was always assigned young man's work. Now the engine job was taken away from me, of course, and I was back to carrying two full buckets of manure all by myself, while men younger than I carried only half a bucket. I was always called on when people were needed for extra work on rainy days and holidays.

One week our company was put to a rush job, harvesting rice and planting the next crop at the same time. We got up at dawn on the first day, went down to the lake and laboured thereafter, day and night. No allowances were made for strength or age. My work was considered light: I dragged the rice straw spewed out by the harvester over to the stacks. At night when the two squads changed shifts, at the blast of a whistle, I had one hour to stretch out on the stacks and take a breather. When the whistle blew a second time, I had to get up and start hauling again. During the morning of the third day, I and two others who were also over sixty finally collapsed. The leader of the brigade passed us without so much as a glance. It was a kindhearted woman comrade from another unit who helped me to my feet and all the way back to the camp.

A doctor at the Wuhan Hospital listened to my heartbeat and looked at my ECG. Then he shook his head, frowned, and wrote three words in my medical record: coronary heart disease.

After that, I was assigned to night duty only. Someone in the company had just died, but Jieruo said that I must go on living no matter what, and although she was sent to the fields during the day, she helped me with my work at night.

At about this time Guo Xiaochuan, a poet who'd been with Mao Zedong at Yan'an, tried to intercede for us all on the basis of his status as a long-time supporter of the revolution. That enraged the leadership of the Army Propaganda Team. Guo was accused of withdrawing his labour, which was heresy and high treason. They were after his blood. Guo had just written a poem to commemorate May Day that contained the line 'I may be in Xianning, but my heart is in Peking'. To us it was clear that he was saying how much he missed the Party Central. But the Army Propaganda Team took this as evidence that he was unwilling to do manual labour. Later on, Peking actually summoned him back to the capital, but his transfer was held up at the local level and this admirable man in fact was never allowed to return to Peking. Taking his grievance to bed with him, he drowned his sorrows in drink. Then he put an end to it all by setting fire to his bed roll. As Tolstoy said, all people are born in pretty much the same way, but they have many different ways of dying. How I wish that a tombstone might be erected for him some day by the banks of that lake. It would commemorate a compassionate Communist and an era that must not be forgotten.

The original intent of the May Seventh cadre schools seems to have been to let us grow old and die there. So, besides houses, we built granaries, schools and stores. But in June 1971, a group was recalled to Peking, highly qualified men who had relatively clean backgrounds. Local government needed skilled administrators too, so provincial headquarters at Wuhan also took several people. By the end of 1972 the majority had been sent back to their professions. That created an anxious state of mind among those of us left behind. The worst thing in the world is not being able to control your own fate. People secretly asked themselves, 'Now that those they wanted to recall have all been transferred, what will they do with the rest of us?'

Our original moronic company captain was of course called back; the new captain was a woman author, Wei Junyi. She was upright in character, led a rough and frugal life, and was a stickler for the rules. She'd come from Yan'an and should have been one of the spotless ones. However, she'd committed a fatal error while running a literary journal – she appreciated talent, and she'd made much of a talented Rightist. She knew she was still stuck with us dregs of the old society.

One day she summoned me to company headquarters for a talk. She said that the cadre school general headquarters had notified her that all workers of sixty years and over could apply for official state retirement. She wanted me to think it over. From her manner of speaking, I gathered that there was room for discussion. That night I wrote her a long letter, not just about my own personal problems. I said that the time of retirement ought to be determined not just on the basis of age, but according to one's line of work. For manual labour, such as mining, it was reasonable to be asked to retire when one reached a certain age because usually one was no longer equal to the task. But many of those in literature and the arts had just reached their prime in their sixties. I cited the example of several foreign authors and composers. I have no idea why I wrote such a letter – I simply didn't feel ready to be pensioned off. Small wonder that her comment the next day was that I'd written a treatise on retirement.

I filled out the forms for Peking anyway and I asked someone to take a quick photograph of me in front of the pig sty. As to where I'd live in Peking and what I'd do once I was retired, all that was unknown. So, of course, was the question of how and when I'd be reunited with Jieruo. But we'd become accustomed to living one day at a time ever since we became second-class citizens in 1957.

Not long afterwards, company headquarters summoned me for another talk. A letter had arrived from the Peking Civil Administration Bureau saying that investigation had confirmed that I had no housing of any kind in Peking. Therefore they were turning down my application to retire to Peking.

What had happened was that after my whole family had been sent down to Xianning, Third Elder Sister Changwei had taken on the little east-wing apartment that we had lived in. In the summer of 1972, Jieruo had sent Tong back to Peking to study. She had also exchanged the tiny east-wing apartment for a room in a little gatehouse south of Northern New Bridge that would allow the children to enroll in a relatively good high school nearby. By then the system of entering school by examination had long been abolished and one attended high school according to one's district.

At the time Tiezhu, our eldest, was away in Jiangxi province, working and living in a commune production team. Our daughter, Lizi, had been assigned back to Peking to be a trolley conductor and lived in the trolley company's dormitory. The little gatehouse was just big enough for Tong and his Third Aunt. There was no space for me to put up there.

But my heart had flown back to Peking ever since I filled out the forms. I wanted to return even if there was no space for me. So in February 1973, on the pretext of visiting my children, I asked for leave and returned to Peking for the first time in three-and- a-half long years. I'd grown up there, but now that I was in my old age, apparently the ancient city didn't even have a bed for me. During the day I hung around in the room by the gateway, spending the nights in the dormitory of my brother-in-law Wen Xuepu. To get there I had to brave the usual gale-force winter winds, pedalling my way from the north of the city to its south-western corner.

Having applied for retirement – even if I didn't really want it – I wanted to remain in Peking. But I couldn't borrow space from my brother-in-law indefinitely. And what about Jieruo? Someone had told her that whenever there were discussions about transferring people back to the city her name was always suggested, but then my name came up also, so the suggestion was tabled. Jieruo herself had committed no crimes that people could drag her down by. But she had married me.

Just then a well-meaning old friend disclosed to me a horrifying piece of information: because of my Rightist past, I was only qualified to retire to some distant province. This alarmed even the unflappable Jieruo. The poor woman was still in Xianning and hated the thought that she might never be able to return to Peking. In order not to keep on dragging down my whole family, I immediately sent a report to my superiors:

> Though I was born and raised in Peking, and though I contracted heart disease at cadre school from rush-harvesting and rush-planting, if only Wen Jieruo can be transferred from her cadre school back to Peking, I am willing to retire to any remote mountain district anywhere, and to stay there alone to the end of my days. So sworn by me today; I will not go back on my word.

Regardless of whether or not I myself could stay in Peking, I decided, I must quickly make a nest for Jieruo and the children. One day my old friend Weng Dujian found a teaching position for me at a foreign languages institute. He said the institute would give me a place to live. This of course seemed like the answer to all my problems. When Weng informed the president of the institute of my academic record, the latter gave the go-ahead. I was almost hired when, as a matter of form, I was asked to write a *curriculum vitae*. In it I mentioned that I had once worked on the same Shanghai faculty as a professor who now taught at the languages institute I was applying for. The next day the school changed its mind. The president who had so wholeheartedly welcomed me backed out of the deal and that was the end of that. I made up my mind to go to the housing bureau responsible for deciding all matters of residence.

The moment it was light the next day, I climbed out of bed and rode over on my bicycle. I had just remembered a Central Committee directive on post-Cultural Revolution normalisation of policy that had been transmitted to the cadre school a few weeks earlier. It said that all residences forcibly occupied during the Cultural Revolution would be returned to their original owners. Moreover, even before I'd returned, the street committee had summoned my children and restored to them some of our confiscated possessions.

Confident that I had justice on my side I boldly strode in through the main entrance of the housing bureau. On the screen wall just beyond the gate were painted three words, in huge red characters: 'Serve the People'. The office was locked. An old man was sweeping out the courtyard. I made an enquiry and he pointed to a notice on the door: 'It tells you everything there. They see people only on Tuesdays and Fridays. Today is Wednesday. Come again the day after tomorrow.'

The old fellow was kind enough. He also advised me, 'Since they're open only two days a week, they're always busy. Be sure to get here early!' I thanked him.

With great difficulty I endured until Friday. I raced over in the haze of early morning light. The main gate of the housing bureau wasn't yet open, but several people were already squatting there and a dozen more were on their way. The moment the door opened we all struggled to be the first inside, as if being first in line might increase our chances.

The reception room was not large. Benches lined the walls. At the end was a little writing desk where the housing bureau representatives evidently sat. The benches had long been occupied by the swiftest. I had to lean against the wall.

A gaunt, middle-aged official pushed open the door and walked in. Once he was behind his little desk, people with anxiously smiling faces moved one by one into the chair facing him and told their hard-luck stories.

'We've got six people in three generations all crowded into one room, including my adult son and daughter. It's really very difficult!'

'Don't the regulations say you qualify as a hardship case if you have less than 2.5 square metres per person? Well, we don't even have two per person!'

'My son is well over thirty and still a bachelor. Won't you do a good deed – give him a room, even half a room?'

Everyone had a tale of woe. The housing bureau person merely spread his hands in gestures of helplessness: 'Even if you have permission for a house I still can't help you. I don't have one square metre to my name, what do you expect me to do? Would you like to trade jobs with me?'

I forced myself to last it out, moving myself sideways along the bench one buttock at a time. The more I heard from those ahead of me, the more depressed I became.

When he came to me, I raised the matter of the Central directive that might return to us the six-room apartment my family had bought with the fruits of its labour.

After listening to me, the housing official laughed and pointed to someone just leaving. 'Why not ask him about it? He had a thirty-six room house confiscated that had been handed down from his ancestors and he's in the same boat. You can try, but don't get your hopes up.'

'Don't get your hopes up' was familiar advice. In this case, other people had owned thirty-six rooms and I only had six, so naturally I had few grounds for optimism.

Every Tuesday and Friday I showed up punctually at the housing bureau, like a Buddhist making his incense devotions to the tutelary god. The seat of my pants was wearing thin from working my way down the benches and I hadn't seen even a trace of a house.

But Heaven never seals off all the exits. One day I ran into a familiar face outside the housing bureau. We stared at each other and simultaneously halted. Seven years earlier, when I was replacing doors and windows in my previous house, he'd come over – in those days he was in charge of repair work for the housing bureau. A young man fond of literature, he'd borrowed books from me and submitted an article that I'd helped him to revise to a major newspaper. They actually printed it. Now he was deputy head of the bureau.

I'd met my saviour. I told him my sad story. He said that the Central Committee directive was entirely authentic; but equally authentic was the fact that, even though his bureau was in charge of housing, they didn't have a single room to give out. He asked me if I had any title. I tensed up and said, in a whisper, 'My Rightist hat was removed in 1964'. He laughed and shook his head. 'What I meant was it would help if you were honorary chairman of or consultant to some organisation.' Now it was my turn to laugh. So that was why people struggled so hard to get those titles. A directive from the Central Committee of the Communist Party wasn't enough; it was still crucial to wear some kind of laurels.

The deputy head knew the state of things within his own sphere of authority like the back of his hand. No sooner had I told him the name of my alley and my house number than he said, 'There's an arched entrance in the wall there, isn't there?' 'Yes,' I replied. All smiles, he said, 'You can always get seven or eight square metres out of an archway. Would that satisfy you?' I told him I'd take it even if it were smaller. But there were several dozen other people in the compound, who went through that archway all day long. How could I pitch my bed there? He'd already thought out his plan: 'We begin construction the day after tomorrow,' he said, warning me to keep it secret at all costs.

I told Tong and Third Aunt this news anyway, on the quiet. After supper, just as I was walking my bike out through the compound gate, an old friend from the fifties came calling. He was now living in Hepingli, and was one of the few friends who had come to visit me during the months since my return to Peking. Unwilling to come in, he said, 'Let's speak together as we walk.'

He told me quietly that a particular organisation related to ours had already issued a transfer order: Jieruo would soon be back in Peking. He said a good friend had told him and that the news was completely reliable.

Of course I was grateful to him for making the special trip just to tell me this, but I still found it hard to believe. A proverb says that blessings never come in pairs whereas disasters never come alone. Could two such wonderful things as a room of my own and reunion with my wife come to me at the same time?

Two days later it was Thursday, the day when people in the housing bureau donated their time to manual labour. The deputy head arrived early in the morning with an aide. Upon entering the courtyard, without waiting to hear any objection, he lifted his pickaxe and hacked a hole in the outer wall beside the entrance gate. The courtyard residents were dumbfounded; the original owner came out of his north-wing rooms to ask the man what the hell he was doing. The deputy bureau chief answered him simply and directly: 'Property rights cannot be exercised by the original owner until we return them to him.' In other words, the bureau could tear down and reconstruct houses when and where it pleased.

At this point, a load of broken bricks, a door, windows and timber was delivered. The deputy chief asked me to be his helper, to stand in the middle of the street mixing concrete and passing him bricks. Not two hours later, a new archway had been built by the side of the old one. Next they bricked up the old entrance that fronted on the street and built windows and an individual doorway in a wall across the opening on the courtyard side. It was now a 'house'.

Just as the construction work was finished and Tong and I were sweeping up, Jieruo suddenly appeared carrying her bags. Knowing that I would be tired from rushing about every day trying to fix up our home, she hadn't told me what day she was returning to Peking, so that I wouldn't go to the station to meet her.

Later I learned that the friend of mine had been right; another unit in Peking had formally requested that Jieruo be transferred into it. Otherwise she might well have stayed at the cadre school forever.

Nothing is perfect though. Beneath our window was a sewage ditch into which flowed the urine of at least fifty people. In the summer we didn't dare open our window the slightest crack, but even so our little room often stank horribly. All our entreaties that the residents of the courtyard dig a proper sewer came to nothing. This was understandable, for in blocking up their entranceway we had incurred the wrath of everybody – including, notably, a carpenter and a bricklayer, members of the working class. Now and then a household would deliberately fling pails of faeces our way.

How much of my time and energy during those next five years was spent in re-establishing that home! Often I rushed about for a whole day, bowing and scraping and all in vain. Returning to my room I'd lie down on the bed, stare dumbly at the ceiling and watch the paint peel off the rafters.

Still, during those five years I also met several warmhearted friends who helped me think up new ideas, even helped me run around looking for a place to live. Sometimes they were in difficult straits themselves, yet they still found time for my problems.

At least, now that we had this hole-in-the-wall, Tong wasn't crowded into the one little room with his aunt any more. We stacked two steel beds up and made a bunk bed. Tong was in the upper berth; I nestled below. Jieruo 'let her office be her home': she worked there during the day and at night she made a bed for herself by placing eight chairs in a row. She came home to our gatehouse only to eat lunch with us on Sunday. That's how we lived from 1973 to 1978.

After Jieruo was transferred back to the publishing house in Peking, I was given a project myself. My May Seventh cadre school disbanded and I was allowed to remain in Peking to take part in a project to translate Herman Wouk's *The Winds of War*. The cadre school kept writing letters urging me to return to them, but I finally wrote a long letter back and to my surprise it was effective. The next year the language school disbanded and I was put into a translating group together with some other foreign language cadres. Our projects were determined by various different publishing houses. The emphasis was on contemporary Western military and political works, not the Shakespeare, Milton and Fielding to which we were so devoted. We translated works like the *History of the United States Navy*, Arthur Schlesinger's *A Thousand Days, John F Kennedy in the White House*, the memoirs of Harold Macmillan and William Manchester's *The Glory and the Dream*. Once, when Chairman Mao sent word that he wanted to read a book on

Napoleon, we got through it in a matter of days by translating round the clock.

Our little gatehouse could only accommodate a little two-drawer desk of the sort used by school children. As I sometimes invited my old companions in distress to my home—one at a time—I invented a makeshift way of entertaining them. I suspended a ratty old cane chair from the ceiling with a rope, to be lowered whenever a guest came in. Thus was filled in the very last space in our little sardine tin. If my boy came home, he would be asked to hang around out in the street for a while.

1976 was the most unforgettable year of all. It marked the passing of Premier Zhou Enlai. Everyone seemed to feel that his death was a personal loss. I myself particularly remembered a ceremonial occasion at the Purple Light Pavilion in Zhongnanhai in July 1957. At that time I'd already been criticised in the papers to the point where I no longer dared to lift my head, yet he singled me out from among the hundred literary guests present and stated his view that although I had made mistakes in my writing, I was not to be branded a Rightist. He was expressing no particular fondness for me, he simply felt that it was better that people be part of the revolution rather than excluded from it. However, even though he stated his position openly and in front of so many people, he was unable to reverse the general trend. It had already been decided by an authority more powerful than he.

Few people guessed that mourning the premier's death in Tian'anmen Square (the Gate of Heavenly Peace) would be viewed as a crime. Yet those in my unit who, during those few days, copied out any memorial poems or took any photographs at the plaza had to go up one by one afterwards and confess. I did not go—my lowly status wouldn't have brought any credit to the premier—but my two children went. One ended up on a black list and the other only narrowly avoided it. So memorialising a leader of the revolution was now a revisionist activity. It made no sense to me.

When the great earthquake struck Tangshan in the summer of 1976, Peking too was damaged: over a hundred people were crushed to death. Jieruo was on assignment in Manchuria at the time, but although our little gatehouse survived, after being shaken to its foundations, we were afraid to stay on in it. At first we slept out in the alley. Later a good friend took us to a nearby research

institute with a big courtyard over which hung canopies made of
reed mats. We stayed under one of them.

In September, funeral dirges sounded again. Chairman Mao was
dead. Soon afterwards, great changes came to the Chinese
motherland. The last hours of the tyrants were approaching. The
night finally came to an end and the first light of morning appeared
in the distance. It was weak, but sufficient to dispel the darkness.

What made me feel that things had really changed was something that happened in the autumn of 1978. Jieruo hurried home
with news from the personnel department that I was to participate
at seven o'clock that very evening in a feast at the Peking Hotel.

China hadn't yet opened up to tourism, so most of the banquets
at the Peking Hotel were for the entertainment of visiting foreign
dignitaries. Since 1957 nobody had invited me even to an informal
supper, but fortunately we had by then been allocated a three-room
apartment near the Temple of Heaven and moved in a few pieces of
our luggage and furniture from store. So Jieruo rummaged
through our wardrobe and brought out the woollen Mao suit that
had been made for me back in the spring of 1957. She held it up.
'Soon after we had this suit made, you became a Rightist! I've used
I don't know how many mothballs protecting it these twenty-two
years, but now it looks like it was worth it.'

I went to the banquet. When I entered the hotel, a middle-aged
man in a Western suit smiled at me and rushed over, cordially
calling me 'Old Hsiao'.

I recognised him right away: Lim Chong-eu, an old friend from
my days in Britain who had then been an Overseas Chinese from
Malaya. He was a medical student in Edinburgh at the time, but he
often came to visit me in Cambridge and London during his
vacations. We'd hiked together in the Trossachs and rowed a boat
on Loch Lomond. We'd eaten cheap fish and chips together and
bought tickets for the Albert Hall, where we heard Sir Thomas
Beecham conduct Beethoven symphonies.

This old friend of mine was now the chief minister of Penang,
Malaysia, and this had been arranged as his departure banquet. One
of my country's senior ministers sat on his right; my friend had
placed me on his left.

During the speech-making the host made a point of mentioning
me. He spoke of the Chinese classes I'd set up forty years ago for
Overseas Chinese in England and he talked of our friendship.

After the banquet he told me privately that he'd asked about me before, every time he came to China, but he'd always been told there was no such person as Hsiao Ch'ien. Now even he believed that China was genuinely beginning to change.

The most important change was that China was beginning to trust its own people.

From 1977 a story had been going round that former Rightists like me might be granted a qualified rehabilitation. I took no notice in 1978, but several friends in similar circumstances came to persuade me to ask for acquittal as a former Rightist. I was dead against it. Then the cartoonist Ding Cong publicly denounced the wrongs done to me in a big meeting. But all I still really wanted was a decent home where I could live quietly and work like an ordinary person.

After that the Chinese Writers' Association actually sent someone to invite me, in not very veiled language, to prepare my case against the political verdict made on me in 1958. I was successful in my defence and afterwards received a certificate of rehabilitation. It said that it had been a mistake to have named me a Rightist and restored me to my old salary, but not back-dated. That was in February 1979.

Early that summer, the Chinese Writers' Association told me to prepare for a trip to America in September. My reaction was mixed. Clearly my political value had increased. I didn't have to be allowed abroad to know that I was trusted, but I was determined to make a good showing on this trip on behalf of intellectuals like myself who in the past had *not* been trusted. I would use this trip to make friends for my country and to dispel misunderstandings, and I'd do it without saying one improper word.

Thinking back on it now, I may have been a bit over-cautious. Before I left, our hostess, Nieh Hualing, telegraphed from the University of Iowa indicating that I should prepare a ten-minute talk for delivery at her International Writing Program. My superiors hadn't asked me to send them a copy for approval in advance, but I wrote it out and sent it to them anyway. My companion on the trip was a long-standing Party member, Bi Shuowang, so I was determined to let him take all the decisions. When we got to America, he decided to throw out the approved text of my speech and started working on it afresh. I voiced no objection. Later, Nieh Hualing found that the speech he had written would last about an hour. Since there were to be ten speakers from Hong Kong, Taiwan and all parts of America for the two-hour session, my original draft had to be put into service. I insisted that it be considered our joint presentation.

I wanted him involved in all of my activities in America. When some universities, Harvard for instance, invited only me by myself, I wrote back politely declining. I accepted the invitation only when they'd invited both of us.

As I think about it now, I know that my cautiousness was not really necessary. From 1983 to 1988, I went abroad unescorted eight times. I visited North America, England, Western Europe, Singapore, Malaysia and South Korea. I was no longer dependent; I had learned to get along on my own.

When I had gone to America for the first time in 1945 as a reporter, I represented only a newspaper. In 1979, I was deeply aware that I was now representing all Chinese writers. For it was the first time in thirty years that Chinese writers from the mainland were to meet writers from Taiwan. Naturally I was rather apprehensive about that at the outset. But, much to my surprise, our common feelings as Chinese immediately dispelled all prejudices. On the very first night of our China Weekend with the International Writing Program at Iowa, we all sang 'On the Songhua River' together, a song that was popular during the war against Japan. It was a moving experience.

When I got back to Peking, it was as if I'd just returned from the moon. The People's Political Consultative Conference, the Democratic League, literary organisations, publishers' organisations – everybody wanted me to speak. But what should I say? Perhaps the old Party members were testing me with all these invitations. My defence mechanisms were set in motion again. I remembered a poet who visited Africa in the sixties. When he came back and made his report, mentioning some of the backwardness and poverty he'd seen, he'd been criticised for his class attitudes. Then there was the case of a colleague who'd been to a country in Western Europe. His crime had been to speak about the affluence there. I decided it would be best not to focus on America as such, but only on how to improve mutual understanding with Overseas Chinese. My first talk was held in the high-rise building that used to belong to the China Federation of Literary and Arts Circles – the building where I had taken my criticism in 1957.

There were many people in the audience. Up on the dais, I looked at the audience, at the amplification and recording devices on the table, and felt a little queasy. Jieruo had copied out my forty-page text the night before, helping me to check my phraseology for political significance as she went along. I read my speech straight from the text.

Afterwards Jieruo told me that most of the audience were disappointed. That's good, I answered; if I had set them on fire, that would have been something to worry about.

I resumed my writing. In China, magazine editors are the people most sensitive to adjustments in a person's current political status. Even before the certificate of rehabilitation was in my hands, journals and publishing houses were asking me for contributions. At the time I felt overwhelmed by gratitude and somewhat at a loss as to how to respond.

The first to contact me was *Shijie wenxue* (*World Literature*), a journal with which I'd had dealings before. I'd lost all of my books in the course of the Great Calamity, but in 1956 I had given Pan Jiaxun four different English translations of Ibsen's *Peer Gynt* to translate into Chinese. He'd never got around to it, but twenty years later he sent someone to return the books to me. So I set to work translating *Peer Gynt* into Chinese myself, working at the little two-drawer desk I shared with my youngest son.

I'd seen the play performed at the New Theatre in London in 1944 with Ralph Richardson as Peer and Sybil Thorndyke as his mother and had immediately fallen in love with it. During the Cultural Revolution, when right and wrong were turned upside down and people were scrambling to ingratiate themselves with the Gang of Four, I had often thought of the troll scene in *Peer Gynt*. Now, as I translated, I recalled the many people and places from the recent past. When I came to the passage, 'It is said, it's best to be howling / With the wolves that are about you' (IV, 13), visions of wall after wall of criticism posters from campaigns in years gone by flashed before my eyes. It was as if Ibsen, writing a century ago, had been aiming his play at China in the Sixties and Seventies. I felt total sympathy with the work, however clumsy my translation.

After that, other journals and publishers asked for contributions. I began planning how to resume my old profession. I was determined to collect my writings from the thirties for republication, and to begin writing my autobiography in instalments, in the form of new prefaces to my old works. Above all, I wanted readers of this new age to decide for themselves whether or not the works I'd written since I started in 1932 were indeed poisonous 'anti-communist, anti-Soviet, anti-people, pro-England, pro-America and pro-Japan' weeds and whether or not I really was a slave of the foreigners as charged. For that was how the Party newspapers and journals had described me in 1957. I wanted to put forward works that would vindicate me more thoroughly than my certificate of 'rehabilitation' had done.

Asked to provide some reminiscences for the journal *Historical Materials on the New Literature*, I decided to start with a safe topic. Best to write about my friend Edgar Snow, the American reporter who had been with Mao on the rostrum at Tian'anmen, the Gate of Heavenly Peace. A picture of the two of them appeared on the front page of the *People's Daily*.

After my article was published, one friend after another wrote to congratulate me. I was no longer a dummy – I had begun to live again. I realised that they weren't so much praising what I'd written as the simple fact that I'd taken up my pen again. Yet, Ba Jin, the friend I've esteemed more than anyone else in my life, wrote to reprove me. That doesn't sound like the real you, he said. The poet Shao Yanxiang also found a remoteness in my work. I was shaken and began to feel anxious: Now that I was allowed to write again, was I still able to write the way I could before? I began to see that while I had thawed quite well on the outside (with much difficulty), it would take time yet before I was thawed all the way through. As soon as I took up my pen, the hideous faces of the Gang of Four rose in front of my eyes. But I couldn't reject this opportunity to resume my old profession. Since 1979, I've published a book or two every year and an article practically every month. That I've come to no harm shows that China is no longer what it was in the 1960s.

Thus, I fully support Ba Jin's admonition to speak the truth. I begin with the facts, although I may hold some of them in reserve. I no longer write whatever may please me; I've drawn my own lines. I only dare to speak as much of the truth as is possible within the range I permit myself. And I came to see that my policy was realistic when my old friend in hardship Liu Binyan got into difficulties yet again in 1987.

This account has dragged on too long, and clearly it has strayed from the subject. I had no idea at the beginning that writing about moving house would call to mind so many memories. Since 1979, people in my circumstances as a rule haven't spoken of the past. It's as if nothing had happened in all those years. People keep a tight lid on them, passing over them all with the four exemplary words, 'Look Towards the Future'. But it's good, I think, that this time I've let my mind wander. It's good that I broke with precedent and took a chance, so that later generations can understand this period in history and therefore treasure all the more the days of stability they now enjoy.

When I returned to Peking in August 1949, I had thought only of returning to my native soil, to build a home there and be a law-abiding citizen. I truly believed that the Party, having undergone reforms and learned from experience, now stood with the vast majority of the people and was striving to make China a good place to live. That was what attracted me to socialism and I wanted to contribute something in return. Again, in 1956, when I was restored to the writer's profession, I was still eager to do something worthwhile for socialism.

And yet in those days it seemed that a giant invisible hand was pushing people apart, alienating them, particularly those who had been abroad. In the end, I myself was thrust aside completely.

On the farm, I loved the Chinese soil and the peasants who lived on it. It seems to me that in time I might truly have overcome the distance between myself and the broad masses of workers and peasants and become a useful contributor to socialism. But in June 1966, that same invisible hand moved again, rejecting and isolating every single intellectual in China. In 1984 I wrote an article recommending the establishment of a hall of remembrance for the national tragedy of the Cultural Revolution and its concentration camps. Subsequently my friend Ba Jin recommended the founding of a Cultural Revolution museum. We say these things, but we both realise that at present the creation of such institutions is still quite out of the question.

We have travelled a long way before arriving at the peace and calm of today. Of course minor storms still blow up from time to time. When the upper atmosphere is in flux, there will be changes in climate. Many a time have hypersensitive weather watchers among us sounded alarms, warned of black clouds, cried that the

Dragon King's whiskers are sprouting again. Indeed, if one interprets the signs in the light of past experience, then the Dragon often seems ready to summon up new tempests. But it never lasts. The sky clears up. And yet, after any major upheaval perhaps not all the destruction can be undone.

Since becoming a translator again in the 1970s, I've discovered to my surprise that many Third World countries, having thrown off the shackles of colonialism in the sixties and won independence – being poised to move to the left – have instead veered right. Nobody can say with any certainty how much they have been influenced by the Chinese model. Since 1983, however, I've had two opportunities to visit parts of South East Asia. Many people there equate revolution with the Chinese Cultural Revolution, so that anything the least bit communistic they have come to view with terror.

Since my qualified rehabilitation, innumerable well-meaning and sympathetic people have said to me: 'You lost more than twenty years, the best years of your life. What wonderful things you might have written if only you'd been allowed to.' I thank them, but I really don't feel that way. When you're encouraged to lie – when you're permitted to do nothing but lie – what's so bad about having your pen snatched away? I couldn't see my friends have their heating systems arbitrarily ripped out and carried off, then lavish fulsome praise on the gains in steel production. An author who is unable to write from the heart had really better go into hibernation. That was particularly true when, in 1966, anything you'd ever written could be used as evidence against you. So, whenever friends in New York, London, Munich or Singapore have asked me, out of curiosity or sympathy, about the time when I was silent, I've told them it was a blessing. That's not just clever talk – it's entirely sincere. My silence kept me alive.

Some people then go on to ask me, with the present policy of getting things back to normal, how can I just be given a 'certificate of rehabilitation' and let it go at that? Was there ever an apology? Were the slurs against me ever taken back? Did I receive compensation for my lost wages? Some even ask the question: How do I feel now about people who slandered and hounded me?

They don't understand Chinese intellectuals. Such questions have no answers. Right now the whole world is scrutinising us as we build Chinese socialism. Will we bring the people of the world to admire it and perhaps to emulate it? Or will we scare people away again?

The film expert who said in the appraisal meeting in 1961 that I was bound to run off to a foreign country was another who misunderstood us intellectuals. He was an artist himself and long ago baptised by revolution, but he didn't know the first thing about his country's intellectuals, what they aspire to, what they dream of, what touches their hearts or what stirs up their resentment.

Now I'm home again, after yet another circling of the globe. This is the place where my ancestors lived for generations. Its history flows in my veins. It's here that I intend to grow old and here that I'll perform my last small labours.

> 1985–1988; Completed in Portmeirion, Penrhyndeudraeth, North Wales, under the sweet nagging of Susan Williams-Ellis

Index